"Hey," John Boothe said, "You want a swig of this beer?"

"If you'll hold it for me," Jill replied.

He hunkered down to her, pouring some of his beer into her mouth, and their eyes locked.

"You were so pretty when I met you," he said. "But, now, now you're beautiful. I suppose you hear that all the time."

She shook her head, surprised, too stunned to speak.

"I keep expecting to see men drive up to the place to take you out," he continued.

Jill sat in her wheelchair, staring at him. This was incredible; she could not believe him. Yet something told her that John Boothe was serious, that he meant every word he said.

Also by
E.G. Valens

The Other Side of the Mountain

Published by
Warner Books

The Other Side of the Mountain Part 2

BY E. G. VALENS

WARNER BOOKS

A Warner Communications Company

WARNER BOOKS EDITION

ISBN 0-446-91322-7

Warner Books Inc., 75 Rockefeller Plaza, New York, N.Y. 10019

W A Warner Communications Company

Printed in the United States of America

First Printing: February, 1978

20   19   18   17   16   15

THE OTHER SIDE
OF THE MOUNTAIN
PART 2

Starring

Marilyn Hassett and Timothy Bottoms

with Gretchen Corbett, Nan Martin, Dabney Coleman,
June Dayton, William Bryant, Carole Cook

A Filmways Production

A Larry Peerce-Edward S. Feldman Film

Written by Douglas Day Stewart

Directed by Larry Peerce

Produced by Edward S. Feldman

A Universal Picture

Contents

Author's Note

Jill Kinmont—now Mrs. John Boothe—was a great American skier who was seriously injured racing in 1955. Since then she has built a remarkably rich life for herself with the help of her family, her friends and, more recently, her husband. She was the subject of a feature article in *Life* magazine in 1964. The article led to a book, *A Long Way Up*, which in turn led to the 1974 motion picture, *The Other Side of the Mountain*. This was followed by a paperback edition of the book with the same title as the movie.

Many people felt that the film was only the beginning of Jill's real story—how it was that she learned to cope with the emotional and professional problems of an eager, sensitive, but severely handicapped quadriplegic. So, in effect, the motion picture led directly to a second motion picture, *The Other Side of the Mountain, Part 2*.

Universal Pictures, the studio responsible for both films, felt that the second picture warranted a second book, which I was asked to write. Jill did not want the second book to be based on the movie. She wanted it to parallel the events in the movie, and she wanted it to deal with the most important events in the past five years of her life—her relationship with John and the rewards and difficulties involved in having two feature films made about her life. So, in a strange way, the book is about the picture and the picture is about the book.

The screenplay was completed before the book was begun, and it was my first source of material concerning Jill's recent life. After reading the screenplay there were several weeks of extensive and intensive interviews with Jill, John, and others who appear prominently in the book. What I had to say in the first book is true again. The wealth of detail in the book, and whatever subtleties may have survived the translation into print, are the direct result of the perceptiveness of Jill and John and their families and friends. The most revealing parts of the story could not have been unearthed without their thoughtful frankness and continual indulgence. Jill and John have displayed a phenomenal memory, always responding with grace, humor, and uncompromising honesty. They endured, and at times even enjoyed, a constant stream of questions throughout the fall of 1977. I am particularly grateful to the Kinmont family—June, Bob and Vikki, and Jerry and Lyn—and to Marilyn Hassett and Larry Peerce, the star and the director of both motion pictures, to screenwriter Doug Stewart, and to Jill's close friends Linda Tikalsky and Audra Jo Baumgarth. I have enjoyed tremendous cooperation and assistance from Sue Foster, who seems to be the person at Universal who keeps Larry Peerce sane, and from editor Annette Welles, vice president of MCA Publishing.

The hardest work of all, I believe, was what went on back here in the manuscript factory, and the credit for holding the book together and keeping the author's spirit and body alive goes largely to my assistant and co-worker, Anne Curtis. Invaluable help came also from Winifred

Valens, David Edwards, and Ann Sawyer. We are all grateful to Jan Mason, author of the original *Life* article. Special gratitude I reserve for my agent and protector, Marilyn Marlow, vice president of Curtis Brown, Ltd.

1

Life

Jill Kinmont wished life could be simple. She leaned back, closed her eyes and breathed in the evening air, still warm, that came up the canyon from the ocean. It smelled lightly of salt and of dry sagebrush and eucalyptus. She could have been sound asleep except that she licked her lips, running her tongue quickly back and forth. Her cheeks were lean and tan.

Her straight, dark eyebrows pulled toward each other and she opened her eyes momentarily. She was beginning a list in her head. Call Dave about the Bishop house. Pack school stuff for the Indians. Pay bills. What about Jerry and his kids? Oil change and check tires. See Dr. Schlumberger again? "Phosphates are high in your urine. That's uh . . . er . . . mmm . . . serious." Do I give up trying for a Master's? The kids at school sure worry about me. "Aren't you ever going to get married?" And still they call me *Mrs.* Kinmont. "You're so pretty I don't know why you're not married." They're so neat. "Who'd marry her? She can't dance!"

"Glass of wine?"

"Sure, Mom, I'd love one," Jill said without opening her eyes. Six-thirty already?

June Kinmont, shorter and slighter than her daughter, had a glass of white wine in each hand, and she set one of them on Jill's tray. "What's the trouble?"

"No troubles."

"I know better than that."

"Just thinking you're sixty-five now and when I'm sixty-five you'll be ninety and we'll still be having coffee at four in the afternoon and a glass of Gallo's white Rheingartener at six-thirty." They both laughed.

"Don't worry, you'll meet somebody."

"I already met somebody."

"Too bad he was married. He would have been just right for you."

Jill laughed. "Mom, I'm not talking about six years ago."

"Who?"

Jill shrugged and reached forward for her wine with both hands. She held the glass between the heels of her hands and raised it carefully to her lips.

"You mean Chuck?"

"Well, I don't mean Bill, and I don't mean Dick McGarry. But that's not the point, Mom." Her voice became level and very calm. "I do have a pretty full life and I'm not constantly feeling, oh, am I ever going to find someone? That just isn't part of my framework."

"You certainly can look out for yourself."

Jill looked startled.

"Always in control, Jill. Almost never cry. I remember you at eighteen months sitting up straight in the front seat, not about to snuggle up to anybody."

"Yeah, I do have a pretty strong image of myself. And like they say, the idea of being single just isn't all that bad."

June reached for the newspaper and scanned the front page. Still reading, she said, "Chuck spent a lot of time here, and driving you to Bishop and all over the—"

14

Jill stopped her with a breath and a penetrating glance. She set down her glass deliberately, and it struck the tray at an angle, almost falling over. "So he stops by on his way to Thailand, picks up a few things of his, says well, so long. And that's it!"

Both were silent as June wiped up the spilled wine. Jill said quietly, "I'm still crushed. I'm sure that's why I was so sick for six weeks. He really didn't care." Her deep-set eyes were narrowed and glistening. She made an explosive little laugh and said, "Don't worry, Mom. I'm still looking." After a sip of wine, she said, "A neat thing I meant to tell you. I have a student, Claudia. She's seven. She said, Are you glad? I don't mean are you glad you're in a wheelchair, but are you glad you're getting all that attention?"

"There are low clouds," June said, looking out through the glass door that was open onto the deck. "Sunset should be pretty tonight."

Jill was facing her at the table, and she turned her head, half expecting to see the sun. But of course she couldn't see much because of the Brazilian pepper tree that hung over the deck. She was sitting very straight in her wheelchair, rather like Queen Victoria. Formidable. If you had asked her about that, she would have pointed out that this posture was what kept her from toppling forward onto her face.

She lifted her left arm and swung it outward in a graceful gesture, neatly avoiding the large plastic bottle of distilled water that stood on her lap tray. She lowered her palm onto a ⅜-inch wooden dowel sticking up by the arm of the chair. She pulled backward with her shoulder and the chair promptly backed away from the table with a soft purring sound. She spun it around and took off at once. She slowed for the threshold and then wheeled out to the far corner of the deck. Her mother followed.

From here they could look down at the Pacific, less than a mile away. Not that they could see much of it, but the sun's red, red reflection off the water was unmistakable through the trees.

15

The telephone rang and June answered it. "Long distance," she called. "I think it's Jan."

Jill wheeled into the living room, and her mother put the telephone on her tray. She thrust at the receiver with her left hand, jamming it between her thumb and forefinger. She had no use of her fingers, but when she relaxed her wrist and let it hang, the fingers separated from the thumb enough to encompass the receiver. She extended her wrist, which automatically tightened the tendons enough to give her a grip. Then she lifted the receiver and bent her head to meet the earphone.

"Hi, Jan," she said. "Sorry I banged the phone around. How've you been?"

After listening for five minutes and murmuring a few times, she said, "Yeah, still working with the Indians again this summer, but it's no big deal, Jan." She listened again and said, "Well, I'd have to sound them out first . . . yeah, the whole family'll be in Bishop mid-July. Jerry for a visit, and Bob and Vikki all summer."

After she had dropped the receiver back into its cradle, she said to June, "Think we can handle another round with *Life* magazine?"

●　　●　　●

The article would bring the magazine's readers up to date on Jill Kinmont. Today was June 20, 1972, eight years after the 14-page spread in *Life* which had chronicled Jill's long struggle to become a teacher, and nearly 18 years after her accident. In 1954, at the age of 18, Jill was women's amateur slalom champion of the United States and a sure bet for the 1956 Olympics. Early in 1955, she fell in a race at Alta, Utah, and broke her neck. Since then she had been a quadriplegic, paralyzed from the shoulders down, with limited use of her arms and no control of her fingers. After a year of hospitals and rehabilitation centers, she enrolled in college and eventually earned a teaching certificate at the University of Washington. The University of California School of Education in Los Angeles refused to allow her to study there because she couldn't

16

stand in a classroom or walk up and down steps. Her applications to teach in Los Angeles schools were later turned down for the same reason, but in 1967 she was hired as a Reading Specialist at the Hawthorne Elementary School in Beverly Hills. Life was saddened in that year by the death of her father, Bill Kinmont.

The following summer she organized a summer reading program for Paiute Indian children in Bishop, California, where she and her two younger brothers had grown up. She moved to Bishop every summer to work with the Indians, and during the school year she taught at Hawthorne and lived with her mother, first in West Los Angeles and then in nearby Pacific Palisades.

*　　*　　*

Jill brushed her teeth with an electric toothbrush and wheeled into the bedroom. The double bed was an electric crank-up bed, and she maneuvered as close to it as she could. The covers were already folded over to the far side of the bed.

June removed an arm of the wheelchair, pulled off Jill's blouse, and slipped a nightgown over her head. Then she faced the chair and pressed her knees against Jill's. With one arm around Jill's back and the other under an arm, she leaned back, lifted, and swung her daughter onto the bed. She eased her onto her back and undressed her, rolling her to one side and back in order to remove the corset that kept Jill from slumping when she was in the chair.

Jill didn't enjoy drawing on others all the time, depending on them so totally and always asking for help. But to cope with the world, you have to use whatever you've got. Like shoulder muscles and biceps and a good head and a lot of help every day. If you have to worry about your basic needs all the time, you can't do anything else and you can't lead a very normal life.

June removed the flat plastic urine bag which was attached to Jill's catheter. She rinsed it in a mild disinfectant and put it in the washbasin to soak overnight. She

17

then attached a drain tube to the catheter so it could drain into a cider jug on the floor. The next step was to shove a pillow under Jill's legs so her heels were suspended. Finally, she forced a heavy board between the balls of her feet and the end of the bed. This procedure served to keep Jill's Achilles tendons stretched during the night so they wouldn't atrophy.

"Remember that guy at the rehab center in Tucson?" Jill said. The man had an injury much like Jill's, and when he heard that this famous young woman was visiting the center he insisted on showing her what he could do. What he could do was transfer himself from his wheelchair into his bed without any assistance. It was a prodigious feat, and it took him half an hour, with heaving pauses to catch his breath. He made it, and it left him utterly exhausted.

June laughed. "You sure let him know your priorities." Jill had told the young man: "Me, I'd rather be doing something else than spending thirty minutes every time I want to get out of the chair. I can get someone to do it *for* me in thirty seconds, and I get to spend that time studying or reading or whatever."

June tucked in the blanket and fitted the pillow snugly around her daughter's neck. Jill sighed with pleasure. "I don't think a husband could ever tuck me in this cozily," she said. She had no feeling below the shoulders except for some sensation on the inside of her arms. Having the pillow around the back of her neck and the blanket up under her chin was as close as she could come to feeling really tucked in.

•　　•　　•

"We only need somebody to get me up and drive me to the Indian Center," Jill said at breakfast. "But it's got to be every day."

"And we can't afford much."

"True!"

"How much do you think?"

"I don't know."

Half an hour later Jill telephoned the Santa Monica

18

Outlook and placed an ad: Girl; 2 hours work daily; 6 weeks Sierra vacation, room and board; $25 per week.

Ten women answered the ad, and the interviews were disappointing. Then Dana walked in, introduced herself, took in the situation at a glance, and said, "I'd like the job." She was a small, pretty girl with gold-rimmed glasses, a khaki tank top, and faded Levi cut-offs. She was a sophomore at UCLA, wondering whether to go back in the fall or look for a full-time job. Jill said, "You're hired. We leave in a week."

• • •

Jill and June lived on a steep street that sloped down into the town of Pacific Palisades just northwest of Los Angeles. They had been in their small frame house for a year. Jill's brothers Bob and Jerry had built large decks at the back and front, a wheelchair ramp at the back, and a walkway from there around to the street. They had also constructed a "loading dock" in the side of the garage so Jill could roll directly into the side door of her VW van. A pair of portable ramps bridged the gap between the dock and the van floor. The van's license was DPZ214; the *DP* identified its owner as a Disabled Person.

On the last day of school, Jill wheeled herself into the van at 7:15, as usual. June stowed the ramps, blocked the wheelchair, and drove Jill to the Hawthorne Elementary School in Beverly Hills. Most of the 11-mile trip was on Sunset Boulevard, and the traffic, as usual, was horrible.

June parked in the No Parking zone by the school, a Spanish-style building with arches and olive trees in the courtyard. She helped Jill down the ramps onto the sidewalk and returned home. Jill wheeled along the sidewalk and climbed a ramp that had been built for her at one side of the school steps, always being careful not to tip over the open plastic water bottle on her tray. She went directly to her room, a converted principal's office, and suveyed the chaos she had created the day before. On chairs and on the floor were empty cardboard boxes and boxes half-filled with paperback books and mimeographed word sheets.

19

Posters and word wheels and workbooks were in little piles on the desk and on other chairs. Jill was a resource reading teacher at Hawthorne, and she was in the middle of packing material she was borrowing for her summer classes with the Indians.

A 12-year-old girl appeared in the doorway, smiled shyly, and went to work at once piling books into boxes. "Good morning, Mei Ling. You're early today." Jill reached back into her purse, which was hanging open from the left handle of her chair, fumbled in it for a moment, and drew forth a small hand brace wedged between her thumb and fingers. The aluminum brace held a ballpoint pen fixed securely with a magnet. The brace was on a wide leather strap fastened with a strip of dirty white Velcro. This Jill pushed around her right wrist with her left fist and pounded it down securely. "If you can find my list for me, we'll see how far we've gotten."

Mei Ling brought a typewritten list from Jill's desk and stood by Jill's shoulder so they could go over it together. She was very bright, but could neither read nor write well. She had come from China to join her family here and had only been in the United States a few months. She could print beautifully and had already lettered posters with rules for pronouncing vowels and rules for breaking words into syllables.

"We need a box for each of the worksheets and answer sheets, and thirty to thirty-five sets in each box. You can label what each box is—like Word Family, Flower Wheel, Basic Sight Words, Prefix Wheels, or Reading For Understanding. I've already typed out the instructions—they're on my desk—and there's one for each box. That's so the tutors won't have to come to me every time to find out what to do."

Other children came in from time to time to say hello or to work for 20 minutes to half an hour, but Mei Ling worked the whole morning and rounded up help to carry everything to the van when June returned at 3 p.m. It was a breathless afternoon with a hundred tiny chores to finish up. The principal and the custodian came during the last frantic rush and helped load things. The custodian was Jill's buddy and he always helped. "Don't worry about the room," he said. "You sure you've got everything you'll need for the summer?"

Jill laughed and let out a long, tired sigh. "I'll let you know when I unpack."

     •   •   •

The Kinmont van was on its way by 7 a.m. with Jill in the back in her chair and June and Dana in the front seats. The space behind Jill was packed solid with suitcases and boxes.

The first 75 miles, due east through greater Los Angeles and on to Palmdale, was a crowded superhighway shoving its way through an endless city. But from there it was a free 200 miles north through the Mojave desert and on up the Owens Valley, with all the great peaks of the Sierra standing grandly just west of the road.

They talked about Bishop, and Dana said, "Sounds like you sure love the place."

"It always feels like coming home," Jill said. "We're lucky we can do it every summer."

"Does it bring back memories? Like before your accident?"

Jill didn't answer, and Dana twisted around so she could see her.

"Sorry," Jill said. "I was just realizing. Do you know what? I've now spent as much time *in* a wheelchair as out of it." She frowned and then smiled. "No, I don't see it as a looking-back kind of thing. More going back to my roots. Anyway, my emotions are pretty worn down by the end of the school year, and this is a chance to recharge my batteries."

June said, "No matter what happens, we always seem to manage to come back to Bishop."

The valley was heating up fast, and they closed the windows and turned on the air conditioner. Jill's body could not perspire freely, and once it heated up it stayed hot, which was the same as having a fever.

21

"Bishop is *my place*," Jill said.

"It's the pace," said June. "We're not on as rigid a schedule. We don't drive as fast. We don't try to do so many things."

"It's more than that, Mom. If you have a flat tire, someone will stop. If your child is lost, the whole town will look for her. Even if your political beliefs are way off from theirs."

Jill was quiet then but thought of a lot more: because things are simpler, I don't feel I have to do certain things, such as get my Master's degree right away, or go to every party I'm invited to, or have a drink at every party I go to if I don't feel like it. I don't feel pressured into certain things like I do in the city.

June said, "The teachers in Beverly Hills are all taking extension classes during the year and summer school in the summer."

"If I take extra classes, I'm too tired," Jill said. "But in my job with Indians I have a chance to give some help to people who want it without having anyone pressure me about how things are supposed to be done. In Bishop you don't feel like you should be looking over your shoulder all the time."

Bishop is a vacation town catering to fishermen, hunters, and backpackers. Main Street is U.S. Route 395—twelve blocks of it lined with motels and restaurants, plus a few stores. The other important street is West Line, which runs from Main through the Paiute Indian reservation and on to the western edge of the valley at Bishop Creek. The road then climbs a steep 13 miles alongside the creek to the Boothe's Rainbow Pack Outfit and three beautiful lakes. Trails from the pack station lead to dozens of the more remote High Sierra lakes.

The Kinmont van rolled out West Line to the end, five miles from the center of town, and turned off by a sign: ROCKING K. "Well, this is where we grew up, but it sure doesn't look the same now," Jill explained to Dana as they drove into a small housing development in pasture land surrounded by a great expanse of sagebrush. Up behind

22

the new houses was an old guest ranch. "That used to be our ranch, but Dad had to sell it after my crash. Dave McCoy bought part of it. He was our ski coach all through high school, and now he's letting us use his house for the summer."

"We used to walk around the perimeter every evening," June said. "All eighty acres of it. Way up beyond the corrals and way down to the bottom along Ed Powers Road."

Jill was excited, bending her neck so she could see out through the van windows, looking for old landmarks and new additions. "Right up there's where we'd find our choice arrowheads and grinding stones and . . ."

"And Jerry!" June broke in. "His rattlesnakes. That's where he got so clever at lassoing rattlesnakes and lizards."

"He had this fishing pole with a nylon noose on its end," Jill explained. "He'd hang it out in front of them and they'd pop right in. So that's how *one* oceanographer got started—in the desert."

"He was always making traps and having museums."

"Including Mom's Dutch oven, which he used for a snake house. I'll never forget!"

Dana asked, "Can you get into the mountains from right here?"

"Not really. What you do is drive up Bishop Creek or Pine Creek or Rock Creek and start in from the end of the road."

When the van pulled into the McCoys' driveway, Jill was suddenly exhausted. She had held up well during the last hectic week of school and the past few days of packing, and the drive up to Bishop had kept her adrenaline running. But now that the rat race was over and there was a place and time to relax, her tiredness caught up with her all at once. She wheeled herself into the living room as soon as June had helped her out of the van. It was a huge house, with six bedrooms and five baths, but it looked just as full to Jill as the tiny house the McCoys had lived in at Crowley Dam 22 years ago when Dave first discovered Mammoth Mountain. The living room had large beams,

23

an open loft at one end, and a massive fireplace. It was crammed with antiques and knickknacks and there were plants everywhere.

Two of the McCoy children and a friend were living in the upstairs bedrooms. Roma McCoy was still there, trying to get moved out for the summer, and Jill had the uneasy feeling that she had arrived about three days too early.

Jill wheeled out onto the back patio and found a sunny corner. She put her elbows on her tray, leaned her chin on her left fist, and closed her eyes, hoping to fall asleep for a while. But there was too much still going on in her head. June was exhausted and wouldn't rest until she and Dana had the car unloaded. The Indian reading classes began in two days, and there was a lot to be done for that. *Life* would be here, and she was unsure what Dan Bomberry, director of the Indian Center, really felt about this invasion by the press. Jill was paying again for a familiar weakness —a chronic inability to say *no* to anything or anybody. She knew from previous experience that a *Life* interview for a major article would be an exhaustive, 10- or 12-day affair. The teaching alone would have been enough to keep her busy.

The summer reading classes got underway on schedule in the new Owens Valley Study Center, a portable classroom on Pa Ha Lane. The room was also the Public Library and the medical clinic for the Indian community. A wheelchair ramp at the front door was a permanent fixture.

Late on the afternoon of the first day of school, Jerry Kinmont and his two children, Robin and Jess, arrived from southern California for a five-day visit. He was 29, not quite as lean as he used to be but strong, still able to grab the handles of Jill's wheelchair and go into a handstand on them. He had a new, full beard. The kids beat him into the house and were both trying to ride on the back of Jill's chair when he appeared. He bent over to kiss Jill and gave his mother a hug that made her say, "Jerry ... *uhh!*"

Jill introduced him to Dana and said Bob and Vikki

and the kids would be over for supper. "They're staying in Aim's trailer for the summer."

"Aim Morhardt," June explained to Dana, "was Bob's and Jill's art teacher in high school, and you know where Bob has gone with his art. Aim was their ski coach at the very first, too."

2

LIFE

Two days later, *Life* arrived in the persons of reporter Jan Mason, photographer Burk Uzzle, and Burk's wife, Cardy. Jill knew them well from the article they had done for *Life* eight years ago while Jill was a student teacher in Seattle, shortly before her father, Bill, died. Burk and Cardy were somewhat younger than Jill, both wiry and full of life. They could have passed for college students. Jan was perhaps five years older and looked the part of a seasoned reporter. All three were staying nearby at the Rocking K guest ranch. The ranch looked pretty much as it had when the Kinmonts ran it in the early 1950s, except that the meadows surrounding it had been sold off to developers.

"So what's with the arm?"

Burk turned to Jill and proudly raised his right arm, which was sheathed in a cast. "Little problem with my motorcycle," he said. "Hasn't slowed me down yet."

"That's good, because the Tri-County Fair opens this afternoon. You guys up to it?"

They were, and they accompanied three generations of Kinmonts to the event that Jill hadn't missed for decades except for the few summers in Seattle.

No one spoke or thought about the *Life* article until the following morning, Friday. Jan and Burk met Jill at breakfast, followed her to school, and stuck with her all day long, even though Burk had left his camera at the ranch. For the moment they only wanted to get a feeling for what Jill was doing "back home in good old Bishop." Burk rarely sat down. He was always moving, circling his potential subjects, seeing them in every possible way, from every possible angle. The kids had already discovered that his cast was the result of a motorcycle accident, and they watched him with admiration.

Jill said, "Jan, you two are like Indians. Waiting, watching, finding out what's going on before you say anything." She wondered what they were seeing and whether they understood what was going on with the Indians. Between her second and third classes, she said to them, "What may have seemed unfriendly to you when you came in isn't that. It's more a watchful observance."

One of Jill's first pupils was David Moose, seven, who was having a lot of trouble with three consonants: *F*, *R*, and *B*. He always forgot them. Yesterday Jill had asked him to draw pictures of objects that began with those letters, and he drew a fish, a rake, and a butterfly without hesitation. He had taken the pictures home with him.

Jill now reviewed the three sounds with him, and he knew each one perfectly. "That's great," she said. "Now, will you write me a story?"

While David was writing, Jill explained to Jan that her object was to get the children to incorporate new or difficult letters in their stories.

David brought her his story, which was written clearly in large block letters.

27

DAVED
POW WOW
I WENT TO
THE
POW WOW
AND PLAYED.

"These kids are smart," Jill said. "Notice he made it without a single *F* or *R* or *B* in the whole thing."

That evening after an early supper, Jill attended a class in watercolor technique, still dogged by Jan and Burk. The three-hour class was taught by Bob Kinmont, who had taught in Toronto during the school year and was headed for Lone Mountain College in San Francisco in September. His wife Vikki was also taking the course.

On the way home, Jill was still worrying about the Indians and *Life* magazine. "I don't want to mislead you into thinking my reading program is the ultimate in anything," she said to Jan. "It is a good small program that meets some needs of the community."

"I get that, Jill."

"Okay. But with all your questions, I'm afraid your editors might try to make the program out as some big thing."

Dana said next morning when she was getting Jill up, "I thought you came here because everything was so much simpler and slower."

• • •

Saturday *was* simpler, but it was frustrating for other reasons. Once Jill was dressed, she noticed that her skirt was crooked and her hair looked all wrong. She was unwilling to face the world until she looked attractive—or, at the very least, presentable. She worked on her hair with a comb and Dana straightened the skirt. Dana tried to fix her hair. June tried to fix her hair. Nothing seemed to work. Jill got so angry that she cursed and smashed her hand against the wall.

Sunday's big event was a picnic in a meadow up on the south fork of Bishop Creek. It was a favorite spot because it was open, with hard ground, so Jill could wheel right up to the stream. Most places had boulders or steep banks or soft pumice soil. The outing was a typical Kinmont affair, June and all her children and grandchildren. Jerry with his two. Bob and Vikki with Ben, nine, and Anna, ten months younger. Plus Burk and Cardy and Jan and Dana.

Bob was a short, rugged man who moved quietly and spoke intently. He had been a football star at the Bishop High School, a diver, and junior national slalom champion. He didn't care about winning, yet he had loved to race—until Jill's accident. But that was all half a life ago, and he had since become an accomplished painter, sculptor, and art teacher. The spring issue of *Arts Canada* had featured his work, thoughts, and philosophy of teaching.

Vikki was different. She was physically strong, yet appeared fragile. Her body looked slender even though she was obviously pregnant. She had long brown hair and was wearing light-rimmed glasses and a long dress. She was from a regular army family, yet she was a woman with strong feelings who loved physical affection. She had been amazed at how reserved the Kinmonts were with one another physically.

Bob and Jerry looked more alike than they ever had, probably because they both now had full beards and Jerry, though taller, looked stockier than usual. They went off fly-fishing with the kids. June and Jan and Vikki unpacked the potato salad, fried chicken, potato chips, spice cake, beer, soft drinks, and cookies. Ground squirrels were running about everywhere, trying to steal food.

The sun went behind clouds, and thunder sounded from back in the high valleys. The sky pulsed now and then with distant lightning.

"This is something our family has always done," Jill told Jan. "We used to go fishing with Dad around here and on up in the mountains. South Lake, Horton Lakes. All different places. Dad was so sophisticated in the ways of fishing. He could pull a trout out of anyplace. I usually didn't fish, though. I liked to just walk around."

29

"Do you miss the mountains? Being able to get back into them?"

"Sure, I'd like to be more a part of the mountains instead of just observing it. Other than that, it just gives me a nice feeling to be here. I have the same feeling about the beauty of the mountains as I did when I was skiing."

It began to rain. Bob and Jerry appeared, breathless, and rigged a plastic tarp to protect Jill.

"Is lightning attracted to plastic?" Jill asked.

"Nope," Jerry said. "Only to wheelchairs."

· · ·

Burk was everywhere with his camera now, and people were used to him. He spent Tuesday morning with Jill in the Safeway, which was one of her favorite places because of the smooth floors and wide aisles and grocery cart ramps. "Oh, these doors!" she said, wheeling out of the automatic doors and back in again. "Nobody has to *open* them for you. I get the most fantastic feeling of freedom."

The following Sunday was one long interview. Jan used a tape recorder and also took notes. She started from the beginning, asking how Jill first became interested in teaching Indian children.

The teaching part had a lot to do with President Kennedy. "I was such a fan of his," Jill said. "He led me to believe that each of us had an opportunity to make a difference in the world. And teaching just seemed to fit in. As for the Indians, even that is related to a Kennedy. When I was in summer school in Arizona, Bobby Kennedy was talking a lot about the Indians, so I started thinking about the Indians in Arizona and thought I'd like to work with them. Then I remembered there were plenty of Indians right in Bishop. And they really needed help. The school dropout rate was 40 to 50 percent, and for boys it was 90 percent!"

"What about Indians being encouraged to turn their backs on their own culture?"

"Some Indians," Jill said, "—and a lot of whites—think the best thing for the Indians is for them to assimilate.

30

Become white Indians. But that's got to be up to them. What I try to do is give them tools, which help them to cope with the world and find their own way in it. You can't cope if you are thirty with a big family and have a second-grade education."

"Well, you're sure doing it, according to Dan Bomberry over at the Center. The teachers say the kids speak out in class now, and they never did before. They were unsure of themselves, but now they know what to do."

"Yeah, that's what it's about."

"What surprises you about the kids?"

"Their tenacity, I guess. They stay right with it once you get them started."

"What else?"

"Their quiet manner. Their capacity to learn. The way cousins and brothers and sisters hear about the program and want to join in."

"Is this volunteer work for you?"

"Not any more, but it was the first year. Then the church provided $250 for me. At first I had this do-gooder feeling that I should put it back in. But the pastor, Reverend Byrd, said it would be ten times more meaningful to the community if they could pay me for my services than if I were giving them something. So that was just fine. I took it and used and enjoyed it. And today I'm paid $500, and we're paying the teacher in Lone Pine the same. And the kids—the tutors—get two dollars an hour."

"How valuable do you think your work is here?"

"Gosh, I really don't think in those terms. I certainly don't think I'm 'saving the Indians' or something."

"Have you seen progress in the kids so far this summer?"

"Yes. Every one. Even the two lowest."

"Like what?"

"It's not very dramatic. David—he's the youngest, too—he can almost remember *R*. He can remember that it says *rrrr* and he can remember that rake he drew on his *R* card. And for him it's a big stride. At the other end, two of the tutors now want to become teachers."

31

The interview went on and on, continuing more informally at Jack's Waffle Shop for dinner.

"Do you think about getting married?"

"Sure I think about it. I have a full life without it, but with the right man . . . of course."

"What about your own future?"

"Gosh, Jan, I don't think that far ahead."

Jan laughed into her coffee, almost spilling it. "Fair enough. But I've got another one for you." She checked her steno pad. "In our last Jill Kinmont story, we ended with a quote which said, 'I want to be somebody, if I can be somebody.' What I want to know is, have you become somebody, and if so, who are you?"

Jill took an exaggerated breath and blew it out with a great sigh. She said, *"Wow!"*

"I know, I know." Jan laughed.

"Well, I don't think about that kind of thing too much. Probably, when I said it eight years ago, I meant something very tangible. National Ski Champion, RCA Cowboy of the Year, something like that. Where now it just means do your best and develop as a person . . . you know, just keep your eyes open and . . . in the process you, I guess, become somebody. Jan, *I* don't know!"

"And meanwhile you keep going and stay open."

"Um."

"And stay vulnerable."

"Yeah, I guess."

On the way home Jill said, "I forgot to tell you something, speaking of marriage. I spent last night with Jack Nicholson."

Jan turned very suddenly.

"I had a dream about him. He told me I was what he'd been looking for all his life, that he couldn't live without me. How about *that!*"

•   •   •

The next morning Jill lay in bed, awake, not wanting to get up. It was the last day of the interviewing. It'll be all the questions and pictures they've missed, she said to herself. I feel like I'm a leg of lamb and it's their last meal. Teaching Indians is fun. It's ordinary. A *Life* article about me teaching Indians gets somehow to be extraordinary.

She was glad Dana hadn't showed up yet. When she thought of her classes today she saw two different things trying to happen at the same time in the same place. The teaching—simple, down-to-earth everyday problems and experiences that we feel without having to describe or explain them. And the interviewing—sophisticated and verbal and geared-up, and there gets to be a lot of glamor and specialness attached to it. Put them together and . . . the teaching is supposed to be the same as ever, except that everything's being recorded. We're on record for the world to see. Every little thing.

Jill loved the attention and the acclaim. She also loved the quiet, private warmth of her classroom. She wasn't sure the two were mixing very well.

And on this particular morning, they weren't.

Jill had forgotten that her classroom was doubling as an eye clinic for the day. It was filled with Indians of all ages. They were quiet and warm with one another, but they got more or less mixed in with the children. A mother left her baby with a friend while having her eyes examined, and the baby was passed around among grownups and children as well. Some of the children were students, some not. Little groups were playing spontaneous games. The elders watched it all intently, nodding, apparently commenting among themselves about Jill and Jan and Burk.

Jill didn't know what to do. It was all one big open room, and the few bookcase partitions were only four or five feet high. Humanity seemed to be flowing freely without regard to the dividers. Jill couldn't separate her pupils from the rest of the people. Burk was upset because he needed a few more pictures of Jill teaching. At one point he said to her, "How can anything get done if you can't keep order?"

Jan was concerned by the way Indian girls were answering the Center telephone. She said, "They are just not getting out the necessary information when people call in."

Jill felt Jan was also thinking: why can't these people get with it; why doesn't somebody get up and straighten things out?

The chaos ended only with the end of Jill's classes.

That afternoon they all drove north to Mammoth Mountain to meet Dave McCoy, and Jill scarcely spoke during the 50-minute trip. She was afraid *Life* would come out with a critical article. Jan and Burk both reassured her, but she didn't feel reassured. She wasn't at all sure they understood about the Indians. That night she wrote a note to herself: it was chaos and a disaster; I'm ashamed; Burk gave me hell indirectly.

The next day she wrote in her daybook: Burk Cardy Jan leave. *Whew!*

3

Camera

June and Jill sensed they might be overstaying their
welcome at the McCoys' house—the McCoy kids were in
nd out a lot—and they returned to Pacific Palisades soon
fter the Indian school ended early in August.

Jill still worried about what *Life* would do with the
ndian material. The magazine had already made some-
hing of a legend out of Jill's early life. What a reader got
rom the previous *Life* story was just the high points. "Jill"
neant big skier, big tragedies, big determination, big suc-
ess. A lot bigger than everyday life had been since then.
he wondered out loud what they would make of her
eaching.

"I notice they were with us just thirteen days," June
aid. "Hope you're not superstitious."

Jill laughed. "That's better than fourteen or fifteen. It's
ure nice to be just plain me again after all that high-
owered, exciting, difficult stuff."

"They're *thorough*."

"It never looks quite the same in *Life*, Mom, as it looked in life."

"A lot closer than *some* of the articles that have been written about you."

"By a million miles. I don't like coming off as the Great American Myth or something."

"Still, it does something for people. Remember the letter from the boy in your class up in Washington? We'll be lost without you. You're our hero and you're the only one we've got."

"That was sure neat."

Jill thought again of Jan Mason's uncomfortable and startling question. Have you become somebody, and if so who are you?

• • •

On Monday, August 28, Jill was waiting for the postman. He gave her the mail and she frowned. "How come no *Life* magazine?"

"Looks like your copy didn't show. Something special in it?"

"You're darned right!"

"Hell, in that case . . ." He pulled out someone else's copy for her and waited for her to read whatever it was she wanted to read. He was soon looking over her shoulder and he was rightly impressed. "A Broken Life Made Whole: Jill Kinmont's Winning Battle." By Jan Mason. Photographs by Burk Uzzle. The story was really good, and there were wonderful pictures of the Indian kids. It was a six-page spread. The article, fortunately, was only about teaching the Indians, but the introduction was all too familiar. "It is now 17 years since the day of the accident—the day 18-year-old Jill Kinmont, vying for a place on the U.S. Olympic team, fell during a slalom race, broke her neck and . . ." It ended a bit sentimentally, Jill thought, with her saying, "I do the best I can—keep my eyes open, stay vulnerable."

She returned the magazine to the postman, thanking him, and he walked off, reading the article himself.

Later in the morning, the telephone rang and Jill answered it.

"Miss Kinmont?" said a rather high, thin voice. "I'm Ed Feldman. I've seen you at the Hawthorne School. You've worked with my children. I'm a producer at Filmways, and I've just read the article in *Life* Magazine. I'd like to do a film about you. Could I come over tomorrow to talk about it?"

Jill was very cool. Disinterested and polite. "What do you have in mind?" she said. Feldman replied that he had been taken with the article and would probably base the story on that idea. He asked if she had a lawyer, and when she said no, he insisted that she find a lawyer to represent her in any possible contractual arrangements. Jill agreed to talk with him tomorrow morning.

Jill's manner changed completely the moment she had replaced the receiver. "Mom!" she shouted, wheeling her chair around. "Guess what! You'll never believe this!"

June appeared at the kitchen door.

"That was a Mr. Feldman from Filmways, Mom, and he wants to do a movie. He just saw the *Life* article."

June was not swept off her feet. She nodded, waiting to hear more.

"This man wants to do a *movie!*" Jill repeated.

"Yes, I understood, Jill. I think that's nice."

"The idea doesn't exactly knock you over backwards."

"It's just that we went through the writing of a screenplay four years ago and it never got produced."

"But I think Mr. Feldman is a person who can make it happen. That's the feeling I get."

"Let's see what he has to say."

Jill immediately leafed through the entertainment section of the *Los Angeles Times* looking for Feldman's name. She found it—an ad listing him as producer of a film called *Save the Tiger*. She telephoned Nick Vanoff, a variety show producer and father of two of her reading pupils, to find if Feldman was legitimate. He was. She also telephoned a friend, June Bennett, who had a friend in the business. She telephoned Dave McCoy at Mammoth to ask whom to get as an attorney. Dave was very excited by the prospects of Jill's life being filmed and of her making some money from the venture.

Jill almost forgot that her annual physical examination was scheduled for 3 p.m. June drove her, and on the way she began to have doubts about the whole business of the movie. "Boy," she said to June. "The thought of putting myself up there on the screen . . . putting my life up there . . ." She grumbled. "I thought the *book* was kind of flashy, but this is a lot flashier than a book. This could get to be a kind of never-ending thing. It'll probably be a 'B' movie."

"It might be a good thing," June said. "The money can make it possible to lead a more normal life. And lots of people want to know how you've been able to make a success of your life. Look at your mail."

"But I wonder how much of my life they'll use. They'll probably call it *The Jill Kinmont Story*. Ugh!"

"Well, *Life* ran your life for a couple of weeks, and you survived."

"Yeah. I was their property. Same as with the first story, and same as with the book after that. And all the hundreds and hundreds of letters . . . it's like each one feels I belong to him, somehow. I'm getting to be a public property." Jill remembered another letter from a former pupil in Mercer Island, near Seattle. It said, "I know you must go to California and become that great movie star. Your name up in lights. Miss Kinmont The Spectacular."

Dr. Reynolds's office was on Wilshire Boulevard in West Los Angeles. He knew about the *Life* article because his nurse had seen it and told him about it. The first thing he asked was whether Jill's weight had changed. She said, "I haven't weighed myself for eighteen years." She had been seeing him for nine years. Every time he asked if her weight had changed, and every time she said she hadn't weighed herself since 1954. He wanted her on the examining table, and it took the three of them to do it—he under Jill's arms, the nurse lifting her knees, and June under her seat.

The doctor poked around in the usual way, studied her

38

eyes and ears and nose and throat, and took her blood pressure. The nurse took a blood sample and a pap smear. Jill had already sent in a urine sample.

"How much water you drinking?"

"Three thousand cc's a day," Jill said.

"Whatever you're doing is just right. Just keep it up."

Kidneys are the crucial organ for quadriplegics. Kidneys calcify easily for anyone who isn't physically active. Jill had been drinking distilled water ever since her accident in order to avoid the minerals that cause calcification such as kidney stones. She was also careful to avoid carbonated drinks, citrus, and dairy foods. She had a urinalysis every month without fail. The other big problem is kidney dysfunction caused by infection. Most quadriplegics have an indwelling catheter, which means bacteria are present all the time. One way to keep out infection is to drink a lot of water all the time.

"Say," Dr. Reynolds said, "I went to school with a guy from Bishop. Dr. Sheldon." Dr. Reynolds always mentioned his old school chum from Bishop. "How long since you've had an IVP?"

"I'm embarrassed to say it has been a while—my kidneys were just great!" Jill answered. She had no idea when the last one had been, but she knew that the Intravenous Pylogram is a very uncomfortable procedure. A dye is injected in a vein—100 cc's of it—and a series of X-rays is taken to see how quickly it passes through the kidneys. It always made Jill nauseated and very hot. Most quadriplegics have it done every six months, but Jill knew her kidneys were in very good shape. She put off the IVP whenever she could, and Dr. Reynolds didn't push it.

"You're healthy," Reynolds said as the three of them placed Jill back in her chair. "I'll let you know the results of the tests. Otherwise you're in great shape."

On the way home June and Jill stopped to shop, June for groceries and Jill for school materials—posters, construction paper, a few books from the paperback rack, stick-on shelf paper and three potted plants.

The next morning Edward S. Feldman showed up on

the dot of 10:30. He was a comfortable-looking man, ove[r] six feet tall, amiable. Sort of a big, friendly teddybear look to him, Jill thought. He reached out to shake hands, and she gave him her left hand so he would realize she wa[s] unable to grasp in the normal way. He shook June's hand studying her face for a long moment.

"It would be wonderful if you could play your own part, Mrs. Kinmont," he said. "Would you consider that?"

He said he was convinced that Jill's story would make a magnificent motion picture and that it would have un-limited appeal to audiences of all ages.

"It seems to be girls between the ages of twelve and sixteen that write me all the letters," Jill said.

"Those are the ones who'll see the picture five times."

Feldman seemed not to know much about Jill's skiing background, and he apparently had not read the book about her skiing career, accident, and rehabilitation, which had been published six years before. But he had no doubts about getting financial backing for the film.

Jill realized that Feldman didn't know about Dick Buek or about Audra Jo and her polio or about most of the other dramatic sidelights in her life. She filled him in, and he became quite excited about it.

"If teaching is part of it," Jill said, "I want it to be with the Indian kids."

"You can count on it."

June sat down on the couch, and Jill and Feldman talked for another half-hour. They said nothing about money, but aside from that, the project sounded great. Feldman said he would be in touch with Jill's lawyer, Herb Weiser.

And that's all there was to it. Jill went off to the dentist feeling very good about the whole thing.

That evening she said to her mother, "Isn't that some-thing. Feldman said, 'I must say I have an extreme amount of admiration for your mother, that rises even above my admiration for you.' You know I really believe him."

"He certainly treated me with great respect. But I do

get the feeling he thinks that film-making is something I just don't know about."

"Well, do you?"

June laughed and shook her head.

Jill was thoughtful for a moment. "I got a kick out of what he said about the *Life* article, Mom."

"What?"

"He thought the girl was wonderful, but he didn't think much of the article. I don't think he thought I should want to be vulnerable. I am supposed to conquer the world."

Jill met with Weiser two days later. Weiser met with Feldman two days after that. Weiser telephoned Jill with Feldman's offer, which included a percentage of the film's profits and a job as a technical advisor during the shooting. Jill said she would think it over. She was actually more concerned about school at the moment, for she had been about to leave to set up her classroom when Weiser telephoned.

The following day Weiser called again and said, "Well, do you want to go for it or not?" Jill said she did.

•   •   •

The last third of 1972 went by without further word on the film. There was not exactly a vacuum in Jill's life, however. She was in charge of a new reading lab which the Hawthorne School had put together under her direction. The project originated during a conference to determine how the school could help gifted students who were bored by much of their schoolwork. Jill said, "Well, I can sure teach them to be teachers." She had always used children as teaching assistants so that her reading students would get more individual attention. "I know the honor students can understand simple teaching methods and put them to use with our kids who have reading problems."

The principal promised several thousand dollars to stock a resource center, and the project was soon underway, led by Jill and 27 honor students who met with her once a week. When one or more children in a classroom needed help with reading, the teacher would call for assistance.

41

One of the honor students would check on what was needed, pick up the appropriate material from the resource center, and come into the classroom to work with the children.

This project was in addition to Jill's regular remedial reading classes. There was also a jumble of other projects and minor crises which she duly recorded in her daybook.

6 September—Dr. Lathrop, Loyola U. called re Mar. 12 speech. Refused to speak.

20—Broke my tooth on Jordan almond. Now have to do crown & impression all over.

22 October—Jerry came and we sort of let him have it: divorced with 2 kids, and he gives up his business venture. Jer builds my desk & shelf.

24—Mom leaves 10 a.m. for Bob & Vikki's. Seth Kinmont born 3 pm

4 November—Anaheim luncheon: Alex Haley—fantastic.

5—Mom starts Weight Watchers.

11—Wrote speech for La Habra Presbyterian Church.

14—RAIN poured all morning. Filming commercial at school for HEW: Stop Handicapping the Handicapped. $500. Quite an experience!

15—Holly Hines called Cascade Films for ss# and must I join Screen Actors Guild?

17—Holly Hines called. Don't worry about SAG. Won't call it acting.

23—Thanksgiving day. Mom throws up! Bob diarrhea. But fun day and good food.

26—Sunny warm lovely day. Kissinger unsure of self much of his life.

29—Received check for H.E.W. Commercial. Only $292. ROBBED!

3 December—Filmed Time-Life documentary 12-4. Went well.

4—Jan called. Picture to be in *The Best of LIFE*. RAIN.

6—Had to retape voice-over for commercial and it went just swell.

7—Julie sick and Mom drives.

8—Julie sick Mom drives.

10—Prop tax due $599.22. Period begins. Slept till 10 am. Quiet, easy, cold, windy Sunday.

14—Jerry went whaling & got whales & dolphins.

15—Did sound for commercial again.

16—Anna coming! Yippee! Changed catheter.

18—Mom, Vikki, Bob & I went to Nauman's opening. Fun. Met attractive man.

21—Sick with runs! Ugh!

28—Called Professional Domestic for live-in help. Called back: Guatemalan girl nurse can't drive $175.

• • •

The new year came in heavy. June was feeling the pressure of housework and driving Jill to school and taking care of her morning and evening. They had gone through a series of housekeepers, live-ins and live-outs. Five Mexican girls in 18 months, and usually they couldn't drive and couldn't speak English. Now they couldn't find anyone at all. It was not much better trying to find someone to get Jill up in the morning and drive her to school.

June was slow to complain, so the strain showed first in her body. A rash appeared on the tops of her hands. One day as she leaned forward to readjust Jill in her chair, pain struck her low in the back. She was exhausted by supper time. Without hired help, she still had to take care of Jill and drive and take care of the house whether she felt sick or not.

When June was tired, Jill could not function easily. Whenever Jill decided to do something, it required a lot of setting up. Getting out paints, for example, and looking for her favorite brushes and moving boxes in the garage to find her palette. When June was finally able to relax, Jill felt guilty about asking for additional help.

In the past, if a housekeeper or driver didn't show up, June had had the energy to take over. Now she had no reserves. The situation was getting worse, and Jill felt what she called *the clutch*. This was a tight, hot sensation that

43

seemed to be coming from her abdomen, and it left her frustrated and irritable. Neither she nor her mother felt free to complain.

On the third of January Jill phoned the *Santa Monica Outlook* and placed an ad for a girl to live in. The ad was to run two weeks. On the fifth, June's back was hurting so much she couldn't lift Jill into or out of bed. They were able to get a neighbor, Patty, to pinch hit for a few days. June's rash spread to her neck. By the eighth, she couldn't lift, couldn't bend, could hardly stand. She lay in bed with a heating pad, and Jill telephoned around to find someone to drive her to work and to the store. A boy in the neighborhood, Bruce, took over the driving, and June's sister Beverly came over to help out.

June recovered after four days and Jill found a girl, Julie, to get her up in the mornings. But Julie had an accident and didn't show up for a few days.

Jill and her mother tried to talk about their problems. They didn't get very far. Jill said, "If we just had someone we could *depend* on."

"It's not just that."

"What do you mean, Mom?"

June shook her head.

"Well, *tell* me."

"Well, even when we have help, Jill, you keep asking me to do things." Her voice sounded muffled because she had the flu.

"If I do, Mom, it's only because . . ."

"Because June always does it better, so Jill keeps asking June to do it. It takes more explaining to get the girl to do it, but she could do it."

"Why didn't you *say* something?"

"After all, Jill, you're the one who's paying the help. She's standing right there in front of you!"

Jill realized this was perfectly true. She just hadn't noticed. She also realized that whenever a long weekend came up and June had a chance to rest, off they went to Bishop, with June driving. She said, "There's one thing I do think of, Mom. There's no reason why you can't go

44

out in the evening even when nobody's here. I have **a** phone, and if you want, you can tell the neighbors I'm here alone for a few hours. That way you could take an evening class and be able to count on being there every time. Okay?" Jill was still afraid of being left alone. "Another thing, Mom, it's time you went on a real trip. We've got enough money. That's the only way you can get a real rest."

"I'd like that," June said. "I've been wanting to go to Scotland and check on Kinmont Willie and some of the other Kinmonts who fought in the English border wars."

Julie was able to work part-time, getting Jill up and to school every day. The housekeeping problem remained unresolved.

4

Action

Late in January 1973, Judi Rosner, assistant producer at Filmways, called to say a writer had been selected to do the screenplay. Could she bring him over?

They came to Pacific Palisades immediately after school a few days later. Judi was tall and slim, a bleached dungaree type with a tailored shirt open low in front. Short dark hair. She introduced David Seltzer, who smiled boyishly and said at once, "I've been wanting to meet you, but I feel nervous about it." He was dark and slight, sensitive, with delicate hands. He wore dungarees, a light blue Madison Avenue shirt, and a tweed sport coat. Jill was very much attracted to both of them. They were both about 28, casual, perfectly at ease.

David sat in the big wing chair in the living room. He said he was going to write a beautiful story. He talked of things he had written. The latest was the film *One Is a Lonely Number*. He said he wanted to get together with Jill a number of times to gather material for the screenplay. He understood something about paralysis since his brother had had polio as a child. Also, he had spent several summers in Bishop. Then David asked, with some concern, "Do you remember at the end of the *Life* article you were quoted as saying you were vulnerable?"

"Oh, yes," Jill said. "That was there because the interviewer said to me, 'You mean you like to stay vulnerable?' and I just said I guess so."

David looked puzzled. Jill said, "What does vulnerable mean, exactly? Doesn't it mean open to everything—pain, joy . . . I'm not at all sure I want to be vulnerable."

David was obviously disappointed, but he went on to talk about how he saw Jill's story unfolding on the screen. He wanted to show the devastation of her total depression, without pulling any punches, and then how she managed by sheer will power to pull herself up out of it.

"But David, I never *was* depressed."

"With that terrible handicap, you had to have been depressed."

"There were moments of depression when I was left alone, but no time when I had to say, pull yourself together and let's get out of it. And if I am depressed, it isn't usually because I'm handicapped. The point is, I don't like being depressed and I want to get out of it very quickly. I think that's part of the business of my not ever having a lengthy depression when I was hurt."

David said he *had* to dramatize Jill's reaction to her accident, and he talked a lot about what liberties he might legitimately take in rewriting her life for the movies.

Jill said again that she had never become despondent. She had had so much support from her family and such a good self-image that it just never happened. During her rehabilitation she knew fellow patients whose spouses or relatives couldn't take it, so the jolt of the disabling accident was soon followed by the collapse of love and emotional support from the family and friends and lovers. In Jill's case, her father's reaction had been, "We do what has to be done, and we build around that." And June had said, "After all, the accident happened to all of us. I just hope we can still live as normal a life as possible." And she had taken pains to be on hand *all* the time.

David was still worried about how to dramatize Jill's accident and its aftermath. Jill said, "Have you read the book yet? It's good, and it's really accurate. Crammed with vignettes and details."

"No," David said, "but I'm looking forward to it."

The meeting was over too soon for Jill. She could have talked a lot more, and David was exciting. She was glad he had been chosen for the screenplay.

"I feel real good about it," she told June that evening. "He's a neat guy, and he wants to see a lot of me to talk about the script. He had the idea I must have had a terrible depression, but I explained about all the support I got."

"Well," June said, "each of us knew that if we got really low it would bring the other person down, too, so we didn't allow it to happen. And you were so full of ideas and goals, and you always acted on them. We weren't settled up in Washington for an hour before you were on the phone trying to get into the School of Education."

"And you were there to dial the phone for me, and Dad was there to make it all possible."

• • •

David's second visit was at school on Friday. He was impressed with Jill's bright, cheerful room, with the olive tree in the courtyard outside one window, and with the private telephone the school had given her last fall. They talked at first in her classroom and then in the cafeteria. He wanted fresh incidents to illustrate her skill on skis and later her ability as a teacher. Could she think of any good examples?

Jill told him about an unlikeable pupil who wouldn't work at all and who frustrated her constantly. He would saunter in to class ten minutes late. He would drop his pencil and break the point, go to the pencil sharpener

48

and back to his seat, drop the pencil again. He stared at study sheets he had placed upside down on his desk. One day when he was supposed to be writing a story he stood up and danced around and started bouncing a ball of wadded-up paper against the blackboard. It was the last straw, and Jill took off after him in her wheelchair. He backed away from her, and she backed him right up against the wall and pinned him there. He was literally cornered, and he couldn't do a thing about it. "I said, 'Harry, I want you to do what you set out to do, and I want you to do it now and finish it before you leave. You understand?' He said, 'I'll tell my parents and we'll sue.' I said, 'Okay, but meanwhile you finish that story, is that clear?' Well, I let him out and he finished the story and we've been good friends ever since."

The bell sounded for the end of lunch hour. It had been another good meeting. David said he needed more material and would call Jill Monday.

That evening Dave McCoy's oldest daughter, Penny McCoy Barrett, telephoned from Bishop to see what the chances were of her being Jill's skiing double in the movie. She was a spectacular skier and had been on the United States Olympic ski team in 1968.

"That's a great idea," Jill said. "I'll insist on it. But I don't have any idea when they'll be shooting the picture. They don't even have the script yet, let alone the money."

A girl from Egypt named Sally called about the live-in housekeeping job. She said she would come for an interview tomorrow, Saturday.

On Saturday a copy of *Variety* arrived by mail from Feldman's office. It contained an enthusiastic article about Filmways's plans for *The Jill Kinmont Story*. Sally never showed. Dick McGarry came for dinner, with a gift of saltwater taffy, and took Jill to see *Jeremiah Johnson*.

On Sunday Sally came for an interview. In no way was she going to work out. She couldn't drive, and she couldn't speak English.

On Monday David never called.

On Tuesday June left immediately after supper for a

49

3-hour philosophy class. It was the first time she had ever left Jill alone in the house in the evening.

A week later David finally phoned. He came by to pick up Jill's scrapbooks and notebooks. They had a great time poring through old clippings and photographs and talking about Bishop. David had read the book thoroughly. He had expected to like it but hadn't. It was a great chronology, he said, but it wasn't creative at all.

•   •   •

Jill spent the weekend in Bishop, and she spent some of the time looking at real estate. Secretly, she dreamed of living in Bishop again all year round. At any rate, she needed a home there every summer. She didn't find anything both suitable and reasonable. Back in Los Angeles, she considered house trailers and looked at a number of them.

Burk Uzzle showed up for a long weekend, and he and Jill spent much of Saturday checking out all the motorcycle salesrooms they could find. He took Jill and June to the Motocross races in San Bernadino on Sunday and to Le Petit Moulin on Monday for dinner. They talked about Burk and Jan and the two *Life* stories and about motorcycle racing.

Jill had been waiting for David to show up to talk about the script, but he never appeared. He telephoned several times and wrote her a letter, but that was about it. And on March 24 he announced to her that the screenplay was finished! Jill was very disappointed that he had not spent more time getting material from her about her life. She had expected to work with him a lot more than she had. Until this moment she had never picked up on the fact that this was the way he was going to go—check a few things out with her and then go off and write what he'd had in mind all the time. He said he had rushed it through in three weeks in order to finish it before a writers' strike was called. And that was the last Jill heard about the script for seven weeks.

What she did hear about was the contract. It arrived,

and she read it with some misgivings. It seemed to her that she was pretty well signing her life away. She was granting Filmways the sole and exclusive rights to her story throughout the world, forever. She had wanted script approval, but the contract stated she would have no veto power over any episodes in the script.

She realized that Filmways would have the right to make a film about something she might do next year or who knows when.

"I feel like junking the whole thing," Jill said to her mother. She seemed to be on the edge of tears, but she closed her eyes, breathed slowly and deeply, and lifted her head until she was sitting as straight as a cadet.

"I know it's not going to be easy," June said, "but this is your opportunity to become independent. I'm getting older, and a time will come when I won't be able to take care of you. If you get sick then, you'll need a lot more money than other people."

Jill heard. Jill agreed. But she said nothing. Inside, she felt as if all the busy fragments of her life were jumbled together like pieces of glass in a broken Thermos bottle. Outside, she appeared to be aloof and in command, able to handle whatever it was she would have to handle. Her lips were set and her eyes dead serious. She was poised. She was perfectly, if precariously, balanced. Her thinking was very, very clear. She was in control. But stress had given her face a look of shock, a look of helpless surprise.

"You would need a full-time person to take care of you," June was saying. "You don't want to go on welfare or to the County Hospital."

Jill returned the contract to her lawyer and telephoned him to say Filmways was not to be given rights to anything later than the date on which principal photography commenced.

•   •   •

Jill was still thinking of buying a trailer to live in during the summer, and while she was in Bishop for Easter vacation she looked for property on which to park

51

it. Jerry was in Bishop working as a carpenter, and he also scouted for property.

Jerry later telephoned Pacific Palisades to say his search for property had been unsuccessful. He also reported that he had just had an emergency call from his first wife, Paula, with whom Jerry's two children were living in Park City, Utah. Jerry flew to Park City to help her out and be with the children.

Paula later asked Jerry if he would take the children for the summer, and Jerry was delighted. He called June to say he was going to take them hitchhiking from Utah to Orcas Island, in Puget Sound, and also to Canada to look up Lyn Boyd. Jerry had met Lyn several years before and had introduced her to June and Jill. June had been so impressed that she told Jill later, "Now why can't Jerry pick a girl like *that?* She's warm and easy and has that lovely quality of being uncritical."

Jill still hadn't found a place for the summer, and she telephoned the McCoy's to ask about Kandi McCoy's recent wedding and to sound them out about using the house again. She talked with Roma, but Roma didn't offer the house. "She's been very generous for four summers," Jill said to June. "I guess it's time to find our own place."

David wrote that the writers' strike was over and the screenplay was on its way to Ed Feldman. Feldman himself turned up at the Hawthorne School Open House a week later.

"I have the script," he said. "I love it. You'll love it. Beautiful job. We'll sell it easily."

"I can't stand waiting," Jill said. "When will I see it?"

"It's in the mail."

•　　•　　•

The screenplay came, 128 pages in a sky-blue cover bearing the words "This Script Is The Property Of FILM-WAYS Inc. No One Is Authorized To Dispose Of Same. Please do not lose or destroy this script." Below was the title: *THE OTHER SIDE OF THE MOUNTAIN*. On the title page it said, "A Screenplay Based on the life of Jill Kinmont, Written by David Seltzer. *First Draft.*"

Jill was excited, anxious, eager, and almost afraid to start reading. She turned the title page and read:

EXT. BISHOP, CALIFORNIA—DAWN
That first moment of vague illumination, when vision is but a mirage. Before us, barely visible in a dark blue tableau, is the majestic peak of MT. TOM: stately, silent, its dim silhouette capped with snow.

Jill was hooked. "CAMERA SLOWLY PANNING to a bed where JILL KINMONT lies. She is thirty years old and beautiful." She read breathlessly, wondering what was going to happen next. "CLOSE ANGLE on Jill's face, unmoving." Then we hear her voice, off screen. ". . . I think . . . the hardest time . . . is waking up in the morning. Those first . . . vague moments . . . before I fully remember who I am . . . and dwell instead . . . on who I was. . . ."

Jill whispered aloud to herself, "Beautiful. Just beautiful. Not true, but really beautiful."

She couldn't wait to continue, but she had to wait because she had to teach school. She was amazed at how drawn she was to the story. She flipped through the pages. The film started in the present and was full of flashbacks. Her skiing with Audra Jo, winning the nationals, Audra Jo's polio, her own accident, rehabilitation, Mad Dog Buek and his escapades and his love for her, the fight to get the School of Education to accept someone in a wheelchair, Buek's death.

That afternoon and evening she read the screenplay slowly and carefully. She cried four times. She kept thinking, oh that poor girl, what a tragic life! But she seldom thought of the JILL in the script as herself, *JILL*. A few things she did identify with. She loved "YOUNG JILL on skis, exploding in a spray of snow over the crest of a hill." She was relieved to read what

53

David had written about the Rocking K and how JILL said, "Dad worked his whole life to put a down payment on it, and we ran it as a guest ranch, each member of the family doing his part."

However, it was a shock to read that she had let out a bloodcurdling scream after dreaming of her accident. It was upsetting to find her friend and one-time protégée Linda Meyers coming off as a teen-age pest, and there was an inexcusable scene in which Audra Jo was turned into a hard, sarcastic, sternly lecturing paraplegic.

When June asked, "How is it?" Jill put it down and nodded sagely. "Some of it is pretty hard to accept," she said, "but there are hints of truth all the way through." She realized she was going to have to go over the whole thing word for word and write in corrections and suggestions. "But, Mom, there's the most beautiful scene with the Indian kids. That's the first place I cried."

Jill telephoned David the next day and said, "I read the script. I really liked a lot of the parts." There was a long, awkward silence. Then she mentioned the things she was most uncomfortable about. "The corny lines where Dick Buek and I meet, the made-up conflicts with my friends, Dave coming off like a jock coach. And I worry about how the Indian reservation is depicted."

David asked her to make a list of her objections and suggestions. He said there simply had to be a lot of conflict developed between people to make a dramatic film. He said things had to be telescoped from a whole life down to 100 minutes, and the hospital scene was like that.

Jill sighed, "I suppose . . ." she said.

"Well," David replied, "I'll be over and we'll talk."

Jill spent a lot of time with the screenplay, writing her objections and suggestions in it. She covered some pages with more words than there were in the script itself, writing between lines, in margins, at the top and bottom, and even on the back of the page. In her early days of skiing at Mammoth Mountain, the place was much too primitive to have had showers or locker rooms. Dave never raised his voice while coaching or at any other

54

time. Audra Jo and Linda and Jill were not smart alecs with one another; insults and sarcasm were just not a part of any of them. U.S. champion Buddy Werner never said he wanted to go to the 1956 Olympics with her as man and wife. Dave wouldn't "struggle" to wipe the windshield; he never accomplished anything by struggling. But David Seltzer got Dave down perfectly when he had Dave say, at the start of a big race, "Smooth and pretty. Just go down there and have fun."

Jill wrote OMIT fifteen times in the Jill–Audra Jo hospital scene. She was outraged by the line which had June saying, "Every time I mention rehabilitation, Jill says she doesn't need anybody to teach her to sell pencils." Beside this speech she wrote *"REALLY!??"*, underlined it three times, and surrounded it with a sunburst of angry lines.

Jill and June went to Bishop for the weekend to look at property again, and Jill visited Audra Jo as soon as she arrived, late Friday. Audra Jo had married Jill's therapist, Lee Baumgarth, and they lived with their two children south of West Line Street, close to the reservation. She had skied with Jill and taught swimming with her at Keough's and worked with her in the Rocking K dining room before she was paralyzed from the waist down by polio. She lived in a wheelchair, but she could drive and she had learned to hoist herself into her car and pull her folding wheelchair in after her.

Audra Jo and Jill could have passed for sisters in high school, and they still looked much alike, facing each other in their wheelchairs in the wide green back yard. Jill's face was leaner, and her manner was less formal.

"A.J.," Jill said, "what do you think I've got here?" She turned the blue-covered manuscript on her tray so Audra Jo could see it.

"The works? Looks impressive."

"You'll be furious when you read your part. You come off like the director of a girl's reform school."

"And are you *Beauty?*"

"I'm *depressed,* Josie. The writer—David—knows that

55

all paraplegics become hopelessly despondent before they dramatically save themselves."

"*You* didn't. *I* didn't. Haven't you told him?"

"I told him. And I told him it was mostly due to the fantastic support from my family."

"And the attention," Audra Jo said. "I always had attention, too. Friends. I remember a girl my age at the hospital with a similar injury. She had no friends and had a hostile relationship with her parents. She was bitter and withdrawn. But that's a different movie."

"David seems to have decided I was depressed, and I guess he didn't want to hear anything different. I should have seen that at the beginning. He had my life all worked out before he came to ask me about it."

"You must admit, Jill, it's a lot more dramatic to be on the verge of suicide and be saved by courage or, better, by a handsome prince. What else are you worried about?"

"About the real people," Jill said, "and how they'll feel about how they come off on the screen." She found the hospital scene and read it aloud. "You visit me in the hospital where I'm permanently paralyzed, but they have me insisting that I can walk again. We've obviously had a big argument, and I say: What do you want me to do, give up? Stop trying? And you say: For what, an acting award? Jill: To walk. A.J.: What's so great about walking. For God's sake, a three-year-old can walk."

"I would not say 'For God's sake,' Jill."

"And you wouldn't say this, either: 'Face it. Admit it. There's only one thing that kills cripples, and that's taking themselves too seriously. So quit moaning about your Olympic medals and start thanking God you've still got your head.' "

Audra Jo was upset but seemed to be taking it better than Jill. "If it's about us, why not make us seem *like* us?"

Jill said, "I suppose they've got to have *something* to show that you know something about paralysis that I don't. So what can we do about this?"

"The two of us could rewrite it for them."

56

"Great. Where's the paper and pencils?"

They wrote one page of a new scene and planned to write the other two pages as soon as they could get together again. They eventually finished the scene and mailed it to David.

•   •   •

Shortly after returning from Bishop, Jill had a telephone call from a friend in Bishop saying there was a small comfortable house for rent at $160 a month. A Roy and Beverly Boothe wanted to sublet it for the summer. The owner was Roy's brother, John. Jill called Beverly Boothe and then she called Audra Jo and asked her to check out the house for her. Audra Jo and Lee went to the Boothes', ran her wheelchair through all the doorways and around or between bulky items of furniture, and reported back. The house was ideal but needed a ramp for the two steps up to the front porch. The owner lived next door and would be there if they had any problems.

"Mom, we're in!"

"What?" June said. "In what?"

"In luck. We got a house."

David came for lunch the next day. He returned the pictures and scrapbooks he had borrowed, and they talked about the picture—or the "package," as he called it. There was a kind of poker game going on between Filmways and the studios, people playing against one another. What studio was really going to buy the package? Or would they have to sell out for a TV movie? Feldman wanted to hold out for the bigger stakes.

Wednesday the thirteenth of June was the last day of school. The final version of the film contract arrived, and Jill signed it and sent it to her lawyer. Friday she flew to Chicago where she was a recipient of a "Golden Plate Award" and one of the speakers in a series of seminars at the American Academy of Achievement. The talk went well. On the way home she stopped in Durango, Colorado, to visit Linda Meyers Tikalsky, her husband Frank, and their children.

Linda's first day on skis 22 years ago had been a disaster. She had been a bustling, bundly, bubbly little girl, and Jill and Audra Jo promised to teach her how to ski. Her borrowed aluminum skis stuck to the snow, and she had to point them straight down and *walk* them back to the warming hut. Audra Jo was convinced she would never put on skis again. But Linda learned to ski and trained doggedly. Jill was her idol, and Dave McCoy became her teacher and friend, and soon after Jill's accident she was winning national titles. She later raced for the United States in both the 1960 and 1964 Olympics.

"Linda Mae," Jill said, "I've got something for you, but you're going to murder me . . ." She gave Linda the script. Linda loved it for quite a few pages. Then—Jill was studying her face—then she began to growl. She had reached the "Linda" scenes. She was also outraged by the characterizations of Audra Jo and Bill Kinmont.

"I'm going to write and let these guys *know!*" she said. "Okay," Jill said. "But cool it until they get squared away on all the arrangements. I don't want to rock the boat at this point."

"All right. Just let me know."

Jill was home in Pacific Palisades barely long enough to pick up school materials for the summer program and to call Dave McCoy to ask if he could get a ramp built at the Boothe house. Then she and June were off to Bishop for the summer.

They reached Bishop about noon and drove directly to the house. Jill had remembered the great and beautiful elms that made a canopy completely over the road, and she had envisioned a cool and shady bungalow. However, the elms on Elm Street stopped in the 600 block, and their summer house was at 763.

The house was comfortably small, tan, and it did have a tree in the front yard. Directly behind it, and quite close, was a second house, same size, same color: 763-A. Probably where the owner lived. Some crotchety old bachelor, most likely. A dirt driveway served both houses, and the Kinmont van pulled into it.

58

Part of the front steps was bridged by a brand new ramp, and two boys were hammering in the last few nails. One was Dave's nephew, Mike. They came over to help Jill out of the van.

"That looks pretty neat," Jill said.

"Dave said to do it just the way you want it. He said if she asks for an elevator, build her one."

"All I want is to get in the house, Mike. Let me try it and see if I can make it." The chair slowed as she started up the ramp, but she made it onto the porch with no problems at all.

A young woman appeared at the door with a mop and bucket. "Welcome," she said. "I'm Beverly Boothe. I was just giving the kitchen the once-over."

"Nice place," Jill said. "That's my Mom halfway into the van."

The boys helped June unload the three suitcases and six boxes in the back of the van. Beverly said her brother-in-law was on the road but would be back tomorrow and would check to see if everything was working all right. She excused herself, saying she had the afternoon's work cut out for her down at the ranch.

The house was ready to live in except for food in the refrigerator. June and Jill went shopping for groceries as soon as they had unpacked the suitcases.

Audra Jo and Lee came over for supper. Lee was a husky, serious man, clean-shaven and very good-looking. He pushed his wife up the ramp and went back to check its construction. He approved. Audra Jo wheeled herself inside. Since she had full use of her arms, she had no need for an electric wheelchair.

Jill was in the living room, and June came out of the kitchen, wiping her hands on her apron. "No Watergate tonight," June said. "TV's out. Guess we're going to have to talk."

They did talk. They talked continually before, during, and after dinner. They began with a detailed comparison of schools in Bishop and Los Angeles. Lee was a science teacher in the high school, as well as a physical therapist.

Audra Jo was president of the school board. They envied some of the special programs at the very well-heeled Hawthorne Elementary School in Beverly Hills, but they felt the local schools were keenly aware of what was needed and getting better all the time.

"Well, you know," Jill said, "the truth is . . . I'd really like to come up. Is there anything for someone with my skills?"

"As a matter of fact," Audra Jo said, "there's some talk about wanting a diagnostic-type reading teacher. The salary's not the kind of thing you find in Beverly Hills, however."

Lee said, "I'd think it over twice, Jill. You thrive on pretty sophisticated stuff, and the cultural scene up here just isn't that great, and social opportunities are nothing like what you're finding down south."

"Well, I do have friends in Bishop who are stimulating, Lee."

"Thanks," he said and laughed.

"And when I just go down the street and know most everyone I meet, well, I really feel good about that."

"There's also June's adult education classes," Lee said. "She's been studying art and psychology down at UCLA and . . . what else, June?"

"Philosophy right now, Lee. At one time or another, it's been woodworking, early child development, water-color."

June was not enthusiastic about the idea of moving. Bishop was heavy with old memories of living here with Bill. The Rocking K was still there and pretty much falling apart. For her, there were problems with Bishop. She didn't have the same feelings her children had about it.

"Just look at all the smog and traffic down there," Jill said. "We can still go down for visits and concerts and things. And there *are* extension classes in Bishop, Mom. It must mean something that we never stopped subscribing to the Bishop newspaper."

"It's not very glamorous up here," Audra Jo said.

"I'm getting very tired of the glamour, Josie."

"Another thing," Lee said, partly teasing and partly serious. "There's not going to be as many men up here."

"I'll do okay."

"Yeah, but if you're looking for somebody . . ."

"Lee, I don't need to go around *looking*. Anyway, I've worked out that being single isn't the sign of a loser."

Lee scowled and Audra Jo applauded. Audra Jo said, "I'll find out what I can."

5

John

Shortly after the Baumgarths left, there was a cautious knock on the screen door.

"Come in." Jill moved her wheelchair forward so she could see the slender figure silhouetted at the door.

"I just stopped by to see if there's anything you need."

Jill was wearing a Levi skirt and white blouse. Her long hair was pinned back on the sides. She wished she knew how she looked, and she wished her feet weren't up with the shoes off. "Well, come on in," she said.

A man entered wearing Levi's, laced workboots, and a white T-shirt. He stood awkwardly and said, "I'm John Boothe." He had short hair and black horn-rimmed glasses. Jill's first thought was, oh dear, I thought he'd be too old, but he's too young. He seemed extremely shy and wouldn't look her in the eye.

"Won't you sit down?"

"Oh no, thanks."

"Please." Jill backed her chair neatly to make way for

him. She had two ankle weights on her tray that she used to exercise her biceps and deltoids. She picked them up between her palms and tossed them on a chair.

"I'm Jill," she said, "as I guess you figured. This is my Mom, June."

"Pleased to meet you, June," he said. "I just came in off the truck and saw the lights on."

"Are you a truck driver?" June asked.

"That's right." He sat on the front edge of the couch, holding a yellow cap with a visor and the letters CAT right on the front. His hair curled up slightly at the back.

"Did you drive?" he said.

"Yes."

"How many days?"

"We just left this morning."

"What? This morning? Where'd you come from?"

"L.A."

John leaned back on the couch and rubbed the back of his hand across his forehead. "Gosh, I thought you'd come from Seattle. That's where you were at the end of the book."

Jill laughed. "That was seven years ago."

John shifted uncomfortably. "You sure there isn't anything I can do for you?"

"Oh, no," Jill said. "Thanks." She took a swig from her water bottle.

June said, "Why, yes, John, maybe you could fix the TV. We missed the Watergate hearings tonight."

John frowned and glanced at Jill. "Sure. I'll do it first thing in the morning."

Jill could tell he didn't particularly go for the hearings. "Have you lived here all your life?" she said. She wished he had long hair. She knew that Bishop boys are always conservative if they've lived in Bishop all their lives.

June said, "Oh, yes. You remember who the Boothes are, don't you, Jill? They've run the Rainbow Pack Outfit for twenty years. Bill used to take his guests up there, and Dudley would send the wives and kids down to the Rocking K while the men were out in the mountains."

63

"I was away in the army for a couple years," John said. "Other than that, just driving trucks and working on the ranch and up at the pack station and watching my brother Roy roping at the rodeos."

"You know Lester Cline?" Jill said.

"I do, and I have the greatest respect for him."

"Lester picked me and Dave up once when we were hitchhiking back from Mammoth, and I went to sleep with my head on his shoulder. He was one of the best then, when I was sixteen, and he's still roping. Didn't he get hurt?"

"Oh, Lester's got broken up two dozen times. Last time was when a horse fell on him. But he's tough enough to keep going on. Still does a day's work on his horse even though it must be killing him. He's probably sixty-five now."

Jill thought the sleeves on John's shirt were too short. She half expected to see a cigarette pack rolled up in his sleeve. What a nice guy he is, she thought. Despite everything. He would look a lot better in a different kind of shirt.

* * *

John Boothe walked home—about 25 yards—in something of a daze. He had been uncomfortable at first and hadn't wanted to stay. He was amazed at how neatly and quickly Jill moved around in her chair, how she had gotten out of his way when he walked to the couch. The biggest surprise was how easy it was to be around her. At first he had been on the edge of his seat, looking for an excuse to go. Now he wished it hadn't ended so soon. He could have talked with her for ages. He was taken by the fact that she was a *very* pretty woman.

Actually, John had known a lot about Jill before he walked in on her an hour and a half ago. He had heard about her all his life and had read the articles in *Life* magazine. When he had learned she was coming, he had borrowed a copy of the book about her from Beverly, who had just borrowed it from a friend. The book was

A Long Way Up—The Story of Jill Kinmont, published in 1966. John had read it from cover to cover that same evening. He had strong feelings about it. He was impressed by how small most people's common complaints look alongside Jill's problems. When he met her in person, he was surprised to find she lived in Los Angeles and that she had long hair. The photographs in the book showed her with much shorter hair, and he had never imagined her looking differently. He wondered what it was like to have been famous all your life.

He spoke about her to Beverly on Saturday morning. Beverly said, "When she called, when I knew she was coming, I thought, oh . . . a famous person. But when you *meet* her . . . she's just right there, and warm, and so everyday. Never made a big deal about anything."

"She's got so much going," John said. "Me . . . I'm just living sort of day-to-day and don't give much of a damn about anything."

He walked over to the Kinmonts' house to fix the television set. He sauntered across the room with his head bent forward and his eyes on the carpet as if he didn't feel he was supposed to look around. Jill sat watching him as he knelt by the set. His hands were shaking, and Jill almost asked him if she could help him put the screwdriver in the slot. He said, "It's kind of hereditary. My grandfather couldn't get a screwdriver into the screw. I had to put it in for him, and then he'd turn it."

•   •   •

Jill met with her Indian tutors for several hours to brief them on what their responsibilities would be at the school.

In the afternoon John came by while she was sitting in the yard going over material she had brought from the Hawthorne School for her summer classes. He always walked very slowly.

"Hello," she said. With her left hand she pulled off the wrist brace that held her pen. "How are you doing?"

"You know, my Grandma Rosie was a great fan of yours," he said, sitting on the grass by her chair and lighting a cigarette. "She talked about you all the time. She followed all the champion ropers and she followed your skiing, and when you had your accident she was beside herself. She told me about that right away. She always made me read the articles about you. I stopped to see her in the hospital in Big Pine and mentioned you were coming. She was excited. I hope you can meet her, because you'd really like each other."

Jill was genuinely surprised. Why would an old woman —in her eighties by now—be so interested and concerned with a young girl she never knew? And why would a ranch woman be interested in a skier?

"John, did you ever ski?"

"Tried it once and lost my ski."

"Didn't you ever try it again?"

"No."

"Oh."

Jill asked where John had lived as a child.

"Two miles south of town on our ranch. Used to be the Brierly ranch."

"What was it like?"

"I remember no electricity when I was a kid."

"No *electricity*? That was only twenty-five years ago!"

"I remember when we put it in. And we had a propane gas stove. We had cattle and raised hay. When I was a kid we even raised chickens, and every morning I had to milk the cow."

"Sounds like pioneer days," Jill said. "I've been reading about the old times around the valley in *The Story of Inyo* and in *The Gentle Tamers*—about women of the early West."

"My mother's parents had a ranch in Bishop. Before that, around 1900, they came out from Iowa and homesteaded near Big Pine. That was Grandma Lucy. Her husband was a horse trader. Pretty foxy."

Jill said, "My grandfather came west from Illinois on horseback in . . . I guess 1898, living off the land. He was a romantic. There was still gold being found in the West."

66

"Did he settle around here?"

"California first, then he went to Grants Pass, Oregon. Some machinery had broken down, and he fixed it. Then he went to the Klondike, repairing mining machinery. And then to a heavy-duty machine shop in L.A. and became foreman after two years. That's where my dad got started."

"I love machines," John said. "My brother Roy—horses are his life, but I'd rather work with a tractor or a truck."

The conversation continued Sunday afternoon when John walked west on Elm Street with Jill to the school parking lot and back. They kept finding common threads. John's grandfather Boothe had been supervisor of the Inyo National Forest and had known Dave McCoy back when Dave was just beginning to develop Mammoth Mountain as a ski area. Jill had just been reading about the big fight between the Owens Valley and the city of Los Angeles over water rights in the 1920s. John's grandmother Lucy had something to do with that. Los Angeles had bought up most of the farmland in the valley, torn down the farms, let the orchards and fields revert to sagebrush, and was shipping all the water south in a 270-mile aqueduct. The ranchers laid siege to the new aqueduct, and Grandma Lucy sent food down to the men and baked cakes for them. That was about the time they blew the thing up.

School began on Monday. It was Jill's sixth summer—she had started with twenty Paiute children in the old Presbyterian Church on West Line—and her second year in the one-room Study Center. She now had 48 pupils and 12 tutors—four boys and five girls of high school age and three older women. The Center was run by the Tribal Council to provide educational, medical, and employment services for the local Indians, and all these activities were carried out in one and the same room.

The first day was nothing like the first day five years ago. Then the children had been extremely shy, keeping their heads down most of the time and saying very little.

Today, eight children were waiting when the van drove up, and they rushed to open the door and set the ramps and help Jill wheel down onto the ground. They still said little, but they were grinning and laughing. They carried cardboard boxes in from the car and then unpacked them. They wrote words on the blackboard for the first class—children going into first or second grade in September: *mat sat fat cat man fan tan can ran.* They wrote out the alphabet in capital letters and in lower case.

The Indians were not verbal like the Beverly Hills children. They didn't intellectualize or explain things. It had taken Jill some time at first to understand their quiet, shy, *feeling* way. Her students had no wish to compete. They identified first of all with the tribe and had been brought up to cooperate with friends and neighbors. They might know the answer to a question, but they didn't want to show up their friends.

The first class consisted of a dozen children recommended by their elementary school teachers because of serious reading problems, plus three others who came simply because they enjoyed the class. Everyone was welcome, and enrolled pupils sometimes brought along a brother or sister. The morning got underway with a gusty rendition of the alphabet song. *"A, B, C, D, E, F, G . . ."* One of the girls pointed to each letter as they sang.

"Okay now," Jill said. "I'm thinking of a word that begins like *man.* Can you think of another word that begins that way? If anyone knows how *man* begins . . ."

"Jill . . . I know!"

"Yes?"

"MMMM."

"So what's another word starting with *M?*"

"Me!"

"Great. Now what about rhymes? *Ran* rhymes with *man.* Who knows another word that rhymes with *man?*"

"Mat."

"No. That's another *M* word. A rhyme is when the *end* of the word sounds the same."

"Which end?"

Laughter.

"Bam."

"Not quite. That ends like *am*. It should end like *an*. Can you hear the difference?"

"Ran! Can! Dan!"

One of the tutors added *Dan* to the words on the board.

The class went very quickly, and the children were not at all eager to leave when it was over. It was story day for the third class, and there were some beauties. About a fierce tarbaby lurking in the marsh. About going rabbit-hunting and getting rattlesnakes instead. About the cat that fell into the toilet hole. When the stories were done, a boy named Arnold said, "Don't we still have some time? Can I read a book to my tutor?" A girl, Tracy, asked if she couldn't do some more word lists.

After the last class, Jill met briefly with the tutors. "Monday," she said, "I want you to start making out the assignments yourselves. Figure out three or four activities for each child. Discuss it with the child. Be sure to give him or her a few choices, because you'll get a lot more from them if *they* have made the choice."

Jill's goal was to train the tutors to do the teaching. The program could be considered a success as soon as it could be carried out without Jill's being there. The tutors were hired by the tribal Education Committee. Some of them couldn't spell or read very well, but they took responsibility for that and looked up words they didn't fully understand. They also learned quickly how hard it is sometimes to capture and keep interest or to get a message or a skill through to a child. They always told Jill exactly *why* they chose a certain assignment for a certain child, and they always followed it up. They also handled discipline, often talking with the parents if a child was making a lot of trouble. Sometimes the parents and tutor together chose a punishment they knew the child would really remember, such as not being allowed to come to school for two days.

Jill didn't see John that afternoon or evening, although

69

she heard his screen door bang several times. She realized that he talked with her only when she was working outside or when he had a request for inside work such as fixing the TV. He probably wasn't that interested.

John in fact was interested, but he was afraid he would be a pest. Also he was shy and not too comfortable about being teased. Beverly had said, "John, why don't you leave her alone? You'll drive her away."

On the Fourth of July John asked Jill if she wanted to watch the fireworks with him. At dusk he put a couple of beers in his jacket pocket and they went half a block to the school parking lot where they would have an open view. Jill was lighthearted, and she weaved back and forth along the road. When she came to the big white letters SCHOOL XING, she traced the C and the O's with her wheelchair. John stood watching her, hands in his pockets and a bemused grin on his face.

"I heard you were married before," she said, coming to a stop beside him. "What happened?"

"I sure as hell don't want to talk about that."

"Well, something must have happened. What kind of person was she?" Jill was wondering who she was, whether she was still around, and whether she, Jill, might even *know* her.

John shrugged.

"How long were you married?"

"Let's go," he said, and started walking again. She followed, and eventually he said, "Six years."

"How long since you were divorced?"

"Gee, I can't remember."

"Come on, John."

"Probably about three years."

"Does she have the children?"

"No, we didn't have any kids. And this is the closest thing to a date I've had for years."

"I don't believe that."

"Believe it. You want a swig of this beer?"

"If you'll hold it for me."

70

He held the can while she drank. She said, "How come you decided to be a truck driver, John?"

"Same reason you chose teaching, I suppose."

"I teach because I can't imagine myself doing anything else."

"Yeah. That's how I feel about driving a truck."

"You never wanted to go on in school?"

"Nope. I didn't like school, and I never wanted to leave Bishop."

"We're opposites."

"I doubt that."

"What are you, twenty-eight?" she said.

"I'm thirty-two."

"Oh," Jill said as she rolled off toward the far side of the parking lot where they should have a good view.

"So you're the daughter of the owner of the Rocking K," he said when he caught up with her. "I must have seen you around. Did you ever teach swimming?"

"Yes."

"Maybe I saw you, then. Pretty and kind of stuck-up. I want you to know something. *Now* you're just plain beautiful. I suppose you hear that all the time."

She shook her head, frowning.

"I keep expecting to see men drive up to the place to take you out."

The fireworks began. A little early and not spectacular, but full of wonder. Graceful arcs up into a sky that was still pink at the edges. The Sierra made a clear silhouette to the west that became visible again after each shower of fire.

"How do you like teaching Indians?" John asked when they started home.

"I love it."

"You've got your work cut out for you. I hear they're pretty far behind."

"John, they're not dumb, if that's what you're implying. They may be shy and don't have confidence to speak up in class, but they have a *lot* of potential."

71

"Whatever you say."

"John, I teach in Beverly Hills, too, and the kids down there really know what's happening intellectually. But they are so over-exposed to everything that many of them are very insecure children. In one sense they could never know what the Indians know about simple survival. But the Indian kids—if given a chance, they could know everything the Beverly Hills kids know."

John said, "That may be so. And I know there's a lot of prejudice around here, and I've got my share of that."

"John, do you want to get married again?"

He was surprised but didn't show it. "Sure," he said lightly. "If I can find some cute young thing."

●　●　●

The first week of school went very well, and Jill loved it, but in her daybook it was never mentioned. John's name appeared in nearly every entry. When she didn't see him, she was aware of where he was, because her bedroom faced his house and she always heard his screen door slam when he went in or out. He stopped to talk to her for a minute on the front lawn one Saturday morning on his motorcycle. He only stopped long enough to say he would show her some movies he had taken of Bishop's Mule Day celebration, and then he took off to change the sprinklers at the ranch. He returned shortly afterwards because he had forgotten his cigarettes.

Two days later the telephone rang at breakfast time, and Beth Fawley, the girl who was now getting Jill up in the morning, answered it. "It's your romantic interest," she said, taking the telephone to Jill. John said he had a load to deliver to Aspen, Colorado, and would be gone several days. She watched him leave the house with a suitcase and a Thermos bottle which he set in the back of his pick-up before driving off. Jill did not like watching him go. Two days later Beth surprised Jill by asking, "Isn't your romantic interest back in town yet?" Jill had had no idea that things were so obvious.

John's Grandma Rosie died while he was still in Aspen,

and one of the first things John said when he returned on Saturday was, "I'm sad that you and Grandma Rosie never met. If she'd have known we were carrying on, Jill, it would have been the most beautiful thing she'd ever heard of. Well, maybe she does."

Jill was very much moved, both because she had become fond of Grandma Rosie just from hearing about her and because this was the first strong evidence she had had that John was really serious about their relationship. They were talking by the pink rosebushes near the front porch of Jill and June's house. Jill had been wanting to say something about the film. She was afraid it would put him off, being invaded by movie people, and the word would be out soon. "John," she said, "you know if you cut the seed blossoms off this rosebush, it'll bloom all summer." Another thing, she had just gotten a big check in the mail, and she'd just as soon share her pleasure about that. She said, "By the way, I guess they're going to do a film about me now."

"A film?"

"Yeah. Not a documentary, but a feature film."

"Well, if anybody deserves something like that, you sure do."

•   •   •

The Tri-County Fair had opened while John was away, and he was anxious to make up for lost time, he said. He and Jill first visited the Art Building, and in the afternoon they watched the childrens' fish derby and checked out the pies and home-canned fruits and jams in the Home Ec. building.

"Whenever I was coming back from L.A. in the truck," John said, "I'd stop in Big Pine. Pull that old semi right up in front of the sanitarium and go in and visit for a while. It really pleased her. Poor Grandma Rosie, almost in tears when I'd get there and as soon as I'd say well I better get going she'd start to cry again. I hated to see her so unhappy."

They looked at all the prize animals in the 4-H building. They stopped for Cokes and snow cones at the Boy Scout booth and for Indian fry bread and beans in Chuck Wagon Alley.

"I'd go to her house when I was a kid. Big honey-suckle vine over the end of the front porch. Looking out from the porch at a ridge this side of Coyote, Grandma Rosie always watched for the shadow of the mountain ridge to be just right—it looked just like the profile of a man's face. She called it the Old Man of the Mountains. She'd tell us kids stories. A lot of rattlesnake stories. The one in the outhouse they'd had to shoot. About the myth that if you kill a rattler its mate will come to it, and a man she knew killed one and went back to get the rattles just before dark. He cut them off, and next day the dead snake was still there and still had its rattles."

They wandered slowly through the carnival with twenty booths set up to peddle spun sugar candy and promise prizes to dart-throwers and ball-throwers and beanbag-throwers.

"It does seem funny to see both a white VFW booth and a non-white VFW booth," John said.

"The Cline Howard Indian Auxiliary," Jill said, "is very proud of its war heroes."

John had never been to a powwow, which was the Indians' main contribution to the fair and was held on the reservation. Jill persuaded him to take her, and they bought fry bread and beans and beef and home-made ice cream at the U-shaped booths made from willow limbs. They watched the dancing in a circular arena, at the center of which was an open drum house made of willow poles. The dancers were mostly semi-professionals who traveled around the powwow circuit, just as ropers and riders travel around the rodeo circuit.

Jill met several old friends. Gerald Kane and his brother stopped to speak with her. He was chairman of the Tribal Council and an old football buddy of Bob's. His sisters had once worked at the Rocking K for Bill Kinmont, and his daughter Lisa was one of Jill's favorite pupils. Josephine Cromwell stopped also. She had been

74

the cook—and therefore Jill's boss—when Jill and Audra Jo had been waitresses at the Rocking K dining room. She told Jill that the years she worked for Bill Kinmont had been the happiest years of her life.

Jill and John went to the California-Nevada Rodeo Association rodeo in the evening. They sat in a box and John told Jill who was good. "Lester Cline still team-ropes with my uncle Orville, and those old guys are still in the money. For calf roping . . ." He lowered his voice. "Leon Campbell's real good. That's him right next to us. And Chop Manzoni and of course my brother Roy team-ropes. And there's Melvin Joseph, but he's an Indian. He's good, though."

"What do you mean, *but* he's an Indian?"

"I think you know what I mean. Let's not get into an argument."

"Is there much money in it?"

"Several hundred bucks at least, for the winners."

A steer charged out of the chutes, and two cowboys were out after him in less than a second. It seemed to Jill that the ropes were flying the moment the steer took off. In seconds they had him stretched out between them. John shrugged.

"Well, John, it looked pretty good to me. What if the ropers come out before the steer?"

"Ten-second penalty. But you know all this stuff."

"I used to, but it's been a long time. It was twenty years ago when I was crazy about roping. The bandstand was down where the calf chutes are now, and I used to sit under the stands right by the chutes. Even when I came back in a wheelchair, I watched from the same place."

Roy and his partner came out and roped their animal in seconds.

John laughed and Jill turned to him, surprised.

"I just remembered what Grandma Rosie used to say. She told me that Dudley, my father, was born on a horse. For a long time I thought it was true. It was a little hard for me to picture, though."

75

"What were you born on, a tractor?"

They grinned at each other.

"I wish you could have seen her gardens," John said. "Beautiful flowers. Huge vegetable garden. She and Grandpa Roy would sell tomatoes and corn to the markets in town. And fun-loving! And always telling raunchy jokes. Like the absent-minded professor who unbuttoned his shirt and stuck out his tongue and wet his pants."

"She meant a lot to you, didn't she."

"I was the first grandchild and the apple of her eye. I used to sit and listen to her play. She never read a note of music but she played the piano and she played the fiddle at the old-time dances. My grandfather called the dances."

* * *

John stopped by on his way back from the funeral Monday. The temperature was 105 degrees and he stood in the sun talking to Jill. He was wearing a gray flannel suit with pleated pants and an old-fashioned black tie, which he took off while he was talking. "I had a talk with Lester Cline at the funeral," he said. "He's real pleased to hear about you and me."

"Oh?" Jill frowned. "What did you tell him about me and you?"

John grinned and shrugged. "I got to change," he said.

A few days later, while Jill was doing school work out on the lawn, John drove his great truck tractor into the driveway. He got the hose and a bucket and a bottle of detergent and a pair of old torn pajamas and began washing the truck, explaining all about trucks to Jill as he did so. June called from the house to say she had a watermelon and was anyone interested. John said, "Sure," and the three of them had watermelon in the living room. John said, "Jill, do you suppose we could go for a ride in the pick-up?"

Jill said, "I thought you'd never ask."

"We could go up Bishop Creek tomorrow and see my

76

folks at the pack outfit. I *think* I can get you into the pick-up."

"All you have to do is put one arm high under my legs and the other low on my back."

Jill later asked her mother if it would be okay to have John in for dinner tomorrow after they got back from the pack outfit. June said, "Well, sure."

John and Jill drove up the next afternoon without the wheelchair. Jill said, "Do you bring the truck home to wash it very often?"

John shrugged and gave Jill a glance which she perceived as sheepish. *"Aha,"* she said. "You've never done it before, have you? And here I thought you did it all the time!"

The Bishop Creek road climbs so steeply that they could see out across the entire valley after the first half mile. After ten miles, the road forks—north to North Lake and Lake Sabrina, south to the Rainbow Pack Outfit and South Lake.

"I guess you know," John said. "We do a great summer business because there's thirty lakes you can get to on horseback in one day or less. It's mostly pack trips. Or spot trips, where you take them in, leave them, and go back for them a week or ten days later."

The pack outfit was nestled in a partly wooded draw downstream from South Lake. It consisted of a complex corral for 30 horses and 20 mules and a beautiful tackroom for saddles and packs—a big building with a peaked roof and no walls. A hundred yards downhill was a large, two-roomed log cabin.

Alice and Dudley Boothe saw the pick-up coming and walked out to meet it. They greeted Jill warmly and walked alongside as John drove carefully down the bumpy dirt road to the cabin.

Jill stayed in the truck, and Alice brought out beer and Cokes and a coffee can of chocolate nut cookies with vanilla icing—a Grandma Rosie recipe that was John's favorite. Alice was a small, well-knit woman who looked

77

rather like June Kinmont. Dudley was a large, slow-moving, comfortable-looking man. He was powerful, but he had an easy way that suggested great self-confidence.

"I remember you as a girl," Alice said. "You taught swimming at Keough's. And I remember Bill Kinmont very well. A remarkable man with tremendous energy."

Dudley didn't say much, but he seemed to be enjoying himself and he seemed to approve of Jill. At least he kept looking at her with a warm and wise expression on his face.

Jill clearly remembered Keough's public swimming pool just south of town. A big pool with new silver paint obscuring the cracks and highlighting occasional fogs of algae, hot springs spilling in at the shallow end, and depressing old gray-green dressing rooms lining the east side. She and Audra Jo had been the Red Cross swimming instructors there when they were 15. She remembered trying to teach a ten-year-old cowboy how to dive. She *thought* his name had been Johnny. He wouldn't go off the board. All he did was look down at the water and fold his arms. "You ride, don't you?" she asked him. "Well, it's just like the first time you got up on a horse. Probably scared you a little, but then it felt pretty great. Right?" The boy had walked calmly back off the board and said he didn't want to take any more diving lessons.

"Johnny was a real serious kid." Alice said to Jill. "We called him Honest John. Roy was only interested in being a cowboy, but John was into all kinds of things. Especially mechanical. Would you like some watermelon, Jill?"

"No, thanks. We just had some."

"Johnny, too?" she said. "Johnny hates watermelon." John was busy talking with his father, so he missed this exchange.

"You would have liked Dudley's mother, Jill. She played the violin and the piano, and she had quite an influence on John. She always stuck up for him. He'd do something I didn't like, and Rosie would say, Well, I don't blame him."

John wanted time to take Jill to North Lake before

dark, so he ended the visit. Jill asked Alice to empty her urine bag. "Do you have an empty coffee can or milk carton?" she said. "Just take the cap off the end." She tapped her skirt with her hand. "It's easy. Let it flow into the can."

John drove to the Bishop Creek Lodge, where he bought small jars of peanut butter and jelly, a loaf of bread, and a package of cookies. Then they went on down to the fork and turned left up to North Lake. A deer crossed the road and ran up the right side into a barbed wire fence. The young buck backed off and then leaped uphill, just nicking the top wire with his hooves.

"He nearly got hung up," John said.

"What would you do if he had?"

"It wouldn't be easy to get him out. You'd sure as hell get cut to pieces by his front feet."

The sun was long gone behind the peaks towering above them, and John stopped to help Jill put on her sweater. He had to lean against her to get her left arm in the first sleeve. Jill thought: this is the perfect excuse to kiss me.

But all he did was put her sweater on.

6

Love?

That night Alice telephoned her son. She said, "Johnny, what's going on?"

"Something pretty nice, I think."

"I hope so, John. I wonder a little bit. I'm scared you might be getting into something you can't handle."

"Don't worry, Mom. It's only once I got into something I couldn't handle, and that taught me what I need to know."

"By the way," she said, "Dudley read the book about Jill. It was too emotional for him to read straight through."

In the morning John left in his lumber truck for Los Angeles. The following morning he telephoned Jill at the Indian Center to say he had to drive away north to Eureka. "I just didn't want you to worry."

Jill could hardly teach the rest of the day. John *really* cared!

When John returned from Eureka, he took her to the

ranch. He ran two planks from the ground up onto the tailgate of his pick-up and pushed Jill's chair up. The pitch was so steep that the battery fell out.

"That was careless," he said. "I'm sorry. I'll fix it when we get down to the ranch."

The ranch was half a mile off 395 on a dirt lane. A big old bungalow with a covered porch and a big cottonwood out front, some sheds in back and a big garden across the lane. There was pasture beyond that, and the arching sprinklers on their great aluminum wheels were visible in the distance. Irrigation ditches separated the fields.

The family was gathered on the front lawn—Roy and Beverly with their boys Mike and Jeff, John's sister Linda, and his sister Janet with her husband Gary and their daughters Suzy and Cindy. Dudley and Alice were in the mountains running the Pack Outfit for the summer while Roy and Beverly took care of the ranch. They all had hamburgers and ice cream from Save Time Burgers. Afterwards, when John and Janet were off picking corn to take home, Suzy said to Jill, "When can I start calling you Aunt Jill?"

John and Jill left at dusk with a sack of fresh corn between them on the front seat. When they reached Elm Street, Jill said, "Why don't we go up to the schoolgrounds and talk awhile?"

They did. They talked for a short while and John reached his arm around the back of Jill's shoulders. "Look," he said suddenly, "this corn's got to go." He threw the sack in the back of the truck along with the wheelchair, climbed back in the front seat and kissed Jill for the first time, a long, gentle kiss.

When John left the next day, he stopped in to say goodbye. "I'm headed for Eureka with lots on my mind," he said.

"And plenty of time to think about it."

"That's for sure," he said. "You know, if you hadn't suggested going to the schoolyard and parking last night, I'd have been too shy. And that time I was putting on

81

your sweater up at North Lake? Well, I wanted to kiss you then, but I was scared."

When John returned he said he needed to know more about Jill's injury. He never looked at her scrapbooks and he had few questions about her past, but the accident and its effects were important to him.

"Okay," she said, "if you don't mind a lecture. My spinal cord was broken at the fifth vertebra in the neck. It was reduced to a fine powder and there was no chance of any kind of repair. So I can breathe and move my shoulders and flex my forearms and raise my wrists when my palms are down. And that's it. My fingers are permanently curled."

"What else?"

"Kidneys—you know about that. Plenty of water and be very careful about infection. The catheter stays with me always except when it's changed twice a month. For some reason my bowels are very regular, once every two days. I have to watch for bed sores. And I have to be very careful not to catch cold. I don't have the muscles to cough, so I can't clear my lungs. The big worry is that a cold could develop into pneumonia. I don't get close to people with colds, especially at school. On the other hand, it could be that my constant contact with kids who have colds has helped me. You know, helped build immunities that keep me from catching anything."

"And there was something about hot and cold," John said, "but I don't remember."

"My body temperature changes with the outside temperature like a cold-blooded animal. When I get hot I can't cool off, and when I get cold I stay cold, and that feels *awful!*"

"Thanks. That's what I wanted to know."

"There's some weird things, too," Jill said. "I don't have feeling below the shoulders except on the inside of my arms, but somehow I can tell when my bladder's full, and I can tell when there's too much sugar in my blood. And I can always feel when it's full moon. I really think the moon *draws* in some way. What it does to the oceans

82

it does to me. I become very sensitive and more emotional. Another thing—I can feel the low pressure when a storm's coming in. I feel weighty. Sometimes it's very exhilarating."

•   •   •

From this point on, John was either on the road or was somewhere with Jill. They ate "at home" with June several times a week. They talked in John's living room, where he always sat in his favorite chair—he could tilt back in it, and there was a broad footrest that pulled out from beneath the seat. They had dinner at the ranch occasionally, and one day they went down to help with the branding: lunch for fifteen with Swiss steak, mashed potatoes, four vegetables, and freshly baked cake. Jill noticed that John talked a lot when they were alone together but was rather dour when they were with others. He became a strong, silent bystander.

Together, the two of them found picnic spots neither of them had known about. They looked at all the old homesteads that had been bought by Los Angeles and had crumbled and gone wild. Swaybacked barns and tilted silos. They also went to the pack outfit and to North Lake again and to Sabrina. John often helped Jill get ready to go out by wetting her washcloth, taking off jar lids, or putting sun cream on the back of her hand. The pickup truck with the wheelchair in the back became a common sight in and around Bishop.

The Indian school was over by the end of July, and Jill had more time to spend with John on his days off. One evening when they were up on the Old Sherwin Grade—the steep, winding grade of Route 395 which had long ago been bypassed—Jill noticed she was slipping forward on the seat. She said, "John, I need a boost in the worst way." He stopped and shifted her back in the seat. She noticed that her urine bag was full and she said, "John, there's something I want you to do for me."

John emptied the bag in the sagebrush. He was perfectly at ease. "Things like this don't bother me," he said, "so don't feel hesitant."

"Good," she said. "Let's stop and get a snack."

"Stop and get smashed?"

"Come on, John, you heard me. Pull my skirt straight and let's go get something to eat."

John spent the next day hauling a bulldozer from the Chalfant Valley to Lee Vining, and he made sure he was back in time to take Jill to The Embers for dinner. It was the first time they had gone to an expensive restaurant together. The only thing that bothered John was that the waitresses and hostess made such a fuss over Jill, giving her a lot more help than she needed.

Studying the menu, he said, "This is where Nancy and I came the night before she left."

Jill sat up very straight and stared at him. "Oh, great!" she said. "So why are you bringing me here?"

John hadn't thought of it this way. "Just because it's my favorite place to eat."

Later it occurred to Jill that perhaps John wanted to talk about his marriage. "I guess the break was pretty tough on you," she said.

He shrugged.

While he was cutting her steak for her, she said, "What kind of person was she?"

John in his own time began to talk. "The night she told me . . . I was finally fixing the air conditioner after having not done it for a number of days. She said, 'I'm leaving in two weeks.' I slung the screwdriver at the wall or something."

"I would guess so," she said.

"It really threw me when she left."

"What was the trouble?"

"Just the way we each did things. No communication. Constant sarcasm and criticism. Both of us. The sexual relationship got to be lousy. She just wasn't a warm, feeling type."

"She must have been pretty difficult." Jill was hoping he would say he couldn't stand her.

84

"I was in love with her. I still have regard for her. But we were always at odds. I got real sore at my family when they said maybe the divorce was a good thing. I know the house wasn't tidy, but after all, she worked. All she ever cooked was meat and potatoes. She always made bread. I really like having people over. She'd rather go out."

"She doesn't sound like your type."

"I don't know, Jill. She's sure the opposite of you in every way. But she had no family life, and the Boothes were always a very close family. When I'd want to express affection, I never knew if I could. Sometimes it'd be fine, another time, no way!"

Roy's wife Beverly often stopped in to visit with Jill, usually with her kids. They became good friends, and Jill found it easy to talk with her about John and to ask questions about Nancy and how Nancy had gotten along with the Boothes. Bev was direct and totally honest, and she always had the time to talk or do errands for Jill or drive her in the van. She cared a great deal about the Boothes and knew all of their idiosyncrasies. The most frequent phrase that she and Jill used when talking about the family was, "Well, that's a *Boothe* for you!"

"Are all of them so impatient?" Jill asked her one day when she was in the pick-up at the ranch waiting for John to finish with the irrigation ditches. Beverly laughed. "John goes crazy when somebody ahead of him is driving too slow or turns without signaling," Jill said. "And some of the language!"

"Yep," Beverly said. "Gets pretty hot under the collar."

"We just had dinner at his house for the first time, Bev. It was so nice at first, John grinning at me from that chair he loves so much, that tilts and has the footrest that can stick out, you know? Well, he got the wine, and the corkscrew pulled out of the cork. He tried to get it back in, and the cork went into the bottle. I couldn't believe what a big deal he made out of it. Swearing at the bottle and cursing the winemakers and throwing the corkscrew on the floor. It kind of ruined the candlelight-and-wine atmosphere."

Beverly nodded.

Meanwhile, John was showing up at the house every day he was in Bishop, and this was getting to be a little too much for June. Not because he wasn't exactly the man she would have picked out for her daughter, but because he was around *all* the time and, as far as June could see, always grumpy. She had welcomed him warmly at first because Jill was having such a great time going places with him, but now she had reservations. She didn't mention her feelings, but she was becoming a reluctant hostess. One afternoon she came back from shopping and found Jill and John in the living room with the curtains drawn. Without a word, she marched across the room, opened the curtains and brushed them straight, and left. She told Jill later, "I felt very silly about that. I guess I resented you two being alone in there with pulled curtains. I'm sorry."

• • •

June and Jill planned to return to Pacific Palisades in mid-August. On the day before they left, John and Jill invited the entire Boothe family to John's house for a Sunday feast. John had everything set early Sunday morning, and he took Jill for a drive up Pine Creek, the next valley north of Bishop Creek. It was an unexpectedly hot day, and Jill finished her bottle of distilled water long before they got back to town. She began to heat up. She soon felt nauseated, and her head began to throb.

By the time they reached Elm Street it was almost time for the party.

"It's like a huge weight on my head," she told John. "I'm getting numb, and it feels like I'm going to die. Put me in front of the cooler and get me some ice."

John carried her into her house, sat her in front of the air conditioner, and went to his house to check on the

86

roast. June came in, and Jill said, "Mom, I'm over-heated."

Jill heard the Boothes arriving, and after another half-hour in front of the cooler, she and June went over to John's house for dinner. She felt awful but didn't want to spoil John's party. Soon after dinner she said, "Mom, I've got to go home. I suppose we ought to call Dr. Sheldon. It just won't go away."

John and June took Jill to the other house, and then John kept running back and forth between his guests in one house and Jill in the other. Jill felt she was ruining the party. John said, "I'm concerned about you. I'm not concerned about the party. So my family realizes there are some weird things that happen to you now and then. So what?"

The next morning before six, John came over and carried their suitcases to the van, buckled Jill in the front seat and kissed her goodbye. She said, "I don't want it to end, John."

"Take it easy," he said. "Are you sure you're well enough for the trip? Call me when you get home. And drive carefully, June. Jill, when will you be back?"

"I don't know, John."

•   •   •

It was a beautiful morning, and there was little traffic. "I sure hate to be leaving Bishop," Jill said. "Don't you?"

"Not really," June answered. Then she added, "I guess I'll have to admit that I'm greatly relieved to be on our way home."

"Our romance getting a little too strong for you?"

"Getting to be too much work for me."

Jill started to laugh, but she realized her mother was dead serious. "You mean being without help on the weekends?"

June shrugged and said no more. After five minutes of silence, Jill said, "Well, what, Mom?"

"Jill . . . I know it means a lot to you, but I'm sick of *waiting* on that man."

"Mom, you haven't been waiting on him."

"An extra person at dinner three or four nights a week, and then you invite him for breakfast Saturday morning. And he doesn't help at all."

"Mom, in the Boothe family there's this sex-role thing and boys just don't do the dishes or carry plates from the table."

"In our house, everybody carries the dishes," June said. "I am always happy to do the things for you that you want me to, but I will not do these same things for John any longer."

"Okay, Mom."

"And your picnics! I've been making *picnics* for you and John. John can make a sandwich as well as I can. Why doesn't he ever offer? What's the *matter* with him? Any halfway decent man would!"

"Why didn't you say so long ago, Mom? I see your point. Anything else?"

June said, "I've tried to be friendly and carry on a conversation with him, but he doesn't even look at me when we talk."

"Hmmm," Jill said uncomfortably.

"And he absolutely monopolizes you, Jill. Your other friends don't get to see you, and when anyone comes in when you're together, he acts as if it's an intrusion."

"I'll talk to him about that," Jill said weakly.

Later, when they were well past Mojave, Jill said, "He has his faults, Mom, but there are other things that mean so much to me. It's getting important to me to keep an ordinariness about everything, and John represents to me a real simplicity and basicness. He understands how his grandparents coped with life, and deals with things in the same way. He was brought up milking cows and living in a house without electricity—in *this* generation! His family is so self-sufficient. And John has that kind of earthy stability. He's totally dependable. And you should like *that*, Mom, after all the anxiety you had about Dick Buek."

"That's true, Jill, but your differences are enormous.

In regard to politics and taste and education and intellectual interests and professional interests and . . ."

"Mom, I'm comfortable with him."

The words stuck with June. She thought about them. She said, "Well, you're right, Jill. That *is* what's important. I guess the political and education part doesn't bother me, really. What I do not like—if you and John are really going to stay together—is the prejudices and the negative moods I see him in all the time. You know I'm used to openness and all the family stuff we've had. Having a lot of fun. It doesn't upset me until I think of you getting married. I want it to be someone who can create an atmosphere that's happy."

June didn't feel up to talking any more about John Boothe, but she said, "You do know what you want, Jill, and I admire you for that." What she didn't say was that she felt Jill was deliberately going after John. She said to herself, I wonder if she's going to make it. To win again. All her life, what she wanted, she had a way to go after it, figure it out. Why not with a man? She's not after a husband, but she *is* after someone she can thoroughly trust.

Jill wrote John as soon as she got home. Within the next ten days she received five letters from him, wrote six, and talked with him three times on the telephone for as long as an hour.

Meanwhile the subject of June's taking a vacation came up again. Jill was enthusiastic. June was excited but reluctant. The problem was getting someone to take care of the house and Jill. Jill said, "Sure it's a problem, but it's not impossible." She called an employment agency and asked what they had in the way of live-in help, a non-smoker to do minimal housework and take care of Jill. The agency had just the woman and would bring her out for an interview at 1 o'clock Friday.

That settled the issue. June would take the trip to Scotland she had been dreaming of, and she'd do it as soon as she could get tickets, a passport, and some travelling clothes. So on Friday morning she and Jill

89

went shopping at the Santa Monica mall. It was a great place to shop because it was all on one level. No stairs or curbs.

Their main project was a dress for June to wear to the ballet, one that didn't make her look too fat, she said. They looked at a lot of dresses, but all they found was a sweater for Jill.

"It's going to look fabulous on you," June said, holding it against her. "But it cries for a skirt to go with it." They bought yardage that matched the sweater. June always made Jill's skirts and the dresses she wore to school.

Jill said, "Hey, Mom, we didn't get anything for Scotland!"

"That's okay," June said. "I'll go to Bullock's tomorrow and see if I can't find something."

They got back home shortly after one o'clock. On the doorstep was a snappily dressed man from the employment agency and a young woman with a suitcase.

"We haven't *hired* her!" June said. "This is just an interview."

The agency man said, "She's very, very good. She's loyal. She's strong. Her name's Maria."

"Does she smoke?"

"Oh my goodness, no!"

Maria sat impassively on the front step, acting as if she didn't even understand the language. The man was her voice.

Jill said, "Would she have any difficulty taking care of me?"

"I should say not, Miss Kilmot. She has been working for a paraplegic who just died."

"Oh," Jill said. "That's a recommen*dation?*"

Maria nodded sharply toward the house. *"Vámanos pues,"* she said. She was about 23, small and fiery with long straight black hair and a pretty, somewhat round face. She was dressed in great style, thanks to Goodwill. She followed Jill into the house, walked suspiciously from room to room, and announced, *"La casa es pequeña. Es*

90

bonita." She went back to the front porch for her suitcase.

June said, "What is the salary?"

"Cheap. Hundred and eighty a month."

And so it was that Maria became a member of the Kinmont household. She moved into her room immediately, closed the door, and lit a cigarette.

Maria got Jill up the next morning with complete ease and efficiency, and she was excellent with the housework. That first afternoon, however, Jill had a major problem—her indwelling catheter pulled out. Jill noticed it and called out, "Mom, the catheter just came out."

June came rushing into the room. Maria held up her hand and said, "No, *señora. Me!*" This was Maria's job, and she understood what was going on and was perfectly capable of handling it.

Communication was not much of a problem since Jill had some knowledge of Spanish and a good Spanish-English dictionary. Maria proved to be, as Jill said, "fantastic," and June soon felt good about leaving her in charge.

Ed Feldman telephoned to say there had been no action on the film. It had been to Paramount and was now at Columbia. David Seltzer called a few days later to reassure Jill. Financing just wasn't that much of a problem with a package like this! The film would make it for sure. He said Feldman was up for a job as V.P. in charge of production at Columbia, and if he got it the film would surely be made there.

•   •   •

Jill and June called Bev to see if they could have the house again for the Labor Day weekend, and the answer was yes. They drove up with Maria on Thursday, and Jill, June, and Maria had dinner that evening with Audra Jo and Lee. John was out of town.

The main subject of conversation was predictable. Jill said, "What do you guys really think about John and me?"

91

Audra Jo said, "At first I thought, you are so opposite, how could this ever work."

"We sure are, Josie. He's a Republican. His hair's always short. He doesn't think at all the way I think. But I think he'll change." Jill sighed. "But he's *so* nice. And he's honest. Completely honest. Completely sincere."

"That he is," said Lee. "Unlike you, he doesn't care what anybody thinks."

"He doesn't even care what *Jill* thinks," Audra Jo said. "In fact, Jill, he's the best thing in the world for you. Because he's not going to do *any*thing just because you say so. If somebody asks him if he likes Indians or blacks, he'll tell them, even if you die a hundred deaths. Most people cater to you, Jill, but John really holds his own."

"He's also possessive," Lee said. "Josie had to withdraw from you this summer because he's so possessive. He wants you all to himself."

"Really?" Jill hadn't realized this. She felt bad and at the same time she was very pleased.

"Whatever else," Audra Jo said, "you two are sure having a good time."

Later, when Jill and Audra Jo were in the kitchen, Jill said, "I want to discuss something with you, Josie."

Audra Jo wheeled closer to Jill. "Well, spill it."

"The fact that I have no feeling, what difference would that make to a man—when he's making love?"

"It shouldn't make any difference. Especially if you're in love."

"What about my catheter?"

"I guess you'd work it out. Maybe you'd want to remove it, maybe not. Many couples have adjustments to make. I don't think it will be a problem, and we know you aren't the first person with a catheter to have these questions."

Lee came in and said, "What's John think of the age gap?"

"Not much," Jill said.

"How about you?"

92

Jill laughed., "It's a good thing because his back'll hold out that much longer."

"He's a good lifter, huh?" Lee said.

"Yes, but I'm afraid maybe he doesn't want to go around with an old broad. He told me once he was looking for a cute young thing."

Bob Kinmont, Vikki, and their three children arrived in their loaded VW square-back the next afternoon, and at 5 p.m. John Boothe pulled in from L.A. in his truck. Jill heard him and wheeled out to meet him. He knelt beside her chair and they were quiet for a long while, looking into each other's eyes. He took her head in his hands and kissed her.

"Mom took off camping with Bob," Jill said. "Maria's fixing dinner for you and me over at your place." They went together into John's house, where they found Maria sitting in John's special chair with a can of beer in her hand watching television. *"Qué cerveza más buena,"* she said cheerfully. Jill introduced John, and Maria nodded. Later, in private, she told Jill, *"Es una buena persona, Jeel, una buena persona."*

John and his best friend Jerry Clark had each bought themselves a Citizens Band radio for their trucks, and both had installed the radios temporarily in their pickups. Driving around Bishop, they practiced talking with each other. John asked Jill, "Want to see how my radio works? We can go up 395 on my regular truck route."

They left soon after sun-up, wheeling north out of Bishop while most of the valley was still in shadow beneath the bright Sierra peaks to the west. John had Merle Haggard on the radio, and Jill smiled at the lyrics. Bob and Vikki liked Country Western, too, but it was new to them. They had gone through rock and Dixieland and a few other places and come out where John had been all the time.

Beyond the top of the Sherwin Grade John tried his CB and managed to rouse Colorado Kid, who lived at Crowley Lake. Soon after that he passed a Shell Oil truck and he switched his radio on again. "Hey, Pumper Three, where you going? This is Muleskinner."

"Muleskinner? Where are you?"

"Just passed you."

"The hell you did."

"Want to back that up with a steak dinner?"

"Naw. You're too sneaky. What gives?"

"I'm in my pick-up."

"Hell, Muleskinner, that don't count."

The valley at Crowley Lake is high, but 395 keeps climbing up past Mammoth Mountain to Deadman Summit, at eight thousand feet, and down through a fir forest to Lee Vining and the back entrance to Yosemite.

"Tree Topper, this is Muleskinner. Do you read me? Come in, Tree Topper."

John said, "I guess the Forest Service is off for the holidays."

They drove on north through the soft green pastures of Bridgeport and as far as Topaz, well over halfway to Reno, before they turned around. They stopped in Walker for lunch with John's favorite cook, Betty, and were back in Bishop in time to catch Jerry Clark heading north in his pick-up.

"Muleskinner, we got Fifth Wheel here. What's with the hitchhiker?"

"Jerry lived with us for a while," John said to Jill. "You'll like Margie, too. Grows and cans her own food, top gal on the softball team, an artist and a den mother."

"Kids?" Jill said.

"Yep. Three."

"You'd like to have kids, wouldn't you?"

"Well, now . . ." John felt just a little bit trapped. "I do love kids, yeah. Nancy and I kept trying, and we never made it. But that's just one of those things, not having kids."

Jerry Kinmont arrived from the Northwest with his children—Robin and Jess—and Lyn Boyd, who had come back with them from Calgary, Alberta. John was included in the Kinmont reunion that evening.

John still didn't have the Kinmont boys pegged. They weren't like his own friends, they weren't like city people he knew, and they weren't even like each other. Bob was terribly serious and used words like "alluvial plain" and some of his wood constructions and plastic sculptures were too far out to even worry about as far as John was concerned. Jerry was anything but serious—full of energy and wild ideas, and for a living he made aquariums or ran around catching real whales. John had never met anyone like them, Jerry and Lyn. A pair of hippies, he thought, and that's different from any of the *other* Kinmonts. Still, he kind of liked them.

As for Vikki, John shook his head when he noticed her unconcernedly nursing her one-year-old, Seth, and letting Anna and Ben run free, making their own decisions and choices. Creativity was highly regarded in their lives. The Boothe kids were used to a stricter code, and they were more disciplined—although no less boisterous.

7

Love!

Just before Jill left Bishop, John said to her, "You know, don't you, what a good thing we have? How happy we could be?"

Jill raised the back of her wrist to her forehead. This was something she didn't want to think about or talk about yet.

"Jill, I can just imagine us . . ."

"But you *cannot* imagine all that goes with . . . all that goes with me, John. You just have no idea of what kinds of care I need and the time it takes to do what I need if I'm going to function in the way I like to function."

"These are things I want to learn about. Let's just not rule out that someday we might be married."

"John, I look fairly normal because I'm so concerned about looking as normal as possible . . . so you may not really understand how much there is I can't do for myself."

"I don't plan to marry you tomorrow, but I want to

96

know all these things. I want to understand, and in time I will. I just don't want to close the door on marriage. I want us to leave the door open and see what happens."

• • •

Los Angeles was a different world, and it wasn't until June went to school with Jill to help get her classroom set up that Jill felt she was back home. School began, and old routines picked up again—work and people and places that Jill had been away from for a long, long while—even since before she had met John Boothe.

The big event now was June's trip. "I got the passport and a letter from Jenny all in one mail," she said when she picked Jill up at school the first afternoon. "It feels like I'm really going!"

Jenny Kinmont was very distantly related. She lived in Australia, had read the first *Life* article, and had written Jill to ask if they might possible be related. Later she had visited June and Jill in Los Angeles. They had compared notes on genealogy and finally established a connection between the two families—their great, great, great grandfathers were brothers. Jenny and June were now planning to meet in London and drive to Scotland together.

"Looks like we're really going to follow the trail of Kinmont Willie," June said. "Jenny knows the castle where he was held prisoner, and we're going to start there. Doesn't that sound exciting? We'll go from Carlisle Castle through all the little towns and villages he went through after his escape." Kinmont Willie was a Scottish hero in the Border Wars with England in the 16th century and was the subject of Sir Walter Scott's poem, *Kinmont Willie*.

"I can see you're going to have a great time, Mom."

"I know I will, Jill. Thank you for making it possible. I wish you could come, too." June wanted to say more, but she never had been very good at talking about her feelings. She had cared for Jill and lifted her and talked over her problems with her for nearly two decades, and Jill had never taken it for granted. Jill always appreciated

97

what June was doing and always went out of her way to do things that would please June. The fact that they never took each other for granted was what made it possible to do so much.

"How was *your* day?" June said when they reached home.

"Nice to be back in the saddle, but it's *work!*"

They unloaded at the dock in the garage, and Jill wheeled into the house. June brought her a hot washcloth. Jill washed her face while June made a fresh pot of coffee.

"Remember Morris?" Jill said. "How bad he was last spring? You wouldn't believe him today. He brought me a bouquet from his dad's flower shop."

June laughed. "Schlumberger's office called," she said from the kitchen. "The usual. Beautiful specimen, phosphates low, no pus cells. And a woman called to ask *me* if you could give a talk to the Candy Stripers next month. You'd be surprised how many people ask *me* if *you* will do something for them."

June brought coffee, and they sat together to talk over Jill's day and June's plans for Scotland. June was full of life and looked positively *young,* Jill thought, in her sandals and white pants and plaid cotton shirt. Her white hair was bright in the afternoon sun. She got out Jill's current scrapbook, opened it on her lap, and trimmed loose clippings so they would fit neatly on the pages. "I want to bring it up to date before I leave," she said. The scrapbooks had always been one of June's favorite projects. They were an impressive record of Jill's successes, beginning with the first time her skiing was ever mentioned in the *Inyo Register*.

The following afternoon Jill bought a second-hand TV for Maria, which she hoped would help keep Maria from getting restless. June and Maria organized Jill's room so Jill could reach things she might need without having to call for help. And Jill telephoned Vikki.

"Just checking to be sure you're still willing to be my

babysitter while Mom's gone," she said. "Are you bringing the kids?"

Maria was wonderful. She actually enjoyed getting Jill up at 6:30 each morning, dressing her, and lifting her into the chair. She usually joined Jill and June for meals, except when they had guests. She had afternoons off and came back to help Jill after school and wash the dinner dishes. When she was late for work, she always had a big excuse. A flat tire on the coast highway. She had been hit by a car while running across the street. One day she said, "Jeel, *soñé de que era un vampiro.*" She always called Jill "Jeel" and June "señora."

"I'm a *vampire?*" Jill said. "Oh . . . you *dreamed* I was."

"*Sí.*"

Someone drove Jill to school at 7:30 every day. It was usually a neighborhood boy or girl, but at $2.50 an hour the drivers were not outstandingly loyal, and the turn-over was constant. Often enough, June had to take over at the last minute.

John drove his pick-up down from Bishop on Sunday the 16th of September, and he took Jill up to Malibu and Topanga Canyon. He drove her to school Monday morning, slept on the couch during the day, and picked her up in the afternoon. They went to the beach, came home for supper, and John left at 9 o'clock to get back for an early morning run in Bishop.

On Thursday, Vikki arrived in the morning with Anna and Seth, and June caught an 8:30 p.m. flight for London.

Saturday morning, John returned in a big truck, which he parked in the Presbyterian conference grounds in the canyon below the house. Since he hauled a lot of materials to and from Long Beach, it wasn't difficult to schedule it on a weekend so he could drive down Friday or Saturday and make the pick-up in Long Beach Monday morning.

Jill was ready when she heard John's heavy, slow step on the porch. He sauntered in, greeted Maria and Vikki

99

and Anna and Seth, piled Jill into her VW van, and they took off.

They drove down to the shore road and then north toward Santa Barbara. They stopped at Malibu. They stopped for coffee. They stopped at another beach. They saw a pair of obviously gay young men sitting together on the sand.

"That makes me sick," John said.

"Come on, John! What do you mean, makes you sick?"

"Queers make me sick."

"You're a hard-nosed bigot," Jill said. "You're prejudiced against *everything*."

"I don't think so, Jill. More than you, yeah, but . . . well I'm in the habit of calling a spade a spade."

"Well, I wish you'd change."

"You wouldn't like me if I changed."

"No, I don't want *you* to change. Just your attitudes."

"Jill, there's more than one way to look at things. I try to look at it your way, but you never try to see it my way, and that's not being fair."

"Yes, but I'm *right,* John."

That took care of conversation for a while. John put her back in the car without a word and drove on. Finally he said, "Honey, I never wanted you to think like me. But I feel certain ways, and you won't understand why."

"It doesn't make sense, John."

"Anyway, I don't think these things are that important. What's important is that we care enough about each other. And the things we admire so about each other."

"But I'm afraid, John."

"Of what?"

"That the differences are so great that I just plain might not like you some time." She thought of something and laughed. "You're one of those people I've been criticizing for years."

"You piss me off, Jill, you know? You're constantly thinking of why it can't work. I'm always thinking of how it *can* work. It never occurs to me that we wouldn't be happy. I just don't think that way."

Jill turned and stared at his profile. She said, "I love you, John."

It was dusk when they reached Oxnard. They drove around looking for a good restaurant and found one. Candlelight, cozy and unrushed, a great menu. John had two bourbons and water. Jill had a whiskey sour. They ordered fried clams and wine.

They had consciously not looked at a clock, but by the time they left the restaurant they knew it was very late. "Vikki's sitting up for you, isn't she?" John said, starting the car.

"What do you suppose we ought to do?"

"I don't know," John said with a beautiful grin. "What the hell, let's spend the night."

Jill leaned her shoulder against his. "Yeah, what the hell." They found a telephone booth, and John dialed the number. He gave Jill the receiver.

"Vikki? It's Jill." Jill looked up at John with a smile. "No, we're okay. Where am I? I'm in a phone booth. Look, Vikki, it's so late that we found a motel, and we're going to stay in the motel tonight." A long silence.

Vikki said, very calmly, "Jill, is John right there?"

"Yes."

"Jill, are you in any trouble? Is he making you do this?"

Jill giggled and turned to John. "John, are you making me do this?" Then, to Vikki, "Yes."

Vikki lost her calm. "Jill, are you *sure?*"

"Vikki, I'm in control of the situation. Everything's fine. We can handle it. We'll see you tomorrow."

"Okay, that's just wonderful. Have a good time."

•   •   •

When they reached home shortly before noon Sunday, John carried Jill into the house. Vikki was embarrassed. Eventually she explained to Jill, "I was worried, Jill. It got later and later, and you were still not back, and I was going to have to put you to bed and it was a terrible program on TV. Then you called and sounded giddy, and

101

I felt so responsible. And after you hung up I called Bob and told him and asked him what to do and what should I tell Anna. He said, 'That's great. What are you worried about?' "

The next day David Seltzer called to say that both United Artists and Universal were seriously interested in the film. Three days later school closed for the Rosh Hashana holiday, and Jill, Vikki, Maria, and Seth headed for Bishop after sending Anna home by plane.

The long weekend was full. Up Bishop Creek to see the fall colors, to the ranch to see if the cows were having their calves yet, out to the irrigation ditch south of town for a picnic, over to the Rocking K for lunch with Dave McCoy, back to John's to cook a meat loaf—and to find Maria in John's favorite chair with a can of beer, watching television. And a great Saturday night dinner at the ranch with all the Boothes plus Vikki and Seth and Maria. John fixed breakfast Sunday morning—eggs, bacon, and tomatoes—before the trip back south to ugly L.A. He wrote Jill a few days later.

Well, it's 2 a.m. and it's time I crawled into the sleeper for a few hours. I left home about one o'clock yesterday afternoon and I have been just sitting on my behind watching that old broken line and thinking of you every inch of the way. I love you and miss you so much.

You should have seen all the smoke today between Walker and Reno. The fires around Yosemite and Sonora are sending smoke over the mountains plus they had one going somewhere around Topaz.

I picked over a dozen cherry tomatoes today before I left. I thought of you out there kidding me about my jungle while I was all tangled up in the vines. Everything reminds me of you, Sweet Girl. It's been so lonely without you to come home to I can hardly stand it. I love you so much.

Oh, I have had something to tell you ever since you left and I keep forgetting. The day you left when

I got back and Howard was waiting for me he was giving me my orders for the rest of the week and his wife was here and she said, "What I want to know is when are you going to sleep?" Howard got a big grin on his face and said, "If he will stay away from that front house he can sleep tonight." I told him he didn't have to worry about that because you had left that morning. I could have slugged him.

June Kinmont returned from Scotland on the 12th of October. The trip had been even better than she had hoped for. She had met Jenny in London, and they had made their headquarters at Jenny's sister Felicity's home. "We saw the window in Carlisle castle where Kinmont Willie escaped," she said. "And in the last town we found a gravestone marked *William Armstrong of Kinmont.* We don't know if that was really Kinmont Willie, but we certainly had a lot of fun."

On Veteran's Day weekend, John and Jill drove to a conference at the Tule River Indian reservation, where they were helping to set up an educational program. The conference was over at 5 p.m. Saturday, and John and Jill went out for an early dinner. They parked behind a young couple who were just climbing out of their camper.

"These college types are really something," John said.

"Sounds like sour grapes," Jill said. "Is there something the *matter* with going to college?"

"Nothing the matter. It's when they don't know anything else, like most of them don't."

"Your prejudices," Jill said, "run all the way from Indians, because they aren't educated, to whites because they are."

"I don't include you, Jill. But if you could see the educated idiots I've had to deal with summer after summer. I have packed so many city people into the mountains, and they didn't know *any*thing except what they'd picked up in college. They knew just *nothing* about taking care of themselves. The younger ones came on like woodsmen with their beards and long hair. They all had big, heavy canteens, and there was running water all around them!"

"You told me about some guy you really admire who has long hair and a beard."

"Sure. He was a man who lived in the mountains and knew what it was all about. These kids I run into, they aren't who they pretend to be at all. Phonies I can't take, Jill, and I never will."

At dinner, over a bourbon and water, John said, "I think we should get married."

"There are too many difficulties, John."

"Look, I'll get a job in L.A. if I have to." He frowned, then grinned. "A much better idea, of course, is you getting a job in Bishop."

"John, we have too many *differences!*"

"So we have differences. When we're together, do we have a really great time?"

"We have a really, really good time."

"So what's about differences? So I think we should have just gone ahead and *won* the war in Vietnam. So I thought McGovern was for the birds. In a democracy, Jill, people can have different opinions."

"It makes a big difference with you and Mom."

"I don't know about June. Whenever I turn up, she suddenly gets real busy, like she sure doesn't want to sit down and talk. I don't know what we'd talk about if we *did* sit down to talk."

"So much of her interest now is in her philosophy class."

"I just think she doesn't like me."

"Well, she thinks that you don't like her. You don't say goodbye when you leave half the time, and she feels perfectly ignored whenever the three of us are together."

"This is getting off the subject, Jill. June and I are uneasy with each other. Okay. But I'm talking about getting married and I don't intend to marry your mother or to live with her."

"The answer is I'm not ready to get married."

"Two weeks ago you were."

104

"I go up and down about it, I know. It's all pretty complicated."

"It's all pretty simple, Jill. It's a yes or no thing."

"Okay, John, but the answer is maybe."

Monday, after John left for Bishop, Jill wrote him a careful list of worries. His ability and willingness to take care of her were not among them, and neither was the fact that they usually had a wonderful time together. But she was afraid they would get into fights because of their different opinions and prejudices, that they would be uneasy with each other's friends, and that their life styles were too different.

The following evening she wrote him that she had no worries. Once she had written them down, they didn't seem so important any more. John's answer came a few days later.

I keep glancing at your pictures. At one time you are smiling at me with that beautiful smile of yours and the next time you are looking at me so serious and emotional. I can almost hear you saying, "I love you, John." I feel so good and sad and lonely all at once. I love you, Jill, more than you could ever know. Even when you get sad and worried like you did for a moment Monday, it makes me feel all warm and emotional and thankful to know that you care enough to be concerned that way. Every time something like that happens, in the end I feel a little more confident that we'll be able to overcome those things in time. I think those moments bring out, more than ever, just how much we really do care for each other. They really bring us closer to each other and to the answer we are looking for than anything else.

I was so relieved to hear you say you were feeling good about what we have and not worrying so much. I never did think that two people who had everything in common were a good match anyway. We have our differences but the fact that we can overcome

105

them with such a deep complete love and so much mutual understanding makes it all that much more meaningful to me. It is such a good comfortable feeling to be able to just be myself and not have to worry about what you will think or to have to try to be something I am not. You love me and accept me for what I am, and I love you the same way. As long as we love each other that way, nothing will ever be too big for us to handle.

At home, however, John was beginning to sense something less than total support from his family concerning his desire to marry Jill Kinmont. His mother had told June how glad she was that John had found such a wonderful *companion* in Jill, which sounded pretty Platonic. And one day at the ranch she asked John point-blank how serious he was about it.

"What makes you think I would ever mention it if I weren't serious about it?" John said.

"I know it's none of my business, John, but I'm worried about what a huge responsibility you'd be taking on."

"I'm not in the habit of taking things on I'm not up to."

"That I appreciate. What I don't know is whether you have any idea how much is involved. Emotionally, physically, financially." John was silent, and the conversation died at that point.

But when John's favorite cousin Boothe Westfall came over from Oakdale for a visit, John brought up the subject himself—not whether he could handle life with a quadriplegic but whether he was expecting too much. "We fight about all kinds of things," he said. "All the time. Politics. Indians and niggers—except you never use that word or you get kicked in the teeth. Education."

"And after you fight, what?" Boothe said. He was six feet six and *big,* and he had a big voice. "You break up forever?"

"Nothing like that."

106

"Then what are you worried about?"

"There's a big difference, too, Boothe, in our backgrounds and everything else. She has a college education and she talks about . . . I don't know, getting a Master's degree, even a Ph.D., and look at me. On top of that she is truly famous, a real big shot. And she has all these brilliant big-shot friends in L.A. and great *Life* photographers that come to see her."

"John, she's a damned good girl, and I don't think you could do any better."

"But I'm talking about all these things that she . . ."

"That's all a bunch of horse shit," Boothe said. "She couldn't do any better, either."

John telephoned Jill and then wrote her a letter.

I told you on the phone about my long talk with Boothe. It really helped me a lot, and my only regret was that we weren't talking to him together. It can all get so complicated-looking and seem so involved from far away, and he has a way of making it all seem so simple. And uncomplicated and right. I've had millions of people tell me what a brave, wonderful person you are, and all I can say is that they don't even know the half of it. Compared to what I know. But Boothe is the first one to express confidence in me and my ability to handle it. Other than you, that is. It's really helped me a lot. He thinks the world of you, sweetheart, and he thinks what we have is right. I sure hope we can get over there this summer and see them.

I'll bet right this minute you're watching the Waltons. I tried to watch it but I'm pretty tired and it looks like about three stories going on at once. I couldn't keep it straight.

I just got my phone bill today. Hold your breath. It was $76.71. There were two phone calls to the guy in Reno about the pick-up. That came to about a dollar-sixty, and all the rest of the long distances were to the same number in Pacific Palisades. Now,

107

who could that be? Would you believe we talked one time to the tune of twelve dollars and twenty cents? You've just got to get that job and move up here, Sweet Girl. If not, I will just have to get a job down there I guess.

David Seltzer telephoned Jill in late October to say that the deal with Universal looked pretty well sewed up. A few days later he called to say it was definitely in the bag.

Jill now could count on the money, and it would be enough for a down payment on a house. June still was not keen on moving, but Jill called Lee Ann Rasmussen at her real estate office in Bishop and said she was ready to buy. Lee Ann had been looking for houses for Jill since Labor Day.

November was a hassled month. Ed Feldman telephoned to say everything was set and shooting would probably start in March. Lee Ann called to say she had the perfect house on Grove Street, two blocks from where John lived. Jill telephoned John and asked him to look at it. John returned the call within an hour. The house was a good one. Jerry Kinmont, who was in Bishop, telephoned. He, too, had seen the house and said it was a good buy. Feldman and his production manager visited Jill to talk about shooting plans. They would start at Mammoth with the snow scenes, shoot next in Bishop, and finish later with scenes in Los Angeles.

Jill and June drove to Bishop the weekend of November 10 to see the house on Grove Street. It was old, small, very attractive, and set well back from the road. A refrigerator, stove, washing machine and couch went with it. Price, $21,500. Jill bought it. Jill's lawyer called on Friday to say that Feldman was having budgeting problems and wanted Jill to accept less money than their contract called for. A week later, Jill was in Bishop for Thanksgiving with John and a big dinner at the ranch. She bought a bed and chairs for her new house.

December was a welcome breather: almost nothing happened.

Jill, June, and Maria took off for Bishop on the 19th. Maria slept all the way, and she seemed to be especially sound asleep when Jill's urine bag had to be emptied. They moved into their "new" house on Grove Street. Jerry and Lyn were living there and had already begun to remodel it. They had built ramps for the wheelchair and were planning to push out the living room wall and to make a kitchen counter.

Jill spent the next day with Audra Jo and tried to find a Christmas tree. All the lots were sold out. The following day John returned from a long haul with a Christmas tree for Jill. Maria flew off to Los Angeles.

Christmas Eve Jill and June spent at the Boothe ranch. After a big dinner they opened gifts by the Christmas tree. Later, in private, John gave Jill a heart-shaped gold locket, and she gave him an attaché case to use in the truck. On Christmas morning, John came over to the Grove Street house early and there were more presents, including a bicycle for June from Jill. The day after Christmas, Bob and Vikki and their children arrived from Woodacre, north of San Francisco, and there was yet another Christmas with presents by the tree.

That afternoon John drove Jill to the Long Valley airport to pick up Maria. The plane landed, and the passengers filed off. No Maria. John said. "That's the last plane of the day. What do we do now?"

Then Maria appeared in the doorway. *"Tuve que encontrar las bolsas,"* she said. In her arms were all the airsickness bags in the airplane. She had collected them to use when emptying Jill's plastic urine bag.

One morning when Vikki was driving Jill into town, Vikki said, "How come John's so glum all the time?"

"I know he is sometimes, but he sure isn't with me."

"Well, with company he's glum. He comes in and doesn't say anything. He leaves and doesn't say anything. We all keep trying to draw him out, saying goodbye when

109

he glums out the door. Well, I'm sick of doing that, Jill. He's a grown man."

"He *is* kind of introverted," Jill said.

"He won't look you in the eye."

Vikki's comments surprised Jill, and when she was alone with John she said, "I sure wish you could be a little more cheerful around the Kinmonts, John."

"You sound like you think I'm picking on the Kinmonts."

"I guess you don't react too much with the Boothes, either, but that's *your* family."

"If I'm not particularly cheerful, Jill, I'm not going to fake it."

"You might at least say goodbye when you leave."

"Who's objecting?"

"Don't get so upset," she said angrily. *"I'm* objecting."

There was a knock on the door, and Beverly Boothe walked in.

"Happy holidays," she said. "Lots of noise going on in here."

"We were having a little talk," Jill said meekly.

Bev laughed. "The Boothe kind. Loud and clear. I brought you some chocolate chip cookies."

All the Kinmonts were invited for New Year's Eve dinner at the ranch, and it was a lovely evening, warm and friendly inside and crisp outside. It started to snow just after dusk.

Bev and Jill and John's mother sat together after dinner talking about Roy and John. "They both tell things as they are," Alice said. "Otherwise they're completely different. Give Roy a job and he'd get it over in a hurry, no matter what. Give John a job, and he'd say okay, but if he got irritated he wouldn't do it at all."

"And there's the horse thing," Bev said. "The Boothes are pretty horse conscious to begin with, and Roy is just all cowboy. John's a loner. He's good with horses, but that's not his big thing. He even played the trumpet for a while. In fact, he fell off a horse when he was a kid and broke his jaw."

"He had some trouble before that," Alice said. "He had a bad curve in his spine, and we had him in a body cast for a while in fifth grade. They thought he might have had polio."

Jill heard John roughhousing with Seth, and she glanced at him just as Roy called across to him, "So when are you getting married?"

"Ask her," John said cheerfully. "*I'm* ready."

Jill smiled and turned to watch the snowflakes coming down just outside the window. She loved John. She loved the ranch house and the snow and the Christmas tree and the big dinner. She said to Bev, "You and Roy are down here a lot, aren't you?"

"We sure are. I don't know why, but we just like to be with Dudley and Alice more than with anyone else."

On New Year's Day Bishop was white and beautiful under eight inches of new snow. John drove Jill and June south in the VW and stayed for five days before taking the Greyhound back to Bishop.

Maria had left Bishop early for a two-day New Year's vacation, but she still hadn't appeared in Pacific Palisades by the seventh. Jill was worried because she had left all her things and hadn't been paid. She telephoned the two numbers she knew of, but no one answered. Maria called the next day from Oceanside to say she had been caught by immigration officials. She had been in jail in San Diego, but she was out now and somehow—the technicalities were difficult for Jill to understand in Spanish—she was going to be all right. She turned up in Pacific Palisades six days later.

Jill had dinner with her old friends Joan and Arnold Travis in Westwood, and she wrote John about it.

Met a girl at Travis' who had been living with an African tribe. It was fun comparing my work with the Indians. I'm always amazed at the intensity of the Travis' lives and others around them. Always talking about how much more *anyone* can be getting from his or her life than they are. I prefer a quieter

111

way that doesn't show so much. By the way, I heard on the radio about a couple who had gone together 51 years and finally decided to get married. Shall we give it a whirl?

Both David Seltzer and Ed Feldman called about the film. The director would be Larry Peerce—*Goodbye Columbus* and *Ash Wednesday*—and pre-production work was already underway. Shooting would start in mid-April.

John came down again on the 24th. He walked in on Jill and June during the *Merv Griffin Show* and—after kissing Jill—he stood between them with his fists on his hips, shaking his head.

"You don't *have* to watch," Jill said.

"Is that some actor I'm supposed to know?" John said. "What an ass he's making of himself."

June said, "Well, John, that's his problem, not yours."

"I like to see what these people are really like," Jill said. "When they're not playing a part."

"You can sure see it. First-class jerks. And here you could be watching *Mannix* or *Barnaby Jones* or *Cannon*."

The next evening John took Jill and June to the Chart House in Malibu for dinner. Jill and June sat across the table from each other, and John was between them. He leaned toward Jill for the entire meal, talking with her, and June ate in silence. "This telephone business has got to end," he told Jill. "My bill was eighty-three dollars!"

"It has *got* to end," Jill said. "Mine was over seventy."

"A year ago, all I paid was a monthly service charge."

"We've been saying this since September, John, and it just gets to be a little more each month."

"Well, I've got a solution!"

"John, we weren't going to talk about *that* until the film gets out of the way."

"Boy, you've got more excuses."

On Sunday John drove Jill to Point Dume, west of Malibu, where they opened their picnic basket and watched for whales. They were searching the horizon

112

when John spotted two spouts of water much nearer than they had expected. Later they saw another plume and then the shiny arch of the whale's body, and after that for a moment the flukes standing straight up in the air.

They were tired when they reached home after dark, but John still had to drive to Long Beach. His truck was down at the bottom of the hill, and Jill asked June to drive him down, which she did. June said nothing, but she obviously was not pleased about it.

Jill wrote John a letter immediately.

I had such a good weekend and feel so much more in love with you than I ever have. How that is possible I do not know, but the warm lovely glowing feeling that's so much joy inside of me, when I'm with you it's so strong. There are really few times now when we let our differences get to us. I guess we have so much love and respect that our differences are understood, more and more.

The next day June spoke to Jill about the evening. "I'm sore at you for asking me to drive him down a few blocks to his truck at ten p.m. when I'm almost ready for bed," she said. "And at him for letting me do it. Why should a sixty-four-year-old woman have to cart a thirty-three-year-old man down the hill in the middle of the night?"

"You're right," Jill said. "I'm sorry." She felt June had more to say, although it was not like her to come out with her worries or resentments. "Anything else on your mind?"

June shook her head, but later she said, "You're getting so close to John, and I can't help worrying. John is such an unhappy person, and I don't want to see you dragged down."

"Not when he's alone with me, he's not unhappy."

"Yes, but you two aren't going to be *alone* together all the time. I wish you could see there's more to it."

"And I wish you could appreciate who John is, Mom.

113

Nobody bothers to see who John *is*. Nobody bothers to look long enough to see it."

"That's hard for me to do when he acts as if I'm not here and doesn't want to talk with me. The other night at the Chart House I almost left. He sat facing you the whole time with his back to me."

Jill dreamed about John for the next two nights. She and John were unable to go some place they wanted to go because they had a tilted trailer with a cot on it and had to set the trailer upright. In another dream, she and John went dove-hunting. In another, they were walking across Siberia in the wintertime.

Maria had not shown up for two days, and June had been left with the chores again. She telephoned to say she had been in an automobile accident and was going to Mexicali for a day to recover. She telephoned again a few days later from Mexico to say she couldn't get back to the United States. *"No es posible. No tarjeta verde."*

Jill was able to hire a new helper who was recommended by a neighbor. The new woman said, when she arrived, *"Tengo gusto en conocerle. Me llamo Maria."*

John wrote from Bishop.

They have pruned the two elm trees and Roy and I have cut the wood and stacked it up in the back of my house. It'll be real good wood next winter and there really was a lot of it. We stacked it up neat along the fence so it won't be in the way this summer.

They had a little excitement down at the ranch yesterday. Dad and Roy were on horseback out on the field getting some bulls and they gave them a lot of trouble. Roy roped him and Dad rode up and hot-shotted him, the bull that is, and the bull hit Dad's horse. The horse reared up and ran away from the bull and Dad went up and landed on top of the bull. I guess he landed right on his head, no horns, thank God. He must have gotten a couple of pretty good bounces there before landing hard on the ground. He got the wind knocked out of him and was pretty stiff

114

and sore all over. Mainly his back, shoulder and ribs.
Roy and I took him to see the doctor today and he
put him in a corset and a belt and gave him some pills
for the pain.

8

The Movies

On January 30, 1974, Judi Rosner from Filmways brought director Larry Peerce to meet Jill. Jill felt he was probably more important than anyone else in the film, and she had been wondering what he would be like. He was dark and energetic with a short, sharp beard. He was excited about the film. At first Jill thought he was coming on a little strong, but he was immediately at ease with her. She got the feeling that he really knew what he was doing.

"I think it's important that the movie is an ordinary thing," she told him. "Me as a person, and what I do, along with everything else, should seem ordinary."

"Yes," he said. "If we can do just that, make the movie seem really ordinary, we will really have something."

Jill said, "I'm glad you don't want to make me out like Superman or Captain Marvel, Jr."

Jill was posted periodically about the film for the next six weeks by David or by Feldman, and she telephoned David to ask when he wanted to discuss changes in the script. He said he would call Feldman and they'd set a date.

Meanwhile, John came down most weekends, and the relationship was getting better and better. Early in March, Jill told him in a letter how she felt about it.

I had the most wonderful weekend with you and I feel so very close. John, you could never know how close and how much need I have for you. The way you can always have your feet so solidly on the ground is incredible. And I love you for that very basic, beautiful quality you have. And I love you for your simple way of seeing things. I began to understand even more on Sunday when we were alone together. It is a whole new life for me now because you are there, and you will never know how much easier it is to deal with problems. Hard, and sad, trying to understand a lot of things in that little bit of time. I love you, John, so very deeply, and I'm growing to know our differences more than I ever thought I would. They are beautiful in themselves. I think it makes us realize we are two different human beings, each complete and individual. And each of us has the chance to intimately know, understand and love not a carbon copy but a very different person. I love our relationship, John.

Linda Tikalsky and Audra Jo Baumgarth telephoned Jill from Bishop on Dave McCoy's credit card. Linda and Frank were visiting from Colorado. They talked for half an hour, mostly about the script. "I'm not going to sign a release for them the way things are going now," Linda said.

"Neither am I, Jill."

"If they won't change things to suit you, Jill, I don't think you should agree to make a movie."

Jill told June about the conversation, and June said, "I think you should think about how it can help other paraplegics and not worry about accuracy unless there are

117

serious distortions. I read the script again, and I think it's good. Most of it is just fine and won't matter at all."

Jill wrote to John about it also.

> I miss talking to you like crazy.
>
> I've been reading the damn movie script all day and it didn't cheer me up a bit. I was cheery before I started worrying about what isn't true and honest about the script. Lordy, lordy! I'm not great at swaying people to my way of thinking, but I know I have to try. Ugh! It really is hard for me to fight for this kind of thing.
>
> You'll have to forgive me carrying on, but saying it to you already makes it an easier task. You are so amazing how you listen away to me and then offer somehow what should be said or done, and then I know what to do next.
>
> Did I tell you I met the director. He's married and has a daughter, Amy, at Hawthorne and doesn't turn me on one ounce. This whole movie business can easily boost my ego sky high, so please be patient. And tell me from time to time that I'm just plain old ordinary Jill.
>
> You are so very important to me, John, that I hope you'll go along with all of this nonsense and my changeable ways. So far, you are so wonderful about it all. I love you so very much and I don't want you ever to leave me. Goodbye.
>
> All my love
> Jill

Feldman called to say they would film the movie on location at Mammoth and Bishop. He made it clear that he didn't want Jill around when interior emotional scenes were being filmed, but she was welcome at outdoor scenes.

"Ed," Jill said, "I have a few changes in mind and I'm wondering when I'll be able to go over them with you."

"What, specifically?"

Jill wasn't ready for that one. She didn't know where to

begin. She said she was upset with Audra Jo's character in the script, and she talked a lot about that. Feldman said they would all get together next week.

And they did. Jill and June met with Judi, David, Larry Peerce, and Ed Feldman at Feldman's home. Jill brought her thoroughly-annotated copy of the screenplay and four single-spaced pages of objections and suggestions which she carried in the neat leather portfolio John had given her for her birthday. She had limited herself to 106 detailed criticisms, since she couldn't bring herself to say, for example, that the very essence of her family's role in her rehabilitation was just not there.

Jill was adamant about some things. "The cabin scene, with Linda and me being so coy about meeting Dick-Buek-the-Famous-Skier?" she said. "That has got to go. And I'm really bothered by Jill's naiveté about the Indian reservation. I do not have a muscle-less brain, and I don't want to hurt my relationship with the Indians." She was referring to an invented scene in which Buek drives Jill to the reservation and Jill says, "What is it? I used to ski right on the other side of this mountain, and I never knew it was here."

David seemed hurt by Jill's remarks, but she went on. She wanted to know why her family almost never appeared in the early hospital scenes. "They were there all the time, and their support meant everything to me." She was thinking of June's endless patience and her father's uncomplaining loss of his beloved ranch because of the hospital bills. She remembered that she had cried heavily when she was first told she could not teach because she was in a chair, and that it was June who had said, "Well, that's the first step; where do we go from here?"

Jill objected to a patient at the rehabilitation center saying to her, What's the matter, teacher, the freak show getting you down? "These people are not losers," Jill said. "They respect each other too much to be so insensitive."

"I'm with you about that," Larry Peerce said.

Jill was particularly upset with Dave McCoy's character in the script. The real Dave was not at all like this macho

119

coach who got all hyped up and told his racers, "You're going to win . . . Take it away from her . . . See you at the Olympics." Dave's way was rather to say things like, "Your skis should float . . . the way a deer runs through the woods, only touching down when it changes direction."

David said, "I wish you had told me earlier."

Larry agreed with all of Jill's criticisms, but Jill wasn't sure that he was really going to do anything about them. Both he and Feldman said they understood Jill's feelings about the script and sympathized. But this is a movie, Feldman said, and everyone cannot be sweet and nice and loving all the time. Larry said, "It's not so much what's in the script but the way it's going to be played."

David listened intently and took notes the whole time, elated at one point and upset at another, depending upon Jill's response to the script and to his alternative suggestions. He was extremely anxious to satisfy her requests, and he promised to rework the script.

Jill felt good about the meeting. "The overall thing is," she said, "I want my life to appear to be an ordinary life. Not spectacular."

Jill later discovered that Linda Meyers Tikalsky had written the following letter to David just a week before the big script meeting.

Dear Mr. Seltzer:

I have reviewed the movie script "The Other Side of the Mountain" and have found it terribly wanting. Succinctly, it is a faint resemblance to the life and personality of Jill Kinmont, grossly inaccurate concerning my relationships to Jill and skiing generally, and grossly inaccurate in its portrayal of both Audra Jo and Jill's father Bill. Bob Kinmont is non-existent.

My major personal objection is my being portrayed as an audacious, insensitive adolescent who peremptorily addresses herself to various matters in her relationships vis-à-vis Jill and Audra Jo. Nonsense! Jill and Audra Jo were my idols. I was awed by them. It was Jill's accident and her response to it

120

that encouraged me to compete, and Dave McCoy's faith that permitted me to hope for success. If you want to use who I am, you must use what I am; no more, no less.

You have portrayed Audra Jo as a berating, cajoling, scolding counselor who somehow brings Jill to grips with reality. This is trite and untrue and it is not Audra Jo's style. The magnificent part of Jill's story is that she didn't need this. If Audra Jo ever played the role of a counselor with Jill, it was done tenderly and subtly. She took traumatic injury in stride and if the "letdown" everyone expected ever came, it came furtively, quietly, and away from public view. If she wept, it is her secret. I suppose that this is hard for most people to believe; however, it is true nonetheless. This very fact is what makes her story worth telling. Jill mentioned to me that you felt that you were the creative artist in this script, but I could not disagree with you more. Jill is the creator; your job is quite simply to tell her story as truthfully and beautifully as possible.

Sincerely
Linda Tikalsky

Soon afterwards, the *Los Angeles Herald-Examiner* carried an article about Universal's plans for the film. Speaking of Ed Feldman, the article stated, "He says that initially there was some effort on the part of her family to idealize the story, thus denying it some of its dramatic conflict, but they soon understood the worth of the whole truth and are now happy with the script."

• • •

The film was suddenly underway, and everything happened at once. The cast was selected. Press interviews were set up. Jill, as the official technical adviser, went to the Universal studios four times to talk about the script, costumes, props, and other details.

The role of Jill was to be played by a 26-year-old

121

unknown, Marilyn Hassett, one of 300 girls who tried out for the part. Jill read in the newspaper that Marilyn's screen test was the scene between Jill and Dick Buek in which they are talking about marriage and not being able to have children. Marilyn was the only one who did not think the scene called for tears and sobbing. She was chosen because of her natural quality of gentleness and what Larry Peerce called "a certain fragility." Also because she was attractive. The news story quoted Feldman as saying, "We wanted a pretty girl. It is my belief that people relate to pretty things that are broken."

The role of Dick Buek was to be played by Beau Bridges, an experienced actor of 33. He came to visit Jill one evening with a long list of questions about who Dick was and how he looked and talked and skied. Beau was lively and looked very young.

"Dick didn't have a black leather jacket and long silver skis like in the script," Jill said. "It was always dirty Levi's and beat-up skis. He dove off the cliffs at Acapulco and flew his plane under the Sun Valley lift line and under the Golden Gate bridge, so people called him Mad Dog. He even signed his letters "md"—in small letters. He was U.S. Downhill champion, had a motorcycle accident that doctors said would keep him on crutches or worse for life, and then came back, skiing with one leg in a cast, to win the downhill title again a few years later."

Beau sat shaking his head slowly. "Tough act to follow," he said. "I mean . . . to re-create." Jill explained how she had skied with Dick before her accident and how he had encouraged her later to take her disability as a challenge rather than as a sentence. He had wanted to marry Jill and he had planned a house to accommodate both Jill's wheelchair and his airplane. He was killed doing power stalls over Donner Lake in 1957.

"Why did he do all these weird things?" Beau asked.

"I don't know. There was mystery in why he did the things he did. He hadn't gotten beyond tenth grade, but he read a lot and was extremely bright and philosophical, as well as impulsive. And he had very definite attitudes about things."

"Like what?"

"Like he didn't care what people would think. Very different from me. And like he had no tolerance for people with self-pity. He had no use for that, and everybody knew it. This was the best thing in the world for me. It was incredible for me. It was really important that he didn't feel pity for me, or let me feel it."

"Doesn't sound so wild," Beau said.

"Oh, Dick would clown and carry on all the time, but he was serious. He said I had a chance most people don't get—to show the world they could become something in spite of huge obstacles. It was his thing to overcome obstacles. He even put obstacles in his own way so he could do that."

Beau stayed until 11 p.m. and he seemed to want to stay a lot longer.

Jill first met Marilyn Hassett at school when Larry Peerce and the casting director and a Universal public relations man brought her over. Marilyn was slender and shy, and she did indeed look delicate in her faded jeans and turtleneck shirt. Jill said at once, "Gee, I really like the way you look." The two women looked surprisingly alike. Similar coloring, although they had different-colored eyes. Same height. Lean, delicate facial features. The same straight, slender noses.

The PR man began taking pictures immediately, but Jill and Marilyn went into a long personal conversation, oblivious of the bustle going on about them.

"What gets to me in the film," Marilyn said, "is that it shows the strength people can have within themselves and the support that comes from family ties. I know my mother was such an incredible inspiration to me when she took care of me for a year after my accident. I was on the verge of a nervous breakdown, and she really kept me going."

"What was the accident?" Jill said. "Is what I heard true?"

123

"All I'd done was commercials, Jill, except for a small part in *They Shoot Horses, Don't They?* One commercial was to have me on an elephant, and the night before, I dreamed about a terrible catastrophe and asked the director to find another girl. He convinced me that everything would be all right. But it wasn't. Bizarre things happened. A dog barked on the set. An engine backfired, and some horses stampeded. It was too much for the elephant. She kicked her trainer in the face and threw me and stepped on me. It was just so awful."

Marilyn's pelvis had been fractured in the accident, and there was some nerve damage to her legs. She spent months in the hospital and more than half a year in a wheelchair. "It was dreadful."

Jill spoke of her own hospital experiences and asked if Marilyn had fully recovered.

"Pretty much," Marilyn said, "but I have a lot of fear in me that's just coming out. I'm trying to see what it is. Fear of rejection, of being wrong, of not being good enough."

A week later, Universal arranged a press conference in the Hawthorne School library. Marilyn and Jill and Jerry and Lyn and the principal and several teachers and two dozen reporters. The press wanted to know how Jill felt about her life being on film and how Marilyn felt about acting in a wheelchair. "I feel pretty great," Jill said. "After all, how many people get to have a movie made of them without dying first?"

Was Marilyn a native? "Yes," she answered. "Born in Hollywood, although I spent some time in San Francisco. I went to a Catholic girls' boarding school and I was pretty conservative. Didn't own a two-piece bathing suit until I was twenty-one."

The elephant accident was good copy, and Marilyn was deluged with questions about it. "I seem to be accident-prone," she said. "I fell off a bridge. I've broken my nose and my leg and my ankles and my wrists." She added that while she was still in rehabilitation after the elephant incident, she was in an automobile accident on her way to an audition. She went head first through the roof and had to

124

have three skull operations. "I couldn't handle it," she said. "I flipped. I said it's not meant for me to pursue a career. I ran away to study music in Paris where no one knew about the accidents and no one could pity me."

"How does it feel to have a starring role?"

"Just the greatest opportunity in my life," Marilyn said. "After the auditions one day I found some flowers by my door and a card which said, 'You are our Jill. Congratulations!' I couldn't stop yelling and screaming and laughing. The only thing I could think of was calling my mother. She's seen me go through so much, and I wanted to share it with her."

Someone said, "Jill, how do you get to have a movie made of you?"

"Just luck," Jill said. "Lucky to be on the cover of *Sports Illustrated* just before my accident, lucky to have the press keep at me all this time, and lucky that Mr. Feldman got this idea for a film."

The reporters finally left, and Jill and Marilyn retired for lunch in the school cafeteria. "I have so many questions for you," Marilyn said. "The big one is, what is it about you that makes it possible for you to deal with your accident and all that came after?"

"I don't really know," Jill said. "Having a good feeling about myself, to start with." She realized that Marilyn seemed quite unsure of *her*self at the moment. "Total support from my family, and a feeling that you don't let down everyone around you, you keep going no matter what." She wasn't at all satisfied with her answer.

"Weren't you depressed?"

"No, and I don't know why not, either."

Jill attempted to explain what went on inside her while trying to accept the drastic change in her life style and in her self-image. "It wasn't that dramatic," she said. "It certainly wasn't nightmare after nightmare or not wanting to see anybody."

The conversation was cut short by the school bell. Marilyn said she wanted to get together soon with June and Jill and her own mother.

125

Jill went back to her room, and Marilyn went off into the courtyard, talking with Larry. Jill felt that life was not easy for Marilyn and that Larry was a great help to her.

Jill was granted an extended Easter vacation so she could be on hand for the filming at Mammoth and Bishop. She and June settled into the Grove Street house and hired John's cousin, Mary Jane, to get Jill up in the mornings. On the second day, Judi telephoned five times, and Dave and Roma McCoy came over to talk about the script. They had read it, and they thought some of it was terrible. They were deeply concerned that Dave was to be shown grabbing Jill's ambulance driver by the collar, spinning him around hard against the wall, and waving *Sports Illustrated*—with Jill on the cover—in his face. "And he says," Roma said, " 'Look, this is Jill Kinmont; Jill Kinmont doesn't die'—or some dumb thing like that."

Jill also traced down an amateur movie film of her accident at Alta, Utah, in 1955. She helped Judi make arrangements to shoot at the Rocking K, and she set the costume department straight on how racing numbers are worn. Meanwhile she saw John on evenings when he wasn't driving. Bob and Jerry were both in Bishop, and John joined all the Kinmonts for dinner on Easter Sunday.

On Monday, Lee Baumgarth was interviewed and hired to play himself in the film, acting as Jill's physical therapist during her rehabilitation. Jerry Kinmont was hired to play himself. On Tuesday the entire cast and film crew arrived, and on Wednesday Jill and her family and friends went to Mammoth Mountain to meet the cast. Jill was very much surprised, after seeing the screen version of the Kinmont family, that she and her family had not been consulted about the casting. The actors didn't look or act at all like their real-life counterparts, although Jill liked the boy who played Jerry and the man who played Buddy Werner. The actor who played Bill Kinmont was on stage all the time, trying to make himself the center of attention. "He's an ass," Jill said. When Bob Kinmont saw who they had cast as Bob Kinmont, he just shook his head. "I can't believe it," he said.

On Thursday, shooting began at Mammoth.

The scenes to be filmed were events that had occurred in the early 1950s here at Dave McCoy's Mammoth Mountain. The mountain wasn't literally his, but the ski development was. It had grown in 24 years from two rope tows to 13 chairlifts and a gondola to the top of the mountain at 11,000 feet. When Jill had trained on the mountain as a teenager, 250 skiers constituted an overflow crowd. Today, the employees alone numbered 820.

One corner of the huge parking lot, however, was clearly Mammoth, 1951. Several young skiers in worn leather ski boots and baggy pants were strapping their beaten-up hickory skis on the roof rack of a black 1941 Chevrolet sedan. It was cold and snowing and bitter, and there was nothing feigned about their shivering. They all piled into the old car under the all-seeing eyes of a motion picture camera on the roof platform of a nearby truck. High on a snowbank to one side were the real, present-day Jill Kinmont and Audra Jo Baumgarth. At one time or another, all the actors came over to ask—lightheartedly but usually with a nervous laugh—"How do I look?"

After the scene had been shot five times, two of the girls walked by the snowbank—Marilyn Hassett, dressed as 16-year-old Jill, and actress Belinda Montgomery, dressed as 16-year-old Audra Jo. Marilyn waved weakly to Jill as she hurried toward her dressing room in one of the film company's trailers. Belinda stopped to talk with Audra Jo.

"Where's Marilyn off to in such a rush?" Audra Jo said.

"Oh, she's always running off to the bathroom," Jill said. "She's real nervous. She was hoping she'd make it through the scene without wetting her pants."

During the afternoon, Marilyn always spoke to Jill when she was coming from the hairdresser or from her dressing room, but Jill felt she was nevertheless aloof and apart. "She's really getting into the role," Jill said to Audra Jo, who was having an animated conversation with Belinda. "I guess she's got too many demands. Too bad, because I'd sure like to get to know her better."

A long, restful weekend was followed by six consecu-

127

tive days of shooting, starting Tuesday morning. CBS telephoned Jill to ask if they could film her and the whole movie-making scene for their show, *60 Minutes*. Plus shots of Jill teaching and Jill at home. The *Los Angeles Times* and the *Examiner* both called, wanting to come up to cover the filming.

In the midst of all this, Jill received a call from the Order of Rainbow Girls, a Masonic auxiliary to which she and Audra Jo had belonged during their high school years. The California branch was interested in Jill's work at the Indian center and wanted to take it on as their annual service project. It would mean $14,000 for the Center, but the money had to be donated to a foundation. "Do you have a foundation?" the caller asked. "No," Jill said. "But I'll set one up."

Wednesday was stormy, which made for some exciting race footage up on the Blue Ox run and a dramatic setting for loading the injured young Jill into an ambulance. All day Thursday was spent filming in the locker rooms.

Marilyn often came to Jill with questions and usually apologized for interrupting. Jill told her she was not "physical" enough. "When I was 17 and racing," she said, "I was full of steam, very athletic, very much on top of things, and obviously proud of it."

Marilyn looked worried. She went to her dressing room to work out ways in which she, age 26, could project this spirit of the young and eager Jill. She wished she could talk with Jill more and get to really know her, but Jill seemed reserved and distant and of course had a lot of important things on her mind.

Jill had a bad night, tossing and turning, worrying about how the "real people" felt about the way they were being portrayed. Audra Jo hated the dialogue, but at least she had become very good friends with Belinda. Dave wouldn't watch any of the shooting, not even the skiing.

Saturday was a great day on the mountain. Sun, blue sky, sparkling snow. It was the day for racing scenes and for shooting Jill's happy days at Sun Valley with Buddy Werner, who was soon to become America's top skier.

128

Jerry commandeered a sno-cat for Jill, strapped her in securely, tied her chair on the back and sent her up the mountain to watch the filming. It was wondeful being back on the mountain again. Jill felt very much at home on the snow in the crisp breeze with the valley spread out below and Mt. Banner standing like a small Matterhorn to the north.

Marilyn came over and sat with her in the sno-cat. They both appreciated the fact that they were two "Jills" who couldn't ski watching a bunch of other "Jills" who could, for today there were "Jills" all over the place. Marilyn had four skiing doubles, all of them Jill's friends and all of them veterans of the U.S. ski team. "They're not doubles," Jill said. "They're quadruples." All were dressed exactly like Marilyn, whose costume matched that of Jill on the cover of *Sports Illustrated* the week of her accident. They saved the crew a lot of camera time because it took each "Jill" 20 minutes to ride up the mountain again on the lift after a take.

Marilyn did a scene that began with a close-up in the starting gate. When the starter said, "Five . . . four . . . three . . . two . . . one . . . *go!*" she pushed out of the gate with every ounce of strength she could muster. She flew down the steep slope like a real competitor and fell into Larry's arms just out of sight of the camera. One of the doubles picked up the scene later on.

It was odd for Jill to see herself—her former self—wherever she looked. She thought of shouting, "Okay, now, will the *real* Jill Kinmont please ski forward!" She had no wish to be back there, back in those great bright young racing days. Her former self seemed to be just about as unreal as all the "Jills" skiing on the mountain today, as unreal and just as much fun to watch or look back upon.

The following Thursday Jill had—or rather Marilyn had—still another double, stuntman Loren Janes. The morning was devoted to the most spectacular shot in the film, Jill's crash, which had actually occurred during a giant slalom race at Alta, Utah, in 1955. Janes was an old skiing friend of Jill's, and Jill worried about the big leap he was planning. So did June and the film crew and the rest of the cast. They had all gone by sno-cat to the Blue Ox area high on the back side of the mountain, along with several dozen extras. Above the Blue Ox run was a rocky cliff covered with snow, and this was where Janes was to make his big leap. He would land on a great pile of cardboard boxes on the steep snow slope 40 feet below. Jill was amazed at all the planning and complex timing that went into this one shot. She and Audra Jo and June had come up together and were comfortably propped up in the snow where they would have a grandstand view of the big act to come.

It was indeed a circus: Larry Peerce, the ringmaster, with a bullhorn . . . honored guests Jill and Audra Jo in their special box . . . "spectators" waiting in dreadful anticipation of the feat they had been hearing so much about . . . newsmen clambering for a better view . . . Larry's cameras trained on the star performer . . . and the CBS cameras photographing Jill watching the Universal cameras photographing "Jill."

Loren Janes stood back from the cliff edge in his Jill Kinmont wig and yellow sweater, running his skis back and forth on the snow as if ready for the starter's *"Go!"* Jill looked up at the image of her former self—a man in girl's clothing about to jump deliberately off a cliff onto a pile of cardboard—and she realized how ridiculous the whole scene was. "It's just like a 1948 Western," she said to Audra Jo. Then she turned seriously to one of the film crewmen and asked, "This is *my* accident?"

"Sure is, Jill."

"In no *way* is this the way it happened. Nobody who's ever skied would believe a moment of it."

"Don't worry, they're going to film it with the camera on its side so you'll seem to be flying horizontally."

"I guess I'll have to see it to understand it," Jill said.

June was pale with fear. She was sure that Janes would get hurt.

The big moment came with everything but the roll of

drums. Janes leaped forward into space, completing a 360-degree layout somersault before crashing onto the pile of boxes. He was unhurt, but he broke a ski. "It was an accident," he said.

The end of Jill's fall was filmed at another spot on the mountain. Marilyn lay crumpled in the snow with spectators beginning to crowd around her. Larry was orchestrating the show, his black hair blowing and the fur-lined hood of his parka frosted with snow. He was shouting through his bullhorn, "This is where Jill breaks her neck. It's terrible, do you hear? Terrible! Look up the hill. I want you to see blood!" Ed Feldman was on the sidelines, bundled up in a sweater and scarf and a big wool cap with reindeer on it, shocks of gray hair sticking out from under the edges. He stood carefully beside a sno-cat, having floundered in the powder snow the day before in a fit of enthusiasm.

The real Jill Kinmont looked on calmly from her seat in the sno-cat. She loved the drama she was witnessing—the drama of re-creating a skiing scene of the early 1950s—but she felt no connection whatever between her own accident and the events she was so avidly watching today. She felt very much in touch with herself the next morning, however, when she received a letter from one of her pupils in Beverly Hills.

Dear Miss Kinmont,
    I miss you so very much. How are you? Are you having fun? Is there any snow on the mountain? Mrs. Kranhouse is very nice to us. I hope to see you soon.

                         Good bye
                         Carol

•   •   •

The first 10 days of May were devoted to shooting in Bishop. The air was still brisk in the early morning, the wild iris was blooming, and the entire town was caught up in the excitement of putting the Bishop of two decades ago on film. Local tradesmen and high school students and Indian children had been cast several weeks before. Enough cars of the vintage of 1939 through 1950 had been rounded up to stage a realistic reproduction of "draggin' Main" in 1952, which was the first sequence to be shot in Bishop. It was filmed at 8 p.m. in a drenching rain.

The wardrobe people and the assistant producers were meticulous about every detail. Everything had to be just as it had been in 1952, clothing, automobiles, ski boots, hair styles. The high school students did their own research and their own costuming, including a number of odd haircuts and several greasy ducktails.

Marilyn's problem was a more fundamental one. In Bishop, where most of the filming was to be of Jill after her accident, Marilyn had to switch from being an energetic and very eager teen-ager to acting the part of a severely paralyzed young woman. This was where Jerry Kinmont's keen eye for detail enabled Marilyn to capture the essence of Jill's physical presence, her way of moving, writing, eating, speaking. She and Jerry got along beautifully. He was very much like a brother of hers, and she felt she was really getting to know Jill through him.

"Raise your forearms," he said. "Okay, you can do that. But if I push on your fists ever so gently, there is no way that you can resist or push back. The only way to get your arms back down is to let gravity do it for you." He explained that Jill was more or less helpless when she was on her back but had a lot working for her when she was sitting up. She could lift her arms. She could lift her left hand at the wrist when her palm was facing down.

He fitted a simple brace on her right hand so she could hold a pen. "Essentially," he said, "you have to write by swinging your shoulder. When Jill began writing, her letters were three inches high, but she has become so skilled and so subtle about it that her writing is neat and small and you scarcely notice how she does it. But if you allow the pen to tilt outward, your wrist will turn palm-up and you're stuck with it that way."

Jerry kept a constant watch on Marilyn and came over to her whenever he spotted something that was out of character or was beyond the physical capabilities of a quadriplegic. "Jill is very conscious of keeping her skirt down," he said one day. "Also, she can't move her hands that way. Look, try it like this. . . ."

Another time he stopped her from lifting a glass of water between her fists. "The hands are fine," he said. "But you've got to remember about her balance. If she leans that far forward, the extra weight of the water is going to topple her right forward onto her face." He also showed her how to work her fingers into the two rings of Jill's specially made fork.

During the rehearsal for a romantic scene between Marilyn and Beau Bridges on the Indian reservation, Jerry showed Marilyn a typical gesture Jill used when she was musing. Jill's right hand had no feeling, but she could feel with the thumb side of her left hand. So she often absent-mindedly stroked her lower lip gently with the ball of her left thumb.

The most fun was learning to operate the electric wheelchair. This proved to be a difficult skill, however, to maneuver as deftly as Jill had learned to do it. The chair's one control lever was simplicity itself—forward to go forward, reverse for reverse, left to turn left, right to turn right. But to wheel at full speed through a narrow doorway, around the end of a couch and up to a table without toppling the open water bottle on the tray . . . this takes practice. "Jill doesn't do this by the feel of it," Jerry said. "She does it by sight, constantly picking her way, totally aware of the terrain and the obstacles, judging just how narrow a passageway is, figuring just where to start a turn . . . and learning how to take bumps without losing stuff off the tray."

"It'd be easier if the tray had a rim on it," Marilyn said.

"If it had a rim, she couldn't push papers and things off the tray when she wants to get rid of them."

One of the most exhilarating days was shooting the high school band at the Bishop airport as Dick Buek flies 18-

year-old Jill back from the hospital in Los Angeles. In actuality, there had been no band and it had been Bob Symons who flew Jill back from the hospital, but it made a great scene. It reminded Jill of *The Music Man.* After Marilyn was carried from the plane and put in her wheelchair, Jill noticed with some concern that Marilyn was sitting up so straight that she looked rigid and uncomfortable. Jill herself felt quite relaxed in her chair, and she decided she had better speak to Marilyn or Jerry about this. However, when she was downtown later in the day, rolling along the sidewalk, she watched her reflection go by in the store windows. She was shocked to find that Marilyn had imitated her exactly! Jill immediately began to think up ways of appearing a lot more comfortable and at ease in her chair.

Jill watched Marilyn more carefully after this. It was a weird experience at times, realizing that she could in some ways see herself more clearly by watching someone else— a woman who was only pretending to be Jill. A second thing she noticed by watching Marilyn was how much she used her hands and how normal her gestures were. How graceful, in fact. Jill had always assumed that her permanently curled fingers made her hands look like paws and that they must therefore always appear to be clumsy. She watched how she moved her own hands, and indeed they were not clumsy at all.

Marilyn could easily have been mistaken for Jill, and she often was when she wheeled along Main Street in her replica of Jill's wheelchair. Several people said, "Good morning, Jill," and many others nodded in the way you would nod to someone you have greeted a hundred times before. Marilyn was uneasy about this. She felt like an impostor.

No one else in the cast was ever mistaken for the real people whose roles they were playing. Jill and June were both disturbed by the casting of Nan Martin as June. Nan was a good actress, but her manner and her voice were, June felt, affected and nervous and harsh.

Dabney Coleman was something else. He played Dave

McCoy, and he was very concerned about doing it well. He didn't look like Dave and his manner was very different from Dave's, but he kept working on it. He did not want to meet Dave McCoy personally, but he asked Jill many, many questions. He even asked how Dave would have delivered specific lines.

Beau Bridges captured a lot of Dick Buek, particularly when it came to clowning and to some of Dick's wild behavior. However, Beau was decidedly more boyish than Dick had been. Dick had had more of a James Dean coolness about him than Beau could project. As Jill said, "There was mystery in Dick, and there wasn't that about Beau."

The most beautiful scene to watch was on the reservation where Marilyn wheeled easily alongside a stream with Jill's Indian pupils running with her, asking questions. The spot was away back in a field by a row of willows, and birds were singing. The children asked questions on camera, according to the script, and they asked even more questions between takes. Was Marilyn having fun in the chair? Why weren't they photographing Jill herself? Could Marilyn open her fingers if she *wanted* to?

The same location was used the next day for a romantic scene with Jill and Dick Buek—that is, with Marilyn and Beau—in a jeep. Jill and June watched from across the creek, and they shared a set of headphones so they could tune in on the dialogue. The scene was very moving and both of them had tears in their eyes.

David Seltzer and his wife, Alice, came to dinner with Jill and June and John, and they talked about Bishop and good fishing spots and film-making. David had been watching the shooting, and he hated it. He always hated watching his scripts getting chewed up and switched around.

John was glad to find someone else who was uncomfortable on the set. "I'm not in the least bit impressed by all this confusion," he said. "And I don't trust them, either." He had watched very little of the Bishop filming and none of what went on at Mammoth. He was completely ignored by the crew and the big shots alike and he felt clearly ostracized. He felt strongly—negatively—about part of the script, but he didn't think anyone wanted to know about it. Also, he had found that criticizing the script was a good way to get into heavy arguments with June and with Bob.

One of the episodes John did watch with Jill was the scene in which Jill's mother and father are looking anxiously up at the sky where Dick Buek was supposedly doing aerobatics with Jill. The father cried out, "I'm going to call Dave," and his wife said, "I think you'd better."

John said to Jill, "Why the devil is he calling *Dave?*"

"I haven't the slightest idea," Jill said.

The most emotional scene in the film was when Dick said goodbye to Jill for the last time before taking his plane off from the paved road just below the Rocking K ranch. Larry was totally involved in it long before the cameras started rolling. Jill and Audra Jo moved up by the camera to get a good view. Larry was pacing back and forth, glancing at them nervously. "Come on, girls," he said finally. "You'll have to sit back where you can't be seen. The scene is too heavy, too heavy."

The scene *was* heavy. Cast and crew and visitors alike were weeping by the time it was finished. Jill herself was moved, but she couldn't identify with it. She looked around at all the tears and she said, "What's the matter with you guys? It's only a movie."

The remark was one that Larry and Marilyn never forgot. When they were alone later, Larry said, "That's her cool, saying it's only a movie. That's her spine that she built around herself. 'I never cry at work.' Same thing when we were filming the accident, and *60 Minutes* was there filming her watching us create the accident and her mother . . ."

"Her mother was hysterical."

"Her mother fell apart. I'll tell you, it was a nightmare."

"And Jill said, it's just a movie!"

"And then you realize that's how she dealt with her life."

136

FROM THE FILM...

Timothy Bottoms as John Boothe and
Marilyn Hassett as Jill Kinmont.

Timothy Bottoms as John Boothe; June Dayton and James (Bud) Bottoms as John's parents.

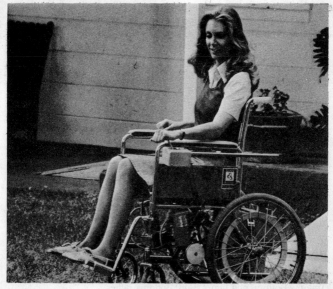

Marilyn Hassett tests her powered wheelchair.

Timothy Bottoms and James (Bud) Bottoms, father and son, as John and Dudley Boothe, father and son.

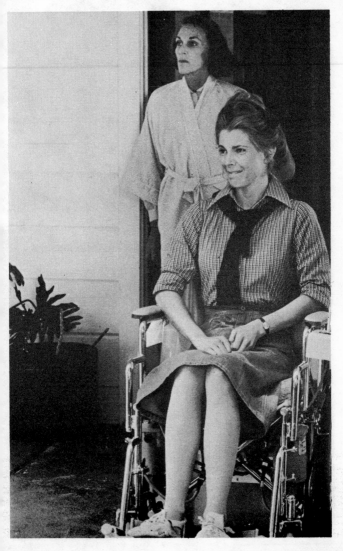

Marilyn Hassett with William Bryant (as Jill's father, Bill Kinmont), and with Nan Martin (as Jill's mother, June Kinmont).

Clockwise: Marilyn Hassett with Dabney Coleman (Dave McCoy) and Myron Healey (Dr. Scott); in the arms of Timothy Bottoms; as a bridesmaid at Audra Jo's wedding (with Dabney Coleman).

Love is patience and understanding—and joy.

FROM JILL'S LIFE...

Jill and her brothers Jerry and Bob return to Bishop Creek.

At the Owens Valley Indian Education
Center on the Paiute reservation,
Jill teaches her summer pupils.

Burk Uzzle/MAGNUM (3)

After watching a Bishop parade,
Jill and John Boothe go shopping.

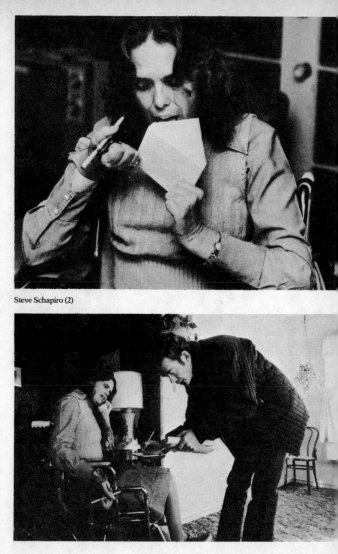

Steve Schapiro (2)

There are invitations and thank you notes to be written, and finally a November wedding.

Jill, John and friend.

They were both relieved to be headed for Los Angeles, where most of the balance of the shooting would be interiors and Jill would be busy with her school. "That woman got to me every time I met her," Larry said. "Like a producer. She came in and everyone stood at attention on the set."

"Every day on the set," Marilyn said. "Zhzhzhzh . . ." she imitated the sound of the electric wheelchair. "Zhzhzh . . . rolling up in her chair."

9

Real Life Again

Jill was due back at school May 13, 1974, and she left Bishop wanting more than ever to teach there rather than in Beverly Hills. She missed John, but she admitted it was nice to be getting his phone calls and letters again. He wrote:

I was really happy to see the story in the *Times* today. It was really good, and I think it did you a lot more justice than the *Examiner* did. I love the picture, too, Jill. That beautiful, honest, suprised smile that only you have. That picture tells so much of what I feel about you and a little bit of what troubles me so much about this movie deal. Your smile is so real and honest and Marilyn's looks forced and phony. Please don't think I'm being nasty again because I don't mean to be. Please help me try and understand all these things that I am fighting with and help me get the best of them like you have been.

138

I loved your Mom's comment about when you marry John. It makes me feel so good when you tell me about those little things, and your feelings about them. She has so much on her mind right now and I know I shouldn't get so impatient and frustrated about her feelings towards me. I admire her so much and want, more than anything in the world, for her to feel good about us and what we have.

> I love you.

Jill had to miss the rest of the filming, but she got a full report on the rehabilitation scenes from Lee and Audra Jo. The Baumgarths stayed in the Kinmonts' guest room while Lee was playing himself on location at the Veterans Administration hospital in Long Beach. Jerry and Lyn were also there. They slept in sleeping bags on the back deck.

Lee rehearsed in the living room the night before. Nobody would take him seriously. He said he was supposed to be in Long Beach at 7:30 in the morning in order to get made up. He thought he could do it himself before he left and save time.

After the first day of shooting, he and Audra Jo came bursting in like children returning from a Christmas party. "We sure got the questions, Jill," Audra Jo said as she wheeled herself in the front door. "There were quads all over! A real peanut gallery while all the filming was going on. *What's so special about being a quadriplegic? Why make a movie about HER?* I said the movie was simply because of what you've accomplished. It's certainly not enough just to be a quad."

Lee came in from the garage and joined right in. "The big thing down there, Jill, was all about pushing their own wheelchairs. Who could do it best. Man, they had races down the hall, and that's where all their energy went. That was the whole pattern in this haven they have for themselves down there."

Audra Jo said, "They said, well, Kinmont's got it made. All that movie money and book money. Does she use an *electric* chair? I said yes and they said, well, it's a Cadillac, what's she need *that* for? I said she uses it to get around. They said that's a cop-out because she's not using what she *has* to push her chair. I said well she teaches every day. It's a matter of using your energies in the best way. Then one of them said, Okay, I can see that. It's okay if she uses an electric chair, and they came to see that."

After dinner, Lee said, "Jill, what do you say if a quad comes up and says, look, how can I learn anything from *you?* You've got it made."

"Maybe nothing," Jill said. "You can't generalize, Lee. I'd have to know where the person is coming from, what does he want. Does he want something my experience could help him with? Does he want what I can offer? You do that with the kids. With anyone. With any new relationship."

"Fair enough."

"Each of them has to figure it out. Not that he has to do it himself, but he has to figure where he has to reach out or open up. We can all make changes. We can have six careers if we want."

"How did Marilyn make out with the tongs in her head?" June asked. Crutchfield tongs had been fitted into shallow holes drilled in Jill's scalp after her accident so her spine could be kept in traction.

"She didn't like it!" Audra Jo said. "They had her in the Stryker frame, and the make-up man attached the tongs with wax and made the hair all around the tongs look like it was matted with blood."

"Did her hair look good?" Jill said.

"What a question," Lee said. "There you are on the verge of death and worried about your hair. That's hardly important."

"It is too important, Lee!"

"You're always worried about what people think."

Audra Jo laughed. "And that's why John is such a good influence. He doesn't care."

June said, "And Dick didn't care."

"*Well,*" Audra Jo said, "neither does Lee."

The next morning Jill's cousin's wife telephoned to say

that her husband, Jimmy Lewis, had fallen out of a tree he was trimming and had landed on his back across two logs. His neck was broken at the sixth or seventh cervical vertebra. He was paralyzed from the shoulders down. Jimmy lived in San Jose and had six children. June flew to Santa Cruz, where Jimmy was in the hospital, to help out. Jill wrote to John about it. "I swear we really don't need another one in our family," she said.

* * *

Jill had hoped to take a leave of absence from Hawthorne and spend the year in Bishop, but she had neither the time nor the energy to follow it up. When she realized it was impossible, she wrote John.

> John, I think I will plan to be here at Hawthorne for one more year. I feel I will have commitments while the movie is being put together, and then when it comes out. I hope you understand, because I never have felt closer to you and my love has never been stronger. I really don't like to think of driving Sunset Boulevard for one more year. Ugh! But for several reasons I think right now it's best. Besides, Mr. Crist, the superintendent at the Bishop school, thought one year from now maybe he could get the funds for my job. Mom is beginning to like the idea of Bishop and wants to start a shop to sell house plants there. In fact she talks about it all the time now. Maybe she'll start it this summer. I went to a political meeting last night and it was so horrible. On and on. I wanted to be with you, damn it, at a place where you would want to be where simple basic open happy contented people were. I hope you will be patient with me because I love you so very much. I know more than ever now I want to be with you. Then I think I'd be happier.

The school year ended in a flurry of activity. Ed Feldman called to say the filming was completed and editing would take nearly a year. Red Valens, author of *A Long*

Way Up, came to interview Jill for two additional chapters. The publishers wanted to bring the book up to date and re-issue it as a paperback with the same title as the movie. Mike Wallace and a CBS crew spent two days filming Jill at home and at school for *60 Minutes*. Jill and her lawyer set up the Jill Kinmont Indian Education Fund with Jill, Audra Jo, and three Indians on the board of directors. And Jill missed the last day of school because her driver never showed up.

On the 23rd of June, Jill and June drove to Bishop the long way around in order to see Jimmy Lewis in the San Jose hospital. He had regained some use of his hands and arms and was in remarkably good spirits. They returned by way of Yosemite. It was a nine-hour trip, the car's engine kept missing all the way, and the air conditioner didn't work, but they forgot their problems when they saw their house on Grove Street. It was beautiful. Jill called John immediately. Jerry and Lyn had pansies growing in a flower box; they had dinner waiting. They had painted the outside a beautiful gray with white trim and had completed all the remodeling inside.

The next morning at John's house, Jill saw his neighbor, Richard Kizer, on the lawn. He was chairman of the town planning commission, and Jill talked with him about the possibility of building sidewalk ramps so wheelchairs wouldn't get stopped by the curbs. Within a few days Kizer held a meeting with Jill, Audra Jo, the head of the Public Works Department, and Howard Knox, a senior citizen member of the town council. There was no tax money or government money available, so they sent letters to service clubs and local merchants, hoping for sponsors. The ramps would be placed at the four corners of the most important intersections, and they would cost $160 each.

After the meeting, John said to Jill, "You, Jill are going to have to slow down and stop running all over like a chicken with its head cut off. You've got to have some time for yourself, and we've got to have some time for *us*."

"John, I can't turn people down when they . . ."

142

"You're so right. You're a pushover for everybody who needs something from you."

Bob and his family turned up early in August, and John barbecued shrimp for Anna's birthday party at the Grove Street house. Bob had spent the day pouring a concrete floor for the shed. That evening after he had cleaned up, John lit a cigarette and turned on the television. It was just his luck to tune in at once on an anti-smoking "commercial." Two men and a woman were saying how great it was that smoking was banned in some restaurants and on parts of airplanes, and they said they did not associate with people who smoke.

Somebody in the room said, "Bravo!" John said, "What do you mean?" Bob and June and Vikki agreed wholeheartedly with the commercial.

John said, "Three or four years ago, smoking was something anybody did anywhere. Then all of a sudden you're no good if you smoke."

"There should be places where nobody can smoke," June said.

"But that's discrimination!" John said.

"Aw, come off it," Bob said.

"They've never really proven smoking causes anything. It's just a bunch of statistics."

June said, "I've heard of people defending smoking, but I never heard before that it doesn't hurt you!"

Bob said, casually, "You know what it does to Jill's lungs, don't you?"

John looked at him but didn't say anything.

"You know she hasn't got the muscles to cough. She can't protect herself."

"I don't exactly blow smoke in her face," John said.

"She can't afford any bronchial problems *at all*."

"Don't worry, Jill tells me what she doesn't like."

"Except when she's too polite, which is pretty often."

John knew that Bob had once smoked rather heavily— before he quit. He said, "It's the ones who used to smoke who are always so damned righteous!"

143

The air was heating up, but Jill sat quietly in the middle of the argument, watching Bob and John. They were so different, yet so much alike. Both stubborn, for sure. Both trying to simplify their lives, but coming to it from different places.

John said, "You know, it's not exactly my aim to make Jill Kinmont either unhappy or sick."

"Perhaps you should think about it a little more carefully, then."

John was extremely upset by this time. "I think about it *all the time*, in case you people weren't aware."

Jill wanted to stop them, but she was afraid they would both jump on her if she tried. John's fists were clenched. He was about to speak, but he cut himself off. Jill said, "If you want to leave, I understand." John got up, kissed Jill goodbye, and walked out, slamming the door behind him.

Jill telephoned him two hours later, crying, to tell him that Bob and June were sorry. June apologized to him the next day. Bob never mentioned it again.

Jill was greatly disturbed by the tension between John and her brother. She had thought they wanted something quite similar out of life, although John had been going in the same direction since he was a kid—toward his idea of what a family should be. Bob had tried a number of ways, studying in Seattle, painting in Spain, teaching in Canada and San Francisco, and now he was consciously returning to a simpler way. Bob talked a lot about simplicity, analyzing where he was going and why, whereas John didn't talk; he just behaved in a direct and simple manner. At the same time, new ideas or changes in familiar patterns were hard for John to handle, and he was easily frustrated.

Jill did know that Bob respected John. Neither of them was in the least competitive by nature, which set them apart from most of their friends. John was a skilled mechanic, and when he worked there were no wasted words and no wasted motion. Just going out to get wood, John's body moved easily and efficiently, each move flowing into the next. When his pick-up got in a rough place,

144

he never overdid it, never spun the tires. Bob had a deep appreciation for this kind of thing. Nevertheless, the two of them didn't seem to know quite what to make of each other.

Jill had been invited to co-host the *Mike Douglas Show*, and she received a call asking her what people she would like to have appear on her part of the show. She had her choice: John Denver, Andrew Wyeth, Georgia O'Keefe, some child behaviorists who were against medication, some quiltmakers, and some Eskimo carvers. And she could invite her family to Philadelphia to be on the show, and several of her friends. Jill said she wanted her mother and brothers to be on the show, and also the Baumgarths. Otherwise, she'd go along with anyone who turned up. There was a lot to do to prepare for her days on the air, and she talked over her plans with Audra Jo almost every day.

At the end of August, Jill and June made chicken cacciatore for the Mammoth old-timers, namely the 1952 Bishop High ski team—Jill Kinmont, Linda Meyers, and Audra Jo Nicholson and Ken Lloyd, who came with his friend Alice. It was the first time John had met Linda and Frank, and Jill was nervous. She was sure they would wonder what John was doing in this crowd, how he was supposed to fit in. Linda hadn't even remembered him from high school.

Linda and Frank each asked John about his truck routes, which ran through a part of Nevada they were particularly fond of. These two conversations lasted about five minutes each, and the talk turned to Mammoth, old ski friends, and physical exercises Linda or Lee had come across. Linda wondered if John were very shy or perhaps just not very bright. She thought, my God, how does Jill ever get him into any kind of deep discussion?

The only positive thing John got from the evening was a slight feeling of kinship with Frank Tikalsky, who was a psychologist. Linda, like Jill, had been a really big-shot skier. John hadn't yet been called John Kinmont, but

Frank had not been so fortunate. He said he had accompanied Linda to her 20th high school reunion, at which event everyone received a little booklet listing the members of the class of 1955 and their mates. Prominent on the list had been *Linda and Frank Meyers.*

Jill said Bob Kinmont had the same trouble and hated it. He had always been a man in his own right, but the press only knew him as Jill's brother. When he had taken first place in three of the six events at the Far West Junior Championships, the story was featured under the headline: BROTHER OF JILL SCORES AT BADGER.

John took Jill home early because he had to be on the road at 4:30 in the morning. Driving Jill back, he started shaking his head.

"What's the matter?" Jill said.

"Oh, just those God damn . . ."

"Well, *John!* Why didn't you just enter in?"

"There's nothing for *me* to say."

"Well, I think it's interesting," Jill said. "I love that kind of gossip."

• • •

The *Mike Douglas Show* was a big event. Jill went to Philadelphia with June to appear as co-host for three consecutive days. Douglas also brought Bob and Jerry and Audra Jo and Lee east to appear on the program.

The highlight of the three days, as far as Jill was concerned, was talking about John Boothe on the air. When Douglas asked if Jill were going to marry him, Jill said, "I don't know. I don't think that if you don't marry your life's a failure."

"What's he like?"

"Tall. A truck driver."

Bob said, "John is very quiet. One time he was leading a string of mules back over Bishop pass at 12,000 feet in the middle of a lightning storm, hauling a load of dynamite. He did it very quietly."

Jill called John as soon as she was back in Pacific Palisades. He thought the show had been great, he said,

146

but he didn't sound terribly enthusiastic. Jill asked why, and he said, "I guess because it's just one more part of your life that leaves me out. It's kind of hard to handle, knowing I mean a lot to you but also feeling I mean little or nothing to so many of the people you're involved with. The same with some of your old ski buddies. I look at you guys and I feel totally opposite. I can't fit in."

Jill could understand that. She thought about old Los Angeles friends who thought as she did and had the same intellectual interests and political concerns. And she thought about the Hawthorne teachers and parents she particularly enjoyed. She became aware again of the stark differences between herself and John Boothe. She began to have doubts about the whole affair—not about how she felt when she was with him, but about the wisdom of allowing it to go any further. June had always been aware of the differences, and she and Jill talked about them again. John was not impressed by a college education. He actually made excuses for President Nixon. He was prejudiced. He was bored by the things their L.A. friends loved to talk about. He distrusted idealists, and he never got involved in causes dedicated to making the world a better place to live in. He was a male chauvinist. What else? "But I always thought he would change," Jill said.

"John? Change?"

"Well, Mom, I don't plan to marry him tomorrow. So what if we have differences? It's something I'm enjoying *right now*."

•   •   •

Jill wrote to John.

You wouldn't believe the way my Mom is talking about living in Bishop now. She read the Bishop paper and noticed they're giving exercise classes at the high school. I think it all began to change when Bob told us about the pains in his chest. Mom and I were concerned and I said flat out, boy, life is too short not to all live near each other for the rest of our

147

lives. I also told Mom she would have much more of a chance to travel if we lived in Bishop, especially when you and I get married. She would be free to come and go as she pleased.

The day she mailed her letter, she received one from John.

We are on a run now where we're hauling material to Salt Lake City. We leave Bishop, drive to Salt Lake and back without stopping, and it takes about 24 hours. A long, hard trip. I got in about 3:30 this morning and Mel sent a new guy back on it. He's an Indian guy named Tom Crowell that I went to high school with. Really a nice guy. I will go tomorrow afternoon and we will probably work it that way now. He told me today that I could either stay on 18, the truck that I've been driving, or work opposite Jerry Clark on 24, the new one. He said he was going to leave 24 on the Utah run and use 18 on that but take care of all the cattle-hauling and odds and ends with 18 also. There's a lot of local cattle-hauling coming up, so I said I would rather stay with 18. It should give me a little variety plus keep me around home a little more.

Mom gave me some lasagne to warm up for dinner tonight so I guess I will rough it here alone tonight.

John often wrote on his steering wheel while driving or in his sleeper, and his letters bore a variety of postmarks. Meyers Flat, Reno, Grants Pass, Eugene, Eureka, Fort Bragg, Medford, Jenner.

One Friday John arrived early in Pacific Palisades, parked his rig in the Presbyterian conference grounds, borrowed Jill's van, and drove to Hawthorne School to pick her up. He put her on the front seat. On the way back, they tried a short cut Jill knew about. He slowed while turning a corner so Jill would not topple over. A Porsche behind him honked angrily and then zoomed by

148

him, swerved in front of him and slowed abruptly so John had to jam on the brakes and grab Jill at the same time to keep her from falling into the dashboard.

"God damned son of a bitch! I'm going to show that bastard!" John gunned the motor and took off after the Porsche. "I'm going to run him right the hell off the road!"

Jill screamed at him. "No, John! John, don't do it!"

John looked at her and slowed down. If he had been alone he would have seen it through. "L.A. drivers are *animals*," he said.

"*He* was, John, but they're not all animals."

"All L.A. drivers are animals."

"June is an L.A. driver!"

"Okay, but watch the road. You're supposed to be telling me how to get the hell up to Sunset."

"John, I'm not sure."

"We'd better figure it out before we end up on the freeway to Pasadena."

"I recognize it, John! We have to make a right right here!"

"Great. Here I am in the left lane in commute traffic on Wilshire Boulevard and we got to go right!" Miraculously, he got across two lanes of traffic to the right curb before they reached the intersection.

Ten blocks later he nodded toward a group of UCLA students and said, "If there's one thing I can't stand to see, it's a white woman with a black man."

Jill blinked. She turned to him with an incredulous frown. "*What?*"

"Didn't you hear me?"

"You're serious. John, how can you say something like that?"

"Look, I wasn't prejudiced in Bishop, but in the Army ... after *that* experience ..."

"John, what difference does it make? All it is is the color of their skins. So he's dark-complected and she's lighter. That has nothing to do with who they are as people, how they relate to each other."

149

He didn't answer.

Three blocks later Jill said, "The fact that he's black hasn't anything to do with it."

"Damn it, Jill, just for*get* it!" he said. "There is nowhere to go if we stay on this subject."

When they pulled up in front of the house after 5 silent miles, John said, "Like to go to the Chart House tonight?"

Jill burst out crying. John said, "What'd I say?"

Jill shook her head and kept sobbing. By the time they had reached the front door, John realized she was crying because of the argument. "I just hardly ever cried all my life," she sobbed.

"Well, cry, honey. I understand. I think."

It was a good weekend, but the next time June and Jill talked about John, Jill said, "It's really something. How come I've gotten so fond of him when he's everything I never wanted?"

In early January, Jill wrote John a mixed letter.

Dick McGarry called and I told him it was probably best that I not see him again. I told him that I had a very special boyfriend, that you and I felt that it wasn't fair to our relationship or to him either. He said he understood.

I called Feldman. The print isn't ready yet because they lost a couple of frames, if you can believe it. Olivia Newton-John's song was one of them and I understand she has to sing it all over again. That information came from Amy, who is nine and Larry Peerce's daughter *and*, she said, president of Jill's fan club.

For the screening I've decided to serve apple cider. No booze because it costs so much. Celery stuffed with peanut butter and cream cheese, and a big round hunk of cheese sliced thin with crackers, too. Does that sound O.K. with you?

My new girl Juli is seventeen and very capable. She drives well and not too fast and is steady as can be. I have a cleaning lady once a week, so that relieves Mom considerably. Jane, my teacher friend, will drive every so often so that is a saving.

The film was in its final stages of editing, and Jill and June were invited to the Universal lot to watch a scoring session. The picture now had a title—*The Other Side of the Mountain*—and an original song—"Richard's Window"—which would be tacked onto the closing scenes and could be marketed independently as a record.

The sound studio was not unlike a blimp hangar. In the pit was a 50-piece orchestra. The film was projected simultaneously onto four screens, one on each wall, so that all the musicians could see what was going on as they played. What Jill and June got to see was the picture—just the picture, without dialogue—plus the background music, live, sounding magnificently into their ears from all sides.

They only saw parts of the film—the scenes with big music—and some of these they watched several times. Jill was overcome by the opening shots of the beautiful mountains she knew so well, accompanied by soaring violins. She was lifted with happiness when the exuberant young athlete swung to a stop in an explosion of snow to cry, "I'm Jill Kinmont. A *skier!*" followed by a cascade of music as Jill Kinmont, Skier, took off again in a swirl of powder. It had been a silent cry, since the voice track wasn't being played, but Jill knew the words and imagined she was hearing them.

The potato-chip scene was a wonder to watch. With soft music building, the newly injured Jill shows her boyfriend Buddy Werner her greatest accomplishment—the laborious task of picking up a potato chip by wedging it between the thumb and forefinger of a hand that is practically useless. "Marilyn does it *so well*," Jill whispered to June. "And that gorgeous apricot bathrobe!" But then, on the screen, Buddy is shocked by the extent of Jill's paralysis and can't handle it. "Oh boy," Jill said. "This really isn't the way it was. I'm glad Buddy didn't live to see it."

The hospital scenes were uncomfortably accurate and were carried off with conviction. There was a long slow pan across plasma bottles and I-V solutions and oxygen tanks and down to a tube running up Jill's nostril. It made Jill force herself to think of something else so she wouldn't get upset. So did the dramatic scene where the injured Jill is turned onto her stomach so her arm falls helplessly and dangles from the cot until someone lifts it for her. In all the scenes, Marilyn Hassett really *was* Jill. Her manner and her mannerisms were the same as Jill's and the effect on the real Jill was uncanny, seeing another self with a somewhat different face doing familiar things in quadruplicate on big screens high on the wall.

Jill still didn't feel she was looking at herself—except at one point where Marilyn is standing on skis on the mountain, facing away. At this moment she was Jill exactly, in every way. Jill was taken back to the mountain and back in time, and she clearly re-lived the feeling she had had high on the cold, bold mountain with the world stretched out below her. In all the other scenes, she went back and forth between recognizing "Jill Kinmont" on the screen and simply watching a good actress playing a part.

Jill and June attended the first screening of the nearly finished film on January 22. The final editing was still to come. The only others there were Larry, editor Eve Newman, and a few of the technical people. Jill was excited and worried, afraid she wouldn't like the picture, dying to see the skiing scenes, wondering whether or not she would be transported back into her own past, particularly into the painful parts of it.

An early scene—Jill in her wheelchair with her Indian students—was handled beautifully. "Oh, there's Eddie Keller," Jill said. The Indian children were playing themselves in the film. "That's where we were sitting up on the bank, remember?"

It was a distinct surprise to see the words *THIS IS A TRUE STORY* flash on the screen. Jill thought, wow, they must have made a lot of changes since the script.

The teaching scenes were excellent because you could

see *why* her pupils loved her and listened and learned. The skiing was wonderful to watch—until Jill's near-fatal accident. Jill felt her shoulders and neck stiffening as young Jill approached the critical rise in the trail. She tried to think of something else, and of course she couldn't. But then the figure on the screen went into a phony fall off a cliff, and there was no way to take it seriously. The tension disappeared immediately from Jill's neck and shoulders. At first the shot made her laugh, but then she was mortified at the thought of what *skiers* would think of this ridiculous clown act. Furthermore, everybody knew she had never fallen off a cliff. That "explanation" about turning the camera on its side so it wouldn't look like a vertical drop had been nothing but a pacifier.

After the hospital scene, Jill whispered to June, "It's got me squirming in my seat because it *isn't* the way it was and because it *is* the way it was."

"What do you mean?"

"I was terribly uncomfortable with that teen-age silliness when Dick and I meet. That's how it *wasn't*. But the part in the hospital made me cringe because it *was* so true."

Jill kept looking for Jerry Kinmont playing the part of Jerry Kinmont, but he never appeared. "Boy, that's a downer," she said. "They edited him right out of the show!"

"I think it's better than what they did with me and Bill," June said. Jill agreed. Her screen parents were severe and stiff, and there was no sense of the spirited exchanges and the warmth that had characterized the Kinmont family. "They got part of our life, up to a point," June said, "but then they went beyond."

At the end of the film, however, Jill had a really good feeling about it. "The overall sense of it was right," she said. "I can't wait to see it again."

"They sure didn't change much since that first script," June said.

"They changed a lot that we asked them to, Mom. And they didn't change a lot. They didn't do a thing about

Audra Jo coming off like a bitch, and *Dave* . . . well, at least there was one scene. I love it where Dave comes to see me in the hospital, and he just says, do you need anything?"

June said, "It bothers me that you don't get any feeling of the strong family support. So now I think, why didn't I *do* something about that when we first saw the script. There's just no indication of all that you got from Bob."

· They talked with Larry afterwards. "Overall, I have a good feeling," Jill said. "That first long hospital scene knocked me out. The tube up Marilyn's nose. And where they flip her onto her stomach and an arm falls over the edge!"

"Did it feel like *you* up there on the screen?"

"There's just one place it felt really real, and that was when I'm talking with the Indian children."

"That scene really works."

"Do you have to have me crying so much? I didn't cry that much."

Feldman telephoned the next day and asked what Jill thought of the film.

"What really bothers me," Jill said, "is that phony accident. You'll *have* to take that out. Any skier who sees it will stop believing in the whole film."

"The audience is not going to be an audience of skiers."

"But it's ridiculous, Ed."

"The audience is going to absolutely love it." It was obviously Feldman's favorite shot.

"It'll just make people laugh, and it's supposed to be the big dramatic climax."

"Uhn . . ." Feldman said. Jill could almost see him shrug.

Jill was about to say more, but she didn't bother. She said to June, "Mom, what's this film going to do to my life? There's nothing but highlights, and some of them aren't even true. What are people going to think?"

"What can they do, Jill? They've only got a hundred minutes."

"My life is pretty ordinary, and that's the last thing anybody'll believe *now*. I'm just a schoolteacher living with her mother."

"How boring can you get?" June said. They both laughed. "I still think it's a beautiful film."

"It is, Mom, overall. Not exactly accurate, but I've got to hand it to them."

•   •   •

Ed Feldman had promised Jill a private preview on February 22nd, and Jill was glad she still had a month's breather before taking responsibility for the way her friends and family were portrayed in the film. The month was pretty well eaten up by teaching, magazine and newspaper interviews, and a long birthday-Valentine's Day weekend in Bishop. She also had to write four paragraphs for the *Richard's Window* record jacket and write invitations for her private screening. She had told Ed Feldman that the preview would be only for a few of her close friends . . . and her list grew daily until it reached 150. She also called Feldman to ask once more that the fake fall shot be taken out of the film. Talking with Dave and Bob and other friends had reinforced her conviction that this kind of melodrama would mar the film.

In Bishop, Jill was met by John with a big heart-shaped box of candies. "We're going on a little trip," he said.

"Where?"

"Up Route 6 to Tonopah, Nevada. I want to show you what I see every day when I'm driving the oil rig. What you need is to get away and forget about all those movie people." John had quit the lumber company and was now driving for a crude oil distributor.

They left early Friday morning in John's pick-up with Jill's water bottle and John's Thermos of coffee on the seat between them. The country flattened out once they cleared the northern end of the White Mountains. The sun rose white and cold, peeking through high clouds. The desert was soft under a thin blanket of new snow, and little whirlwinds spun up like spindrift behind a passing truck.

155

"Hello, Bigshoe, this is Muleskinner," John said on his CB radio. "That was my pick-up. I'm on a busman's holiday."

"Hello, Muleskinner. I caught two of you."

"That's a ten-four, Bigshoe. She's a hot property down in Hollywood these days."

Jill was impressed. She was even more impressed when they passed and talked with Prospector and then Red Frog, and it became evident to her that John knew just about every truck on the highway. "You'd like Red Frog's wife," he told Jill. "Her CB handle's Pink Pollywog." He nonchalantly lit up a cigar.

They passed a herd of wild horses, and the horses took off in the same direction, racing the pick-up. Snow flew up in their wake, sometimes hiding the slower horses from view.

"Don't tell me you see this every day," Jill said.

"Every day. Honest." He honked his horn, and the horses broke away from the highway into the white, flat desert. "It's really like this, Jill. The crazy characters on the CB, the desert, horses, jackrabbits. People wonder isn't it lonely out on the road so many hours, but I love it."

Later, approaching Tonopah, the CB crackled and a woman's voice said, "Muleskinner?"

"How'd you know, Honeybear?"

Jill said, "What's going on? Your voice gets sexy all of a sudden, and we haven't passed a car or a truck for miles."

"But we did just pass a double-wide mobile home, and that's where Honeybear lives with her husband, Packrat, who's on the Highway Patrol. She's got damned good eyes. I never had the pick-up in Tonopah before."

"You always talk to her?"

"Always. I'll call ahead and tell her to cook me lunch. That means she'll order me lunch at the burger stand and I'll pick it up when I get there. She knows about you, too."

"She *does?*"

"Just a bit. I keep her in suspense. I keep talking about my girlfriend way down in L.A., tell her we're going to Laguna Beach or Santa Barbara for the weekend. Sounds real romantic, and on my Monday trip she wants to know all about it."

"Have you met her? What's she like?"

"She's cute. But she's four by four. Not just what I'd been looking forward to. But she's very special, Jill. She monitors the radio twenty-four hours a day. She can tune it out but wakes up if somebody calls her, so if it's two a.m. and you're in trouble, you know she'll be there for you. It's a real responsibility."

The radio said, "Muleskinner, what's going on?"

"Just a joyride with my girl, Honeybear."

"I thought so. By the way, how tall is she?"

"Five feet. Four feet. Hell, I don't know."

"What do you mean you don't know?"

"I'll tell you, Honeybear. I've never seen her standing up."

"I got you, Muleskinner. I heard about that. You've been holding out on me. I've got a question to ask you."

"I'm here."

"Is your girlfriend the same one they're making a movie about?"

"Maybe she is, Honeybear." To Jill he said, turning off his microphone, "You want to talk?"

"Sounds like it's hard to keep secrets on the open road," Jill said.

"Epecially when Honeybear's got her CB open day and night. Tell her a secret and it's all over the state in half an hour."

"John, I can't talk on that thing."

"Oh, come on, now."

"John, I've got stagefright."

"Beats me," he said. "You talk to three thousand people in an auditorium and you won't talk to an audience of one person who's over a mile away from you." On the radio he said, "She won't talk, Honeybear."

"Well, introduce us, anyway, Muleskinner."

"Okay, Honeybear. Honeybear, I'd like you to meet Hot Wheels."

"*Hot* wheels?" Jill said.

"Hi, Hot Wheels," the radio voice said. "This is Honeybear. Glad somebody finally came along to get Muleskinner back in action. When you guys going to get hitched?"

Jill whispered, "John! What makes her think . . . ?"

John said, "Oh, she's going to marry me, Honeybear. She just hasn't said so yet."

John drove through Tonopah and on to the desolate oil field where he regularly took on his cargo of crude oil, and they stopped later for lunch. On the way home John said, "Jill, you know you've been *awfully* busy this winter."

"That's for sure."

"Well, I want you to start taking on less. You don't always have to be *at* something."

"I just get caught up in things, John."

"All you have to do is say *no* once in a while. I want you to allow time for what's really important—us."

"I'd like to, John, but . . ."

"Jill, you're crazy! You've got to admit your limitations and stop using up all your energy."

Jill was silent, but she was thinking hard. She knew the Boothes had a quality of being very aware of who or what they were, but nobody had to do anything with their lives if they didn't want to. There was no pressure from one another, and they didn't respond to pressure from outside.

"You're not responsible for the world," John said. "Things will happen without you, believe it or not."

"Well, it does worry me," Jill said. "How I come off to people who mean something to me, like all you Boothes. You're a pretty unpretentious group, and it worries me that there's too much flashiness around my life. What I really want is to be as ordinary as possible."

"That sounds like your always wanting to look normal

158

and not look like a quadriplegic. You *are* extraordinary, but you don't want to look that way."

"Let's just put it that I'm really tired of that. I want to lead an ordinary life. I want to get down to earth. I don't want to be a darned *myth* floating around up there like the Goodyear blimp with messages written all over me."

10

Fame, of Sorts

The big night was Saturday, February 22nd, the private screening for Jill's 150 most intimate friends. Feldman had called to say they'd had a sneak preview in San Jose and it was a big hit, but Jill was far too nervous to be comforted by this news. Tension mounted in her shoulders and neck as the day went on, and she could even feel it in her face. John was with her, and he was very uneasy, afraid he would hate the movie and have to say so or say nothing at all. Jill had seen most of it twice, and she knew Audra Jo would be very upset about her "shape up or ship out" bitchiness, which hadn't changed at all from the original script. A.J. and Linda both would hate the vigorous, graceless gum-chewing—like speeded-up cows—that went on on the screen. John's family would think . . . what? Dave and Roma were already upset, not even having *seen* the thing yet. June was upset, although of course she had already been through it. Linda would explode when she saw the smart-alec Linda they had dreamed up. Jerry would be really disappointed to find he had been cut out of the film, and Bob would be furious that the actor playing Bob Kinmont had been left in.

Jill felt awful, and her mind wouldn't stop working. The film had been such a lark at first, but somehow it had managed to suck in everyone around her, and there was going to be a flood of hurt feelings. Not many people would come out with them, so the air would be bristling with static. John was certain to be critical, maybe caustic, about the film and the film-makers. Linda would surely get all wrapped up in the past. Dick Buek's mother would be there watching Dick's last days and the effects of his death . . . well, at best it was going to be a *wet* evening. She was glad that Beau Bridges and Marilyn would be there to sort of stabilize things.

June said, "Jill, we're not going to a funeral, you know." They were late, and Jill couldn't believe the size of the crowd. There was room for 120 comfortably, and there were a good 150 in the audience, some on folding chairs in the aisles and some standing along the sides. Audra Jo and Jill's cousin Jimmy Lewis were both there in their wheelchairs. Jill took her place up front with John on one side and Audra Jo and Lee on the other. Linda and Frank and Dave and Roma were in the row behind, along with Gary McCoy and Penny and their families.

Jill watched the audience throughout the film, Linda started crying right off the bat, and Audra Jo said, "What are you crying for? It isn't even sad yet." Jill's aunt burst out in sobs when the words *THIS IS A TRUE STORY* flashed on the screen. Dave McCoy never took his eyes off the screen. Jill whispered to Audra Jo, "Get Linda, A.J., she's getting a real bang out of it!"

Jill studied Audra Jo's face during the "shape up or ship out" scene, but Audra Jo was too contained or too polite to reveal how uncomfortable she was. During the hospital scene, someone in the back fainted and fell on the floor. Jill asked what had happened and someone said it was Vicki Davenport, the sister of an old skiing buddy of Jill's. Jill's aunt who had started crying with *THIS IS A TRUE*

STORY, was still at it at the end of the picture and didn't stop until the credits announced: Technical Advisers, Jill Kinmont . . . Jerry Kinmont.

Jill had cringed at some of the dialogue and had said *ugh* when her body went hurtling off the cliff, but the worst was still to come: the aftermath.

Actually, it could have been a lot worse. Dave came up and gave Jill a big hug. He was pretty emotional, which was not at all like Dave McCoy. Roma left without saying anything to Jill. Mrs. Buek was pleased and tearful, and she gave Beau Bridges a long, warm hug. Beverly Boothe said with enthusiasm, "It was just great!" John liked it better than he had expected, and he was most affected by the scene in which Audra Jo was stricken with polio. Andrea Mead Lawrence, who had been America's great gold medal skier in the 1950s, as well as Jill's main competition in her tragic last race, said, "It's just a beautiful film, Jill, very well done." Jill was pleased. Audra Jo said she liked it. Lee said he hated it because it didn't have a happy ending. Jill should have gotten married or something.

Red Valens, author of the book on which the film was based, had come down from San Francisco for the screening. He said he enjoyed the picture but wondered why they'd had to pour corn syrup over everything. Bob Kinmont more or less agreed, but he said, "The book was more accurate than the film, but the book, too . . . I watched when you interviewed us, watched how different people involved in an event remembered it. Christ! No wonder I don't like history. Because it's not true."

Linda Meyers seemed to have been more affected than anyone else. "They captured the feel of the mountain at the very start," she said, "and I started right there, living my life over again, and I cried all the way through it. I'm utterly exhausted! I just re-lived twenty years of my life and all the emotions that were going on parallel to Jill's life."

"You liked it?" Jill asked, somewhat doubtfully.

"They did a beautiful job with you and Dick, Jill. I can't

162

say the same about all those supporting friends. But it'll do well, and that's what it's all about, I guess."

Later, when the Kinmonts were alone, Vikki asked, "Why did they put in 'This is a true story'?"

"They thought it would make a bigger impression if they said that," June said.

Jill said, "It *was* true, in a way, but . . ."

"But they sure know how to make a million fifteen-year-olds cry their eyes out," Bob said.

"Aw, come on, Bobby . . ."

"I'm serious, Jill. I have tremendous respect for Feldman. His job is to make a movie make money, and he really knows his business and lets nothing get in his way. He's a master."

"You know what Baba Ram Dass says," Vikki said. "When a pickpocket meets a saint, all he sees is his pockets."

"Why not?" Bob said. "Feldman is making a movie and he's not going to lose money. What pisses me is why they didn't at least choose someone who looks a little like me to play me. It's embarrassing. He's flippant and . . . so if they don't cast the Kinmonts as Kinmonts, how can I believe they want *anything* to be like it is?"

In the end, John asked Jill how she felt about the preview.

Jill looked him in the eye and said, *"Whew."*

*   *   *

Jill recovered quickly, and on Monday she went to work on the plan she had been hatching for a long while. She wanted to teach in Bishop, but she wasn't sure how it would work out, so she figured a way to keep her options open. She wrote to the Bishop Elementary School saying she was interested in the newly created job of Reading Specialist. She did not mention that she might return to Beverly Hills if the job wasn't rewarding. Then she asked Hawthorne for a year's leave of absence, but didn't mention that she might stay. The school was thoroughly cooperative, and she was also granted a short leave to plug

163

the film in Houston early in March, a week before its première there.

The Houston schedule was heavy. Radio interviews Monday afternoon and a live show on television channel 26 at 7 p.m. Tuesday, a live show at 11 a.m. on channel 39, lunch with the *Houston Chronicle,* and afternoon interviews with three university newspapers. Wednesday, a videotaped interview at channel 26, lunch with the *Houston Post,* and catch a plane for L.A. at 5:45.

On March 14th, *The Other Side of the Mountain* opened in Houston, Denver, Minneapolis, and Memphis. It was very big indeed, and brought a rave review in Denver: "An inspiration to anyone who sees this film . . . a credit to all involved." Jill planned to celebrate with a weekend in Laguna Beach with John, but she developed a bad urinary infection and had to postpone it. Beau and Marilyn telephoned from Memphis, where they had gone to push the movie. They'd had a great press, and the picture was a sell-out.

Easter vacation began at the end of the week. Jill was off to Bishop and an interview with the school superintendent to find out just what the Reading Specialist position would involve. The school wanted to evaluate the reading abilities and problems of all 1500 students. Jill, if she got the job, would have to personally check out about 350 students during the year and work with the 45 or 50 most severe cases. She would also work with the Indians and the white community as a school liaison officer. The teaching job would involve reading workshops with teachers and presentations to parents. It was definitely going to be more work than her job in Beverly Hills, and the salary was less.

It was a very big step to take, but Jill was more than ready. If she could just get this big move taken care of, she knew her life would settle down, her emotions would stop swinging like a wild pendulum, and her relationship with John would become clearer.

She applied to the school board for the job and was told she would be notified by mid-June. Audra Jo, as president of the board, disqualified herself from the task of choosing among applicants for the job. John was uneasy about Jill's application because he felt it might prove to be too much work for her.

By the time Jill was back in Pacific Palisades, the reviews of the film were pouring in and the ad campaign was burgeoning. Several approaches had been tried, billing it in one city as a family movie, in another as a ski movie, and in a third as a love story. The love story won, hands down. The thrust of the campaign settled on the unfinished sentence, "NOT SINCE LOVE STORY . . ." with a close shot of Beau leaning tenderly over Marilyn, who had been carefully posed to resemble Ali McGraw.

A big local ad for the Avco Center Cinema in Westwood said, "IT TAKES A RARE AND SPECIAL MOVIE to each week attract larger audiences than in each preceding week. "Mountain" is such a movie . . . when you see it, we think you'll agree with every wonderful word you've heard about it." Also, looking hopefully in the direction of an Academy Award, an announcement was sent to academy members which called the film "a gift of love and inspiration from all who made it to all who see and share it."

The reviews were mixed but never mild. *Variety* and *The Hollywood Reporter*, the two weekly bibles of the entertainment industry, were split down the middle. *Variety*'s "a standout in every department" was matched by the *Reporter*'s "emotional grotesqueries and impossible lines." When Jill went through the stack of reviews, she wondered if the reviewers had really seen the same picture. It was "tender, powerful, touching," and it was "an avalanche of mush." It was a "salute to the human spirit." Larry had directed "superbly" and he had directed "heavy-handedly" and "with great doses of moral uplift and sentiment." The screenplay was "a compassionately-written insight in human suffering and heroic resolve" and it was "a travesty of cliché'd writing." There was consensus on the overall effect, however. It was a wet weepie, "the first

165

guaranteed three-hankie, doomed-love story since *Love Story*." Moviegoers were warned: "substitue beach towels for handkerchiefs."

All the reviews made great reading.

Variety: Perfect casting, fine acting, sensitive direction, imaginative photography. Seltzer has woven a continuity of stunning appeal. Stunt coordinator Max Kleven rates a high hand, too, for his realistic handling.

Hollywood Reporter: Seltzer's corny dialogue and hard-sell emotional plotting are compounded by director Larry Peerce's stilted over-dramatization, static staging and bland casting.

Los Angeles Herald-Examiner: That rare film which manages to be unabashedly optimistic about the human condition without resorting to easy sentiment or by avoiding reality.

Denver Post: You will have to be made of stone not to become emotionally involved in this drama, and not to be affected to the point of tears.

Time Magazine (regarding Buek's death): It is some indication of the hollowness of "The Other Side of the Mountain" that this piece of real personal tragedy comes out looking like the last desperate invention of a weary and rather mechanical scenarist.

Los Angeles Free Press: The film triumphs over its own emotional base and becomes a powerful testimony to individual strength and the value of life because the film makers have kept the true story factual, unlike many Hollywood biographies.

Washington Star: "Mountain" is guaranteed to neither play up to your kids nor talk down to them—but rather, to give them some genuine and not always pleasant insights into the overwhelming frustrations and small, hard-won victories in the life of a paraplegic.

Memphis Press-Scimitar: On the other side of filmdom's mountain of sludge lie occasional pockets of art and truth and honesty . . . a sensitive script and superb direction tell Jill's story without either avoiding or bathing in the tears that naturally flow from it. The essential drama of the story is the overcoming of self-pity, and Peerce has devised marvellously affecting scenes to illustrate that drama. . . . Jill says, after her fiancé's death, "How lucky I am to have known somebody, and something, that saying goodbye to was so damn awful."

Jill was thinking, not only am I a very different person to Larry than I am to the CBS director, but even Larry's version is very different for different people. I wonder, what pieces of me are the real ones? And which are the ones John sees?

The most thoughtful reviews were those in *The New York Times*, *Skiing Magazine*, and the *UCLA Bruin*, but they were largely critical and this always made Jill feel bad. Vincent Canby of the *Times* wrote:

The movie seems to have less interest in Miss Kinmont than in the devices of romantic fiction that reduce particularity of feeling to a sure-fire formula designed to elicit sentimental responses. If you go to see "The Other Side of the Mountain," load up on handkerchiefs and leave your wits at home. Should you have even half a one with you, you'll be ahead of David Seltzer's screenplay at almost any plastic point. The movie also contains a couple of moments of genuine feeling—all set in a Los Angeles center for the rehabilitation of the handicapped—that raise the over-all tone."

The *Skiing* review was entitled "An Extraordinary Jill."

Jill Kinmont's life is the stuff of which "B" movies are made . . . they did make a movie, and it's not all bad. It is not a *good* movie, either. The producers were unable to resist the temptation of turning Jill's life into a catalog of tragedies and triumphs, a barren cliché of a pretty girl who overcomes her handicap and devotes her life to others. The film overlooks the mental and emotional struggles that changed the girl crumpled at the bottom of the mountain to the independent, self-confident woman whose wheelchair seems merely a place for her to sit.

The story of Jill Kinmont is indeed an inspiration to us all, but not for the sentimental reasons the movie suggests—the plucky girl who perseveres over her handicap. Jill has done much more than merely persevere: she was a girl who lived only for skiing; with skiing taken away from her, she carved out a rich, full life for herself, and she has done it on her own terms.

The *UCLA Bruin* review, entitled "The Other Side of Sugar Mountain," echoed some of John's feelings about the picture.

The true story of the championship skier Jill Kinmont could have made a profoundly moving, even an inspiring motion picture. As presented in short form on CBS's *60 Minutes* a few months ago, the story was both fascinating and heartwarming. But leave it to Hollywood to take a basically promising story and embellish it until it becomes little more than schmaltz. With swelling violin music behind the love scenes and trite dialogue throughout, *The Other Side of the Mountain* manages to make a near laughing stock of the brave woman it set out to immortalize on celluloid. . . . The script goes on to embellish and "improve upon" the accident itself. It is not visually impressive enough for Miss Kinmont to hit a tree, so Seltzer has her ski over a fifty-foot cliff instead.

John Morely Stephens' ski and stunt photography using a hand-held camera for a skier's eye view, is both startling and stunning.

A title at the beginning makes the bold-faced claim

168

"This is a true story." Unfortunately, the names weren't changed to protect the innocent.

The last line made Jill sad because of Audra Jo and Dave and June and because of Bill Kinmont and Buddy Werner.

The crowning irony, however, arrived in the mail in the form of the paperback edition—just published—of Jill's biography, brought up to date and re-titled *The Other Side of the Mountain*. In bold letters on the cover of this factual biography, the publisher had engraved the words

see
the film
READ THE
NOVEL

When a fictionalized version is labelled *True* and the original biography is labelled *Fiction*, who will ever know what really happened? Jill envisioned an endless progression of more and more people knowing less and less about her. Once upon a time a few friends knew her rather well. After the flood of romanticized news stories about her ski titles and her accident, a lot of people knew a lot of things about her that weren't reported very accurately. *Now* she was destined to become more and more famous for things that had still less to do with who she really was. Unless she really *was* getting to be like the image people had of her, living up to what her Mercer Island student had predicted: "You must become that great movie star, your name up in lights, Miss Kinmont The Spectacular."

Things were getting to be *too much*. The month was a flurry of activities that had nothing to do with daily life—with Jill-and-John or with teaching. Jill set up a special screening of the film for teachers. She went through six more newspaper and television interviews. She attended a Hall of Fame dinner in Chinatown, which was a bore and left her exhausted. She said to June, casually, "Oh, by the way, John's coming down."

June said, in a very dead voice, "Oh, is he?" and went off to the kitchen.

"You don't want him to come down?"

"There are just *too* many things going on right now Jill. You're too tired, and a quiet weekend is what you need. In fact, we're both exhausted."

"You don't like him. You really don't like him."

"I don't dislike him, but . . . it's just one more person He doesn't cook for me. I cook for him."

Jill telephoned John and asked him not to come down this time. He was upset. Jill cried. And her obligations went on and on. She attended the opening of the film a the Avco Center Cinema in Westwood. She sent out invitations for a benefit preview at the Director's Guild Theater which raised over $6,000 for the Indian Education Fund She was a hostess at the wine-and-cheese reception that followed. It was the fifth time she and June had seen the picture. June had wanted to watch it as "just another new film," but this was impossible. She was quickly swept back into her own past, re-living the real events as Jill's story unfolded again on the screen.

Tourists were beginning to approach Jill in stores or on the street. "Say, we saw you on the TV." One afternoon on the Santa Monica mall a man in shorts and a flowered shirt walked over and said, "Oh, you're Jill Kinmont?" Jill nodded. The man turned, cupped his hands and yelled down the block, "Hey, *Mabel!*"

Jill whispered frantically, "Mom, let's get out of here!"

June said, "Oh, Jill, be nice, it'll only take a minute."

"Mom, it's getting to be a zoo!"

•   •   •

Ed Feldman telephoned Jill to say he had a marvelous idea. He knew that a television sequel to *The Other Side of the Mountain* would sell. They could do a TV pilot which would lead to a television series, or they could even do a movie for television, which again could lead to a series.

170

Jill said, "I have no interest in doing another film of any kind. The answer is no. Just no. Not now."

Jill mentioned it to Audra Jo, who said, "You did the right thing. You'd be crazy to do another film." Jill and John talked with Bob and a friend of his, Ron, who said, "Well, at least talk about it with him."

"She just plain doesn't want to do it," John said. "We just don't want to get involved with the film people any more!"

"Maybe you could produce it yourself and have some control," Ron said. "It could do a lot for paraplegics, a TV series. If you had complete control, it might be worth while."

"You'd never get control," John said. "They're thinking of their own financial gain and not about us."

Feldman called again and told Jill that a movie for television, plus a series, could make her financially independent for the rest of her life. "Think about yourself, your mother, your brothers," he said.

Jill said she was dead set against it.

At last Jill got around to two things she had been wanting to do for some time—buy a new car and get to Bishop for a breather. She put down $1,000 on a Chevrolet van and initiated it with a weekend in Bishop for the annual Mule Days celebration.

A much bigger event than Mule Days was the acceptance of her application to teach reading at the school. She immediately made plans to move from Pacific Palisades the day after school closed. The move wasn't to be permanent yet, however. She wanted to give teaching in Bishop a year's trial and also see what effect living in Bishop would have on her relationship with John.

Jill left Hawthorne with some regrets and a number of small presents she had collected over the years and couldn't bear to part with. One of her favorites was a poem written for her by Mei Ling's 13-year-old brother, Kwok Fong, who had arrived from Hong Kong with minimal knowledge of English three months before writing it. The poem read, in part:

171

At the first time in my world
The land full of happiness
The sky is no end, the sea is no end
I, can do what I want
My friend, some is good, some is bad
But! Both are good.

I lose; my world is changed . . .
I don't know where I am
In this new world anywhere just me.
No sky, no sea, no anything . . .
My friend some is good some is bad
But! both are bad . . .

Ocean, it is no end.
All is beautiful.
I stand in the middle
I see the changing ocean
From sunny days become to raining
From raining become to storm
From storm become to raining again
From raining become to sunny day again
Never stop
Ocean is the start of the world
And it is the end of the world, too.
Ocean it is no end
All is beautiful.

John and his friend Jerry Clark showed up in Pacific
Palisades with a big moving van on the evening of Friday,
June 20, 1975. It took six hours to load the truck Saturday
morning and three hours Sunday morning to unload it at
the Grove Street house in Bishop.

Jill and June settled into the house Sunday afternoon,
and on Monday they left for Washington, D.C., aboard a
Lear jet to help launch a national campaign to do away
with architectural barriers in the United States. There was
a press conference and there were sessions with several

senators and with Casper Weinberger, Secretary of the Department of Health, Education and Welfare. A photographer took a picture of her with a very tired Senator Ted Kennedy. He later gave her a print with a note attached: "Hey, friend, who is this wrinkled-looking 'BUM' you are hanging around with?"

Back home, Jill finally settled down to a reasonably paced summer of teaching the Indian children, seeing old friends, and spending a lot of time with John. John designed a folding wheelchair ramp which could be fastened permanently just inside the side door of the new van. Dave McCoy had the ramps made in his machine shop at Mammoth.

Bob Kinmont had decided it was time for him and his family to settle in the country, and he meant "settle" in the sense that early settlers had homesteaded the American west. He bought 20 acres of desert 12 miles north of Bishop and drew up plans for a house and student building with several studio rooms, a common kitchen, and a common workshop. He planned to have a small number of students living and working in the building for periods of three or more months.

There was only one other house to be seen in any direction, and there were no trees on or near his property. Only sage and bitterbrush. Bob began work on the foundation with the help of Vikki, Ben, Anna, and any friends he could find. Jill and June loaned him money to help him purchase materials and equipment. It was a hot, hard undertaking. The family was now living in a large teepee, and they planned to have at least one room finished to live in by the time of the first freeze. The entire project would take about two years.

Jill spent a lot of time at the Boothe ranch, and the entire Kinmont clan was often invited down for barbecues or roast beef dinners. John struck up a lively friendship with two-year-old Seth Kinmont, and Jill was impressed by his manner. John didn't *move* into a relationship with a child as many adults do, anxious to get something going.

173

He was simply *there*, open and matter-of-fact, and Seth felt at ease with him at once. Vikki thought John was playing too rough, but Seth loved it. When Vikki was putting Seth's cowboy boots on after lunch one day, John said, "You know, Seth, cowboys never have their mothers put their boots on."

Vikki said, "Seth, he's just kidding."

"No, he's not!" Seth answered, and immediately moved away from Vikki and finished the job himself.

• • •

School began four days after *The Other Side of the Mountain* opened at the Bishop Theater. Just before the school day started, and at every recess, curious children flocked to the windows of Jill's room to stare in at her. Whenever she looked toward the window she would see 20 or 30 heads ducking out of sight. The smaller children had trouble at first because of the high windowsills, but they quickly solved their problem by propping picnic tables or benches up against the outside wall.

Teaching was difficult because the children were all new, the other teachers Jill had to work with were new to her, and the job itself was more complicated than her work in Beverly Hills. Jill had to recruit all new helpers so the children would know to pop in during recess to see what they could do. Few of them realized how much she was unable to do for herself. At the end of one particularly long day, she wheeled home in a cold wind without her jacket zipped up because she couldn't bear to ask yet one more favor from someone. At least it was a great relief to be able to wheel home by herself—it was only half a block—rather than having to arrange for a driver every morning and afternoon. It gave her a wonderful feeling of independence.

The teachers were more outspoken than the Beverly Hills teachers and less impressed by Jill's reputation. Some of them asked her pointedly what her job was, exactly. What special service was she supposed to be bringing to the district? The myth of Jill Kinmont didn't mean anything to them, and there had been no fanfare—fortunately—when Jill first showed up at school. If anything, there had been some resentment. The man in charge of special services for Bishop schools said he was being accused of granting special privileges in regard to Jill's job, and so was Audra Jo, as president of the school board. Jill, after all, did not have a Master's degree, even though she had accumulated far more credits than the degree itself required. Another problem was that many teachers refrained from referring students to Jill because they feared it would be a "burden."

Jill worked with the relatively few students who had already been referred for help, and she was immediately successful. When the regular classroom teachers saw what she had accomplished, they sent her more students.

Friends in Los Angeles began sending Jill little clippings from newspapers and the trade magazines that hinted at a possible sequel to *The Other Side of the Mountain.* Jill was rather surprised by this but didn't do anything until she read a small story which said there *was* going to be a sequel and David Seltzer was going to write it. Jill couldn't believe it. She telephoned David.

"How come I haven't heard anything about this?" she said.

"Well, *I* surely haven't heard anything about it, either," David said, "and I wouldn't want to do it, anyway. I've already told Jill Kinmont's story."

Jill telephoned Feldman to ask what was going on. Feldman didn't say much, but the implication was that Filmways and Universal did after all have the rights to the story of Jill's life, both film and television rights, and they just might go ahead and do something anyway. Jill would have more to say about it if she went along with it.

Jill called her attorney, Leonard Glusman, and said, "Look, they want the rights to my life again!"

"That seems to be what they figure they bought," he said.

"Well, what rights *do* they have? What rights do *I* have?"

Glusman said the contract for the first film gave them the right to make a sequel, but they had no right to use incidents from Jill's life that had occurred later than 1972, which was as far as the first film had gone.

Jill felt somewhat better. At least she could argue that the contract wasn't valid after 1972. She decided to let it ride until they took the next step, which she supposed they would do.

Meanwhile, more people were stopping to chat with Jill in stores or on the street. A surprising number of old-timers "remembered" the band at the airport when Dick Buek had flown her home from the hospital. She never bothered to remind them that he hadn't flown her home and there had been no band—except in the movie. Also, more people were telephoning on business or to ask for favors, and more tourists were stopping to stare at her and whisper among themselves. Jill had to protect herself, and she began to avoid friendly conversations and to make herself difficult to reach on the telephone. People reacted at once and started to tell each other, "Jill's changed. Jill's not as friendly as she used to be."

Jill said to June, "What can I do, Mom, when everybody keeps bugging me and there's no time for anything else?"

One day a family from the Midwest telephoned from downtown. Jill had once written that it would be okay for them to stop in and say hello if they were ever in Bishop. Could they come on over?

They came over. They bounced in the front door, Mom and Dad and the four kids, all scrubbed and polished and the girls with bright hair ribbons, and proceeded to put on a show. They had a whole *act* worked out. The children lined up and each one recited his favorite passage from the Bible while Dad scurried around taking flash pictures. When the recitations were over, everyone sang two long hymns, collected autographs, said goodbye a dozen times, and took off for Kansas.

176

Jill had a letter that day from a young boy in the East. He wrote, "I wasn't allowed to go to the movie, but I did anyway. I found there *is* a Mt. Tom and there *is* a Bishop. Now I want to know, is there a Jill Kinmont?"

Jill wondered.

11

Honeymoon

The biggest disappointment connected with being settled in Bishop at last was that the relationship with John was becoming less clear instead of more clear. Every time John was away for a few days, Jill began to doubt her own feelings. Several times she decided to forget it, to just back out of the relationship. But each time, she said to herself, how in the world am I ever going to be able to tell him? And she never did. When she was with him again, she was happy with that.

Jill talked John into going to a pot luck supper for the old Mammoth gang, which this time included Norma and Toni Milici. Toni had coached Jill at Mammoth in the early days and still ran the huge Mammoth cafeteria. Norma had been one of Jill and Audra Jo's constant skiing companions. John felt somewhat more at home because Toni was a staunch Republican and liked to smoke. Toni said, "Hey, I'm so glad you're still smoking," and they both lit up.

Everyone got into a hot discussion of *The Other Side of the Mountain,* pretty much tearing it apart, until Linda said, "There's one thing don't forget. A teen-ager was visiting us when we were kind of running down the film, and she said, look, I don't care what you say, that picture meant a lot to me and it is what made me decide to become a teacher."

But then the conversation turned to Nixon and Republican maneuvering, and John was silent again. Afterwards he told Jill, "Their whole point of view makes me mad."

"It's a democracy, John, like you told me. You don't want everybody to turn out just like you, do you?"

"No, but I'll tell you one thing. Every time we all get together, all you guys ever talk about is what's wrong in Washington or what you all did together twenty-five years ago."

"They're my *friends,* John."

"You and your friends! It's as though I'm not even there."

"Don't you talk about old times with your friends? What's so different?"

"I don't know. My friends are everyday ordinary people with no frills, but they'll give you the shirt off their backs and expect no return. There's no flashiness."

The next morning Jill was in a foul mood, and June asked what was wrong. "Nothing, Mom. A little talk with Silent John."

"He keeps to himself, all right," June said.

A few days later, when Bob was visiting, June said, "John just doesn't acknowledge you. And he looks so *down* all the time."

"He's not down all the time," Jill said. "He's just quiet, like his father—and you all like Dudley."

"Well, yeah . . ." Bob said.

Jill realized that she really did have reservations about John, and she decided she would have to explain her feelings to him. He listened without comment, and at the end he said, "Well, why don't you just go back to

L.A., where everybody behaves just like you want them to?"

Jill didn't want to talk with June about it this time. June was always fair . . . but very unfair in a way because she wouldn't just *say* she wished Jill would find somebody else. She would only say: make sure you've thought it out well. When people asked her about John, June would leave the question trailing: I always thought it would be nice if Jill would find a man.

Jill went to Audra Jo to talk. "It's getting pretty serious, and I have a lot of doubts, Josie. What do you think?"

"Do you enjoy his attention?"

"Yes, I really do. And I love to have someone to hold me in his arms."

"Well?"

"But I don't think you and Lee really approve."

"It's something only you can decide."

"But what do *you* think?"

"It's just that I was surprised he could be so different from anyone I'd ever considered would be . . . you know. Lee simply thinks it's silly to go on year after year without *doing* anything about it."

Jill was thoughtful. She frowned and seemed to be talking to herself. Then she said, "I'll tell you a secret, Josie. I got a letter from a man I didn't know. From Boulder. I liked it, so I answered it. He sounds so interesting. He has all the right credentials. And money. Divorced. He'd kind of wanted to make a change, so he sold his business a little while back."

"Aha! The truth will out."

"His letters are so nice, but I don't want John to know."

"Sounds promising."

"Actually, he telephoned me while Bev was doing my hair, and if you think *that* wasn't frustrating!"

"Exciting, too."

"But I can't just go on with John, then, if . . . well, in his last letter, this man said about our phone conversation . . . I can tell you didn't want to talk with me."

Jill felt somewhat relieved just from having talked about

180

it with Audra Jo, and on her way home she halfway decided maybe she had better just forget her relationship with John Boothe. The only hitch was that she didn't know how to go about it. She tried to talk with June about it, but tears kept welling up. Trying to stop the tears left her too choked up to talk. "This is so hard," she said. "He cares so much. I know it."

June was very sympathetic. "Whatever you decide to do," she said, "it's your decision, and I know it will be the right one."

•　　•　　•

Feldman called a number of times to tell Jill about the film. It was surprising everyone. It was in its 32nd week in Denver and playing citywide in Los Angeles. It had just opened in Australia and was opening in Japan this month, December 1975. Jill got a letter from a girl who had seen it in South Africa. A clipping from Canada said "Skiers' Weepie Grosses More Than *Jaws* in Ottawa." Larry Peerce called, and even *he* couldn't understand why it kept running on and on and on in theater after theater. In Minneapolis, a man named Everett Lawton had seen *The Other Side of the Mountain* 125 times. He wrote Jill a note, which she answered, asking him why. He wrote back. He didn't know why; he just kept having to see it again and again.

Newspaper reporters telephoned to ask Jill what the secret was, but they seemed to know as much or more than she. One of them said, "Jill, you've got it made. Whatever the reason is, the picture's really taking off. That means Jill Kinmont is Box Office, and that's what counts in Hollywood. They'll be wanting a lot more of you."

Jill could easily visualize—as if she were watching still another movie—*Jill Kinmont The Spectacular*: The *Jill* who has just realized the American Dream; the *Jill* who has what everyone desires; the *Jill* who has just been awarded the *America's Most Valued Person* award, for isn't that what it means when they make a movie of you

181

in your lifetime? Twice valued, in fact, since they want to make *two* movies.

Jill could picture this "Jill Kinmont" clearly, but she couldn't identify with her. It was not the Jill of 731 Grove Street or the Reading Specialist Jill of the Bishop Elementary School or the Jill who was deeply worried about her relationship with a fascinating, frustrating local truck driver.

Why *was* the film taking off? Why was it drawing blocks-long lines of hopeful viewers? Lots of lonely people looking for a hero? Probably not. Lots of lonely people looking for a *lonely* hero? Well, that could be. My God, maybe even *John* is looking for a lonely hero! Maybe it's an even *more* particular kind of hero that everybody needs —a lonely hero they can look up to and still feel superior to. Maybe that was one reason Jill had gotten along so well with the Indians. They had been through something and been looked down upon, and they could see at once that she had been through something. Furthermore, she was no threat. They could literally look down upon her, and that made them equals in a strange way. To have a hero you could feel equal to might be quite a thing.

Jill appreciated the irony of her situation. She felt her love life was going to hell, and she was being grossly manipulated by Hollywood, but in a funny way she did indeed *have* the American Dream. Maybe it's: the American Dream's got me. Or: the American Dream, what's that? But whatever you cared to call it, the big question was: *now* what?

Jill sensed what the trouble was. She felt obliged, somehow, to act the part. To *be* Jill The Spectacular. To feed into the myth. Otherwise, people were always going to be let down when they met you because you turned out to be nothing but a real, everyday human being.

Long ago, the more attention Jill had received, the better she had felt about herself. Now, the more attention she got, the more problems there were and the more confused she felt about herself. How do you escape it? What is the saving grace? What do you do *now*?

She thought of the values the Kinmonts had come to Bishop for to begin with. To connect with the land, to connect with history, to gain a solid sense of family. Jerry's life was the simplest of all, living off the land on a remote Canadian island, planning to build a log cabin from trees on his own land. Bob was trying to get back to this kind of thing with his own "homestead" out on the bitterbrush flats. His life was direct and simple. The Indians, too, are simple and direct. No, not really direct. There is a quiet, watching warmth that you come to respect. They have great staying power. They know what they have in mind, and they wait for the right time. What Jill longed for was to live simply, to live in a very ordinary way and find pleasure and support in the unadorned, everyday business of living. Like John.

•   •   •

Jill was still seeing John regularly. It was a habit she didn't seem to know how to break. She liked driving with him. She loved the family meals down at the ranch. She was uncomfortable with the feeling that everyone was expecting them to get married. Bev said to them one day, "I've just got to ask you guys something. Everybody's asking *me* and I'm getting tired of putting them off. Are you going to do it?"

John said, "You know *my* answer."

"Bev," Jill said, "you and June'll be the first to know."

Audra Jo came over to Grove Street for a visit a short while after Christmas, and she said, right off the bat, "You're still with John."

Jill leaned her head back and closed her eyes. "It's a turmoil, Josie." She was silent for some time before she said, still with her eyes closed, "Big frustrations. Always these petty arguments. And he's so *stubborn!*"

"You mean he won't change like you'd planned for him?"

Jill opened her eyes in a hurry. "What's *that* mean?" she said. Audra Jo returned her stare calmly, and suddenly they both laughed. "Moment of truth," Jill said. "Wow. I

183

really always counted on that, didn't I? I really thought I could change him. He is just plain *not* going to be changed."

"You're a powerful woman, Jill. You're not used to people who won't do it your way."

Jill had never thought of herself as powerful. She had only thought of herself as dependent but able to look fairly normal. She reflected a long time on Audra Jo's words. "I guess I'm a basically selfish person," she said.

"In some ways you are, Jill. In order to survive. You told me about that once. I think it had to do with Buddy Werner."

"Yeah. Bob told me Buddy was all for Buddy, and I said no he wasn't, and Bob said sure he is, and why not? You've got to be a very self-centered guy to be a great skier. You've got to be an egotist to go out and do what most people can't."

The telephone rang, and June answered it. "It's Ed Feldman," she said.

Jill prepared herself while June was bringing her the phone. She decided to be blunt with him, right off, let him know she knew exactly what rights she did and didn't have to her own life.

Feldman sounded extremely cheerful. "Did you get your check?" he said.

"Yes, I got the check, thank you."

He said the picture was doing wonderfully and they were marketing it worldwide under the title *A Window to the Sky*. He had heard from Universal again and they really wanted to do another film. How did Jill feel about it now?

"I don't want to do another film, Ed."

He mentioned having the rights to her story, and she said, "You do not have the rights to my life. You have the rights to my story, but only up through 1972."

There was a pause. Feldman said, "Well, we'll just have to fictionalize, then."

Jill said with a groan, "Oh, no . . ." After a considerable

184

silence she added, "I'm going to have to think about this whole business."

Jill telephoned Glusman. He went through his "Mountain" file and called her back. *Could* they legally fictionalize Jill's life without her permission? Glusman said there was no clear answer.

Jill talked the situation over with John and Audra Jo, who were against doing another film, and with Bob and June, who thought it would be a good idea. Bob wanted to divorce himself personally from the film, but he and June both felt it was extremely important for Jill to take this opportunity to resolve her major financial worries. June felt a second film was important for a number of other reasons, as well. "You know how many people have told us the first film stopped at what was really the beginning," she said. "They wanted to know *how* a quadriplegic could become independent. There are so many people who want to know more. And people want to know about your teaching career, which was barely touched upon in the first movie."

Jill felt the same way about the teaching. She loved teaching and wanted people everywhere—young people especially—to know just why it was so rewarding for her. But basically, she did not want to get involved in a film again.

Her teaching career meanwhile was clearly a success. She was especially talented when it came to motivating children to learn, and all the Bishop Elementary School teachers were now aware of this. They were discovering that all the children they referred to Jill did learn to read, or greatly improved their reading—even the few "impossible" cases they sent Jill as a last resort. Jill, for her part, had learned to work well with the teachers—something she had not always been able to do. For years she had expected all teachers to be responsible, extremely mature people. "I finally discovered they have hang-ups just like *I* have hang-ups," she told her supervisor. "It's a heck of a job to work out differences, but it can be done."

185

The Tikalskys had moved to Mammoth Lakes, where Frank was now director of the Mono County Mental Health Center. Frank sent children to Jill for reading evaluations, and he had her work with some of his very difficult Special Education cases. One of these was a boy whose IQ had dropped suddenly. The county staff psychologist feared he might have a brain tumor. Jill tested the boy, talked with his family, and told them he definitely had a problem with visual perception. Another important factor was that it could be a direct result of family tension. She was right. The family had put up a pretty good facade, but, as Frank put it, "Jill has super intuition, and she poked in the right spots."

Shortly before Christmas, Frank invited her to participate in a conference on mental health problems among Indians. Some of the panel members, learned professors in their field, were patronizing at first, saying in effect, isn't it nice that the lady in the wheelchair was invited. They soon discovered that this lady knew as much as or more than they did about the psychological problems of the Paiutes. Jill was not very much impressed with the conference. The talks by psychologists, archeologists, sociologists, and anthropologists were academic and boring, and there weren't even any Indians on the panel.

• • •

By the spring of 1976, Jill had decided to go ahead with a second film. John still didn't feel comfortable about it, but Jill said, "If they're going to do it—and I know they *are* going to do it, one way or another—then I want to be there and not sitting in the background." She told Glusman to see what he could do about getting a good contract. That day she told one of the teachers at school—with a groan—"Guess what! We're going to do *another* film."

Jill felt resigned but anxious. She knew from long experience that whenever you take a big step of any kind, everyone around you is drawn in. She knew that all her close friends and relations would be affected by the film, and this time she knew that some of them would inevitably be affected adversely. Good or bad, what happens to Jill happens to everyone. She remembered what her father had said when he first learned how serious her injury had been. "I guess this is the point where rehabilitation really begins . . . I mean for the whole family." He had seen how deeply the accident would involve the personal emotions and practical affairs of each one of them.

So Jill called everyone in the family, told them she had committed herself to another film, and asked how they felt about it. June and Jerry were excited by the news. Bob approved of it. Vikki was upset. "How could she *do* that?" she said to Bob. To Jill, later, she said, "I feel strongly about someone coming into your life and filming it. But everyone seems passive, let's let it ride. Gosh, am I the only one with negative feelings?"

She was not. Audra Jo and Lee thought Jill was crazy to go with another film. They remembered how dead set against it Jill and John had been a few months before, and they remembered well what the first film had demanded of Jill in terms of time and energy and in terms of a continuing loss of privacy.

The *Los Angeles Times* reported the decision, taking note of the fact that *Mountain* had now earned Universal more than 15 million dollars worldwide. The new film would be called *The Other Side of the Mountain, Part 2.* Feldman was quoted as saying that *Mountain Two* would deal with the last 10 years in Jill's life. "We'll be paying particular attention to her fight against exclusion of the handicapped from the teaching profession. Basically, we will be telling the story of her fight against the city of Los Angeles. The city refused to allow her to teach because it has a rule that teachers must stand on their own two feet."

• • •

Aside from the decision about the film, the spring's two big events were two trips to Canada, one to make a speech and the other, a month later, for a long vacation. The speech was in Edmonton, Alberta, where Jill was invited

187

as guest speaker at the Amateur Sports Hall of Fame dinner. June went with her and they were joined by Lyn's mother and her sister Gae, who came up from Calgary. Jill's introduction was greeted with resounding applause, but she was not prepared for the total silence that followed it as the large audience waited expectantly to hear what she had to say. This left Jill feeling more nervous than usual, and she scanned the crowd for some one person to talk to. She spotted the Canadian Women's Olympic Basketball team of—she thought—1920, a group of big women in their seventies. She focused on the largest of these women and directed the entire speech to her. She talked about skiing, about her accident, and her teaching career, and about the obstacles she had encountered. "The obstacles tended to give me a real incentive to outdo them," she said, "whether they were the dean at the School of Education, or the mountain, or retraining a usable muscle." She said she had never been depressed. "The only time that really happens is when I can't balance my bank statement."

The Canada vacation was Jill's idea. For nearly three years she had been going back and forth about John, deciding one day to get married and the next day enduring a flood of misgivings. Or her feelings would say "Just do it" while her head was saying "Look, objectively your chances of a successful marriage are *zilch*." But then she couldn't imagine not being with him.

Jerry and Lyn had been married at Christmas and were now living on a beautiful little island on the Inland Passage in British Columbia. They had begged Jill and John to come visit them, and one day Jill said to John, "Let's go to Canada."

"I sure like the idea," John said. "Fly, or what?"

"I mean a long trip . . . driving . . . two or three weeks. Because then . . . well, many things. You'd have full responsibility for understanding all the things that need to be done for me. And we'd find out what it's like being together *all* the time."

"What better way?" he said. "I was really beginning

to give up. What I wanted seemed to get farther and farther away, like I was just expecting too much."

"It's really important to go away together, John. In three weeks, most everything's going to come up that's likely to come up if we get married."

They talked about the trip every few days, and they got out maps and studied them. John wanted to show Jill some of his favorite truck routes—299 west along the Trinity River through Weaverville, where Grandpa Roy Boothe had lived, on through Willow Creek to the coast and the Trees of Mystery, where it feels as if your car were coasting uphill. Then north through the big redwoods to Crescent City and either along the coast to Gold Beach, Oregon, or inland to Grants Pass. Finally north to Seattle, Vancouver, and Cortes Bay by way of winding roads and big ferryboats.

"Kind of a honeymoon," John said, and kissed her. "Are you sure about it?"

"Let's do it and just see how it goes."

"Anxious?"

"A little. Are you?"

"No, Jill. I don't have doubts, like you. I *know* what our feelings for each other are. Our differences don't have to be that important."

John's photography was improving steadily, and Jill wanted him to make a photographic record of the trip. John was feeling the limitations of his old camera and he spent a long time shopping for a new one—a Canon TX.

On the last day of school, June 4, 1976, John picked Jill up at school with suitcases and camping gear already piled in the back of the van. They drove home and were on their way within half an hour. June wished them well with tears in her eyes. Tears of love that were undoubtedly compounded of fear for her daughter's health and safety and joy from seeing Jill so happy.

"John," she said, "you're pretty brave, I think. I know Jill is in very good hands. I wish you a beautiful journey."

John and Jill felt a soaring sense of freedom as they roared past the familiar Mammoth turn-off and on toward

Bridgeport and Reno and points north. The trip already felt like a true honeymoon.

They stopped for the night at a motel, and John asked for a downstairs room because his wife was in a wheelchair. He said to Jill, "If anyone asks you, you're Mrs. Boothe. Okay?"

"I like it."

He carried her over the threshold into the room and sat her in an armchair facing the television monitor. "Shall I turn on the TV?" he said.

"*TV?*" Jill was startled.

John laughed. "Okay. I was afraid you might want to catch one of your late talk shows."

"You just come here," she said.

"First, since I don't want you to escape . . ." He locked the door, then came and knelt beside her. He put his arm around her shoulder and rested his head on her breast. He kissed her neck and then her lips. He carried her to bed and undressed her.

"You are so gentle," she said.

"I like taking care of you. And if I overlook something I ought to do, let me know." He stopped to kiss her eyes. "You are beautiful, the way you look at me."

"I love you, John."

He undressed and turned out the light and got in bed beside her. "I love you," he said.

They made love and they slept and they came half awake again.

"Jill? How are you?"

"I'm wonderful, John. I feel . . . womanly. Did I satisfy you?"

"Yes. Did I satisfy you?"

"Yes. I'm so happy."

As John finished dressing her in the morning, Jill said, "Be sure and get the slip *straight*, John!"

"It's as straight as it's going to get, sweetheart. Let me give you a lift." He moved her to the edge of the bed and lifted her into her chair. Then he pulled on her blouse and tucked everything in.

"John, the waist has got to be pulled lower. I don't want to look like a slob."

"Okay. There you are."

He brought her toothbrush, a cup of water, cleansing cream, and a washcloth. He brushed the tangles out of her hair. Jill brushed her teeth and then worked her fingers into the large rings attached to her comb. She was more tired from the effort of identifying with John than if she had been doing it all herself, but John was neither hassled nor hurried. "You look pretty neat," he said. "How about some cologne?"

"You look pretty snappy yourself in those fancy boots and slim brown pants. And I like the new glasses."

They drove until they found a sun-filled diner for breakfast. They had no immediate goal and no hard and fast route to follow. They stopped whenever John wanted to take a picture, they ate when they were hungry, and they stopped for the night when they were tired or when they came across a motel that particularly appealed to them.

The ferry rides in Canada were exciting, even though John had to carry Jill from the car deck up steep narrow steps to the passenger section. The view and the salt breeze were well worth the effort. The best part of the trip was the visit with Jerry and Lyn on Cortes Bay. The days were bright and the nights as clear as nights had ever been up at the pack outfit. Jerry knew where the salmon were, and he took them by boat into the most beautiful coves and by pick-up to his favorite places in the deep woods.

John was impressed with the way of life Jerry and Lyn were making for themselves. Jerry was now a landed immigrant and planned to become a Canadian citizen. He worked as a carpenter and also as caretaker of a summer lodge, and he often commuted to work by motorboat.

John and Lyn hit it off immediately. They were alike in some ways—quiet, slow-moving, slender—and they were both concerned with the present rather than with past or future. Both were good listeners, although John was far more critical. They thought of themselves as realistic compared with the Kinmonts, whom they saw as idealists who couldn't give up the belief that anything and everything is always possible if you just keep at it. "I think they are more concerned with how things should be than with how they simply *are*," John said.

It interested them that all three Kinmont children were now trying, in very different ways, to simplify their lives or get back to their roots—Bob by building his own personal community in the bare desert he loved, Jerry by moving to the edge of the wilderness in a new land, Jill by . . . well, it wasn't clear with Jill yet. She was far behind her brothers, still caught up in a gregarious, overbusy, sophisticated urban life.

Jerry and Jill meanwhile were talking about John and Lyn. Jerry thought they both placed great value on practical skills and keeping things in order. "They seem to have the same Midwestern ethic, too," he said. "You don't charge at stores, you pay cash. And neither of them are very demonstrative. Lyn's not one to kiss and hug."

"They're both *so steady*," Jill said. "And I don't think you and I are."

"I've never been, anyway," Jerry said. "I've always been so impulsive. If I want something, I want it now!"

"Me, too, I think. And I can't sit still and relax like John can."

Jerry added, "But you should see the meticulous books I'm keeping now. You couldn't believe the new order in my life."

"I can see it, Jer, and I just think it's great!"

•   •   •

The trip back south was no less exciting than the first half of the journey, and John and Jill talked at length about their immediate future and how the new film might affect their lives. There would be more work with the scriptwriter than in the first film, and it would require a lot of effort to keep the script on the right track, to stay with the aspects of Jill's life that she felt were most im-

192

portant. It became clear that there was a great deal John could do, and he began to see the second film as an opportunity for him to share in Jill's life. He had been off on the sidelines the first time, and he had not enjoyed it.

They returned to Bishop by way of the UCLA campus where Jill, along with several other UCLA graduates, was given an award for special achievement. The award dinner was a sober affair with many very distinguished guests who talked a lot about their own impressive academic achievements. A woman asked John, "Are you a UCLA man?"

"No."

"What do you do?"

"I'm a truck driver."

The same exchange happened twice again. John got a kick out of it, and so did the chancellor's wife. She had only recently returned to college to finish her education, and she and John seemed to be the only guests who couldn't take the dinner-table conversation or the long-winded acceptance speeches very seriously.

Jill's award was presented by Beau Bridges. Her acceptance speech was very short. As she told Beau ahead of time, "UCLA wouldn't even let me *in* to their School of Education, so they're going to get a short talk. They're giving me an award for doing what they wouldn't let me prepare myself to do."

• • •

The final drive back north to Bishop was a tired and happy one. The trip had lasted three weeks, and every day had been a good day. Jill was joyful because everything was working out. There was no problem with John caring for her, and he was completely willing. When they stopped for lunch, John said, "Have you decided to marry me?"

Jill smiled. Softly, she said, "I guess so, John."

He embraced her gently, and tears were in his eyes. "It's not only a perfect trip," he said. "It even has a perfect ending."

193

Home at last, Jill told June, "It all went so easily. Nobody was hassled, Mom. John did anything that needed to be done with ease and good humor, and he made me feel good. Not like I was being a burden. And in that whole time, we just did not have any differences."

"Do you think you'll get married, then?"

Jill hedged. "I think so, Mom. I'll see how I feel after a week or so at home."

Jill knew June wasn't sold on the idea, and she began to feel that in some strange way she, Jill, was having to choose between John and June. Whatever she did, she couldn't make both of them perfectly happy. In fact, it was like being caught in a classic love triangle: she had been living with June for years, and now a man has showed up who threatens to take her away and break up the family.

Feldman telephoned to say he had been hearing rumors that Jill and John were getting married. "No, Ed," she said. "But if it happens, you'll be the first to know."

John and Jill were hand in hand all the time at the Tri-County Fair early in July. On the last evening they were returning to the van when they stopped to watch a stage show near the Home Economics Building. It started to thunder loudly, and soon a downpour hit. The spectators scurried under the eaves of the building. A staggering, obviously drunk Indian man in the crowd recognized Jill and inched his way over to her, stumbling on her foot pedal as he arrived. He fell over her, bending her head and shoulders forward before he caught himself. Jill was uncomfortable. Not knowing what else to do, she said, "Hi."

John was furious. He pushed the man away. Jill said, "John, he's not that bad. He'll go away."

The man moved away for a moment but was soon back with his arm on Jill's shoulder. John shoved him back again. Jill said, "Well you don't have to be so rough." When the man came back a third time, John pushed him back, hard.

"We've got to get the hell out of here," he said.

194

John opened the van door, slammed the ramps down in place, and helped Jill's chair up the slope into the car. He clomped around the front and climbed into the driver's seat without a word.

Another Indian came over to the car, perfectly sober, and said he wanted to thank Jill for the work she had done at the Center. John was still angry. He started the van noisily. "Come on, come on," he said to Jill. "We can't hang around here!"

Jill said, "John, damn it . . ."

He was silent for a block before he said, "What are *you* so upset about?"

"Because you hate Indians."

"I don't hate Indians. I just don't want anybody falling all over you. I don't care whether he's black, white, green, or red."

"John, you didn't have to do that. He just wanted to thank me for teaching his kids."

"That's a hell of a way to do it!"

"What *is* the matter with you, John?"

"Nothing's the matter with me. I try to protect you and all I get is a kick in the ass."

They rode on in silence. Jill was talking angrily to herself inside her head. He gets upset with something I do: so I get upset with him; so he gets upset with me being upset. Out loud, she said, "Well, I'm sick of it. I'm through!"

"So what do you want me to do?"

"Just stop telling me our differences don't make any difference!" Her voice was loud, and she could feel the hair standing along the sides of her neck.

"There are *not* that many differences that make any real difference."

"You stop shouting, John! We have political differences, social differences, emotional differences. You don't accept my friends. You're jealous of me and my time. Sure, it's fine on a beautiful trip where you don't have to share me with *anybody*."

"Oh, go to hell."

"And you're critical of my ideas and my ideals," she

195

added. "Like crusading for human rights. To you, that's *dumb!*"

"You mean like *amnesty?* You and your friend Carter just want to pat all those draft dodgers and traitors on the back and say, come back home, Sonny, Mommy knows you didn't mean to do it."

"Your sarcasm drives me right up the wall!"

"I'm just telling you that I'm of the opinion that you take care of yourself and don't go off and help the world if you haven't got yourself in order."

"Thank you, John Boothe."

"So you don't want to get married?"

"No."

"*Oh baby!*" John said. They were already home and parked by the house. "*Up* and down. *Back* and forth. I don't *want* to marry a God damned yo-yo! You've been stringing me along for . . ."

"John . . ." Jill said. She had turned cool and reasonable, and he felt like a child about to be lectured. "Relationships don't develop in a nice straight line. So often you're carried away with each other . . . and then certain things dawn on you."

"Don't talk to me like a *teacher!*"

"Okay, I won't. I'm just saying it's a big trouble. As soon as we get very serious, all these differences flare."

"*That* again! If it isn't sweet and pretty all the time, it's no good. Well, let me tell you about differences. When there are two people close together, there are differences, and they flare up. Maybe it's not the way people *should* be, but it's the way people *are*. You can either ignore it, or bust up the relationship, or you can listen to it and confront it and learn something about each other from it."

Jill said, gravely, "John, I've never heard you so serious."

"Well, I'm serious. And I need an answer from you, and I need it now. Are you going to marry me?"

"John, don't push me *now*."

"It's always *wait . . . not now . . . some other time!* Well, I'm tired of you not deciding. It has to be decided. I

196

can't go on. I can't handle it. I can't stand it day after day like this. We have to decide."

"But I'm confused, John. I need time, John. I don't know *what* I want. I don't know what to do."

John reached out and turned her face toward his in the dim light. "I am going to tell you what you can do," he said in a voice that was low and level and fierce.

Jill was scared. Very quietly she said, "What, John?"

"You are going to shit or get off the pot."

Jill was astounded. She choked back her automatic response, which would have been: *what* did you say? She had heard clearly, and this was no time for word games. She said nothing more. John said nothing more. He took her to the door and left.

• • •

Jill couldn't talk with June, but she lay awake for a long while before she could sleep. She had never before realized how deeply serious John was. Or perhaps on some level she did know but was frightened, so she hadn't allowed *herself* to be that serious. She had never before seen how much John needed her or how much she needed to be needed.

She and John were together several times in the next few days, but they never mentioned the night of the drunken Indian.

One afternoon while John was driving her down to the ranch, she said quietly, "Let's get married."

She was in the back of the van in her chair, and John looked around suddenly. All he said was, "Okay."

That evening, driving back, he said, "You know, Jill, I'm a lot closer to the Indians than you think. Quiet. No wasted words. No wasted motion. Able to wait and listen until the time is right. The Indian way."

12

The Knot

They decided to ease into the business of announcing their engagement and to let the news soak into June for a while before they spread the word any further. Jill said to June, off-handedly, "When we're married, Mom, we'll want a house with a view of the mountains." June didn't even pick up on it, and the next day Jill said, "Maybe John and I will get married." June went on about her work—she was rearranging dishes in the cabinet—and didn't seem to notice anything unusual. Finally one day Jill said, "Mom, John and I have decided to get married."

June said, without stopping what she was doing, "Hmmm. That's nice." Jill figured that she must have talked about getting married or not getting married so many times over the past 3 years that it had gotten to sound like "good morning" or "good night." But June stopped suddenly in the middle of pouring a cup of coffee. She turned to Jill with a surprised expression on her face. "Are you and John getting married?" she said.

"Yes."

"Well, that's wonderful!"

Next they told Beverly Boothe, but asked her not to tell anyone else. "Hardly a surprise," she said. When they told the Baumgarths, Lee said, "It's about time!"

They attended a Boothe family gathering at the ranch, and Bev said to them, "I *wish* you'd hurry up and tell people." She confessed that she had already told John's younger sister, Linda.

Shortly before dinner, Jill was sitting in the dining room while the women were setting the table and working in the kitchen. The men were in the living room with their drinks, talking about cows. Roy went to the kitchen for something, and when he came back through the dining room, Jill said casually, "Well, John and I decided finally to do it."

Roy stopped. Talk in the front room ended abruptly. The women stopped what they were doing and all of them came into the dining room. Nobody said anything at first. They just looked at one another.

Somebody said, *"What?"* Roy said, "I figured as much." Alice came and gave Jill a big kiss and began to cry. Dudley, from his big chair in the living room, said, "Well, I knew it would happen one of these days."

Jill telephoned Jerry about the engagement. He was deeply pleased, and he said, "There's one thing very important, Jill, and that is that Mom doesn't feel *not needed*."

"You really think so?" Jill said. "I thought it was going to be just wonderful for her to be free, finally."

"Yes, but not completely. All of a sudden, after twenty years, that's too much of a shock."

Jerry was right, of course. He had always been sensitive to what was important to other people. Many times he had run up from San Diego when things got out of hand at Pacific Palisades, and he was always the one who brought flowers when someone was sick.

Jill and John and June together talked about living arrangements and decided that the ideal set-up would be

199

for June to live alone in a separate house close to John and Jill. By good fortune they soon found just what they wanted, a pair of houses on Sunland Drive, off West Line half a mile from town, with an unhampered view of Mt. Tom and the neighboring peaks to the south. Both houses needed a lot of work, but there would be time for that.

Except that there wasn't time, from June's point of view. She wanted to have the wedding reception in her new house, and it wouldn't be ready before early 1977.

John said, "I want the wedding to be in October."

"We can't!" Jill said. "We've got to think about Mom. You just don't understand."

"I understand, and I don't want to wait."

"John, we're being married forever, so I don't think that time is *that* important."

They settled on Thanksgiving. Then Jill and June decided that Christmas would be better.

"Your family is trying to keep us from getting married," John said. "It's final. We're getting married Thanksgiving." June was disappointed, but she went along with it. Neither Jill nor John wanted to be married in a church, and when Audra Jo offered her house for the wedding they were very pleased. They decided to ask the Reverend Bee Landis to marry them. She was the minister at June's church, the Science of Mind Church, and Jill liked what Bee had to say at the few services Jill had attended. Bee's philosophy was that you get out of your life whatever you put into it.

The ceremony would be limited to the family, but the reception was something else. By the time John and Jill and June were finished with the list they had 160 names. June insisted on giving the reception herself, and the McCoys offered their house. It was probably the only house in town that could handle 160 guests gracefully.

•   •   •

Mountain 2 became a reality to Jill and John with the arrival of Douglas Day Stewart, his wife Joannie and his two children, in August. Stewart was the new screenwriter. He had just written a television film, *The Boy in the Plastic*

Bubble, about a boy raised in a sterile plastic cage because he had no natural immunities and any germs whatever might kill him. Jill had watched it on the tube and had thought it was very well done.

Doug Stewart was a young man with a suntanned face and an easy, quick smile. He introduced his family, sent them off somewhere, and got right down to work interviewing Jill and John. He was thorough, for which Jill respected him, and he was capable and sensitive and very easy to talk to, even though some of his questions became increasingly personal.

Jill wanted him to see her and John as distinct individuals rather than as a couple, and she suggested that he spend some time talking with them separately. Doug took Jill to The Embers, leaving John at home. He delved right in, clicking on his tape recorder and asking Jill what kinds of problems she had. Jill said she didn't have any problems. "You must have had uneasy times," he said. "Rough times! Can't you remember any?" She mentioned a period seven years before when everything was getting to be too much for her and she became very sick for six weeks.

"What kind of problems had you been having? Romantic problems?"

"Just trying to do too much, and trouble finding housekeepers and drivers and a girl to get me up in the morning."

Doug said he knew there was more to it than that. What was she repressing? How was she feeling *inside* at the time she was so sick? What kinds of dreams was she having?

"I had a dream about hollowness. As if there were no substance to my body, and it disturbed me."

Doug asked a string of questions about romantic episodes in Jill's life, particularly about what had been going on when she was so sick.

"Nothing big," she said, "but there was a guy I sort of liked—Chuck—who just kind of disappeared on me."

Jill began to see that Doug was always looking for heavy situations, conflicts, romantic entanglements. When Jill thought of a man she had once had a crush on, Stewart lit up. "It didn't materialize," Jill said.

201

"Why didn't it? Was it because of your handicap?"

"I don't think so."

Jill felt that Doug wanted her to admit that men were turned off by her paralysis and that was why relationships didn't happen. But she didn't feel this was true except in a very general way. "Well, sure I was aware that I would have had more men friends if I wasn't in the chair. But the real turn-off—and many dates were this way—the real turn-off was how intolerant I am of any man who has no mechanical ability and can't fix things with his hands."

Doug said, "Let's call John and ask him to join us after dinner for a drink." He excused himself, and when he returned and pushed the buttons on his tape recorder he discovered that it wouldn't work.

"It's probably something simple," Jill said. "Too bad John isn't here."

"Yeah. Probably. I don't know anything *about* these gadgets."

When John arrived, extremely quiet, Jill asked him to take a look at the tape recorder. Even in the dim light he could tell what was wrong, and he fixed it.

At home after Doug had left, Jill said, "What's the matter, John?"

"It's kind of dumb," he said, "but you know it bothers me that you go off to talk with him and leave me out of it. And I'm not sure I trust these reporter types, anyway."

"I think he's okay," Jill said. "Give him a little time and I think you'll like him."

The rest of the weekend was one long interview. It was tiring, but Jill was relieved to have a writer this time who asked searching questions and really listened to the answers. Doug was always sincere and was obviously impressed by what they could tell him. However, he got stuck on the idea that Jill's handicap must make any man Jill was dating feel good. "You are so dependent," he said. "So when a man is with you, he is placed in the position of feeling like a man. Haven't you noticed this?"

Jill could only think of the time Andy Lawrence's

brother had accidentally dumped her out of her wheelchair while pushing her across Main Street.

Doug talked a lot about what he wanted to do with the script. First of all, he wanted to make it honest, to show things as they really are. To do that, he would have to ask a lot of probing questions. He wanted to come back for an entire week, go out with John on his truck, talk with June and with Bob, and spend a lot more time with Jill. By the time he left, both John and Jill felt very good about him, and they said they would give him all their free time when he returned.

Camera crews moved in on Jill and John in late August and early September. Producer John Cosgrove had filmed Jill in the spring as part of the television series, *Medix*, but the film was so good that he decided to make it into a special feature, *Jill Kinmont: From Tragedy to Triumph*. His cameramen followed Jill to school, to a ramp committee meeting, and to an Indian Education Fund meeting. They filmed her teaching and recorded John and Jill shopping, picnicking, driving together, talking. They also interviewed June, Bob and Vikki, Lee and Audra Jo, and Jill's boss at school, Don Calaway. Jill talked Cosgrove into staging a special benefit showing of the program for the Indian Fund.

On September 14, Jill went to St. Louis with June to give a speech before a conference with an impressive name: "The National Bicentennial Conference on Woman's Pursuit of the American Dream—A Creative Middle Road." Jill called her talk "The Courage to Be a Woman," and preparing it was an unexpectedly rich experience. The speech turned out to be a summing up of her entire life, a perspective which connected the memories of her childhood with her life and work today.

"I want to share some of my experiences with you," she told the large, attentive audience. "My childhood, the fierce desire to compete athletically, the new unexpected challenges during early adulthood, the barriers that for some puzzling reason kept looming up, and finally, new adven-

203

tures. I'm not sure all this has to do with courage, but I do have this urge to persist."

The part she loved involved the early days on the ranch and at Mammoth. "We grew up on eighty spacious acres we called the Rocking K, an old Indian land grant with streams running freely, green pasture land, willows, cottonwood and locust trees, wild roses and blackberries. It was a wonderful place to find ourselves. My mom and dad had an incredible ability to provide an environment which would enable us to accomplish just about anything my brothers and I set out to do. We had family work projects. One of them was to clean the fence lines to allow for new fences. And the treasures we found stuffed along the fences were incredible. Cast iron frying pans, bed springs, old treadle sewing machines, mattresses, plows. We had no running water or even electricity on the ranch in those early days, but the pond became a skating rink in winter, and the sledding down our frozen, sloping pastures was fast and scary."

She described her skiing career and her recovery from the accident. "I was lucky to be able to handle it," she said. "I have a family who were totally supportive, and they had an uncanny way of seeming not to be sacrificing during many years of great sacrifice. My family has a great sense of humor, and my incredibly cheery, energetic, understanding mother helped enormously. Also I had a crazy boyfriend, and my injury, to him, became a great challenge. All of this craziness, nonsense, and wisdom made handling my new state of affairs a little easier."

•   •   •

Jill and John talked a lot about the new film, and by the time Doug Stewart showed up for his week of interviewing, John was beginning to take to the idea of getting into the act himself. He now felt that his relationship with Jill should be a part of the movie, even if Jill's teaching were to be the main focus.

Doug wanted to write a big scene about John's oil rig and the CB radio, so the two of them set off for Tonopah in John's truck. Doug turned on his tape recorder and launched into some very personal questions about Jill's handicap and how it affected John. He asked also about John's relationship with his first wife. This didn't offend John, because Doug talked freely about his own personal problems. He compared Nancy with his own first wife.

They were approaching Benton, California, and John picked up his CB microphone. "How about it, Chevron?" he said. "Have you a copy on the Muleskinner? Chevron, have you a copy on the Muleskinner?" He turned to Doug. "Yeah, it was pretty much the same with me. Nancy put me down a lot."

"Muleskinner, where you headed?"

"Tonopah Town. Just wanted to say I'll stop for coffee on the way back."

"I'll be here. Keep your shiny side up."

John told Doug all about Honeybear and how she looked out for everyone on the road. "You should have seen her place when she had her last baby. It was full of flowers from truckers all over the West."

Doug said he wanted to include a lot about John's relationship with Jill, and he wanted it to be a truly adult love story. They talked about that all the way to Tonopah. He asked John how the physical side of the relationship was going.

"Oh, hell . . . you know how one thing leads to another."

"Like . . . ? Can you give me some examples?"

John shrugged off the question.

"What I'd like to do," Doug explained, "is maybe end the film where the two of you first come together. With you two sitting on a couch, or in a bedroom. End the film at the bedroom."

John said, "Hmmm." Then on the CB he said, "Honeybear?"

"Come in, Muleskinner. What's the latest?"

"Guess who I've got here, H.B."

"Hot Wheels."

"Guess again."

"You mean that nosey guy that gets to ask all the personal questions I never get to ask you?"

"You hit it. He wants to meet you."

"Why didn't you let me know ahead? I'm tied up with the kids. Am I going to be in the picture?"

"Sure, but you're going to have to play your own part."

"Muleskinner, I *couldn't!* Look, I got a call. Catch you later."

John said to Doug, "You're going to want a blow-by blow?" Doug nodded cautiously. "Look, Doug, something like that would be a pretty personal moment, and it's not something I'd want to share."

On the trip home, John introduced Doug, by radio, to Black Sheep, Yogi Bear, and Super Mex and, in person, to Chevron, where they stopped for coffee.

"You know, I met the first writer," John said. "Nice guy, but not one I'd pursue as a friend. But I've met you and Joannie, and you are guys I'd like as my friends. It'd be nice if that worked out."

"I hope so, too, John."

Back in Bishop, Doug got out where he'd left his car. He rewound the tape on his recorder and played back enough to check the conversations he had recorded. All he could hear was the truck motor.

Doug worked hard for the rest of his visit, flooding John and Jill with questions. He went out to see Bob and Vikki, who did not want to be bothered with yet another film. He took June out to dinner at Whiskey Creek, ordered wine for her, and began to probe her feelings. How did she feel when Bill died? What was it like being a widow? How did she feel about having a daughter in a wheelchair? He was thoroughly sympathetic. He said, "What do you have that makes it possible for you to deal with all this?"

June said later to Jill, "He got me into a teary mood and asked about all the types of things that you don't like to dwell on. I was never aware of things being bad until I talked with *him!*"

Doug left Bishop in good spirits and told Jill and John he knew it was going to be a good script.

"I really liked him," John said after he had left.

"We really let him in on who we are, didn't we? I think he knows more about us now than we do."

"I talked about things it was never easy to talk about with anyone."

•   •   •

The Cosgrove special—*Jill Kinmont: From Tragedy to Triumph*—was previewed at a big party arranged by John Cosgrove. Tickets were $15 a head, and the proceeds were to go to the Jill Kinmont Indian Education Fund. There were cocktails and plentiful hors d'oeuvres. The program appeared on four large television monitors on the stage.

Universal put John and all the Kinmonts up at the Sheraton Hotel with all expenses paid. Interesting, Jill thought, since she was still sitting on the unsigned contract for *Mountain 2*. "This is the time when everybody is being nice to everybody," she said to June when she spotted a Universal publicity man and the whole Feldman family. She and John Cosgrove each spoke briefly, mostly to explain what the money—about $4,000—would be used for.

Later, she and John announced their engagement. She thought Feldman would go wild, and in fact he did later tell the newspapers, "It's hard to believe she keeps coming up with these plot lines."

Jill signed the final version of the contract late in October, after holding out for a clause guaranteeing that Jerry would be paid for coaching Marilyn Hassett. In the first film he had been paid for acting his own part in the picture, but his work with Marilyn had been on a volunteer basis except for $250 Larry Peerce had given him out of his own pocket. The contract represented two important compromises between Jill and the company:

> Miss Kinmont shall have a right of approval of the fictional events to be depicted in the sequel photoplay referred to herein, which approval shall not be unreasonably withheld.

> Miss Kinmont shall be consulted with respect to

207

the performers selected to portray the members of her family. However, we will have the right, after such consultation, to select such performers.

• • •

A teacher at the Indian Center telephoned to ask if Jill would give a short talk to a class in childhood development that was being given for tutors at the Center. They wanted to know something about learning disabilities. Next Thursday at 6 p.m.

Jill said she would, of course. But when the time came, she had been so busy trying to plan for the wedding that she had had no time to prepare a talk. She was nervous when John drove her to the Center. "It's just going to have to be impromptu," she said. "I guess I'll get by." Several tutors came out to meet the van, and one of them said to John, "Why don't you come on in? It won't take long." So Jill and John followed the girls inside.

There they found 50 people with a pot luck dinner already laid out. It was a while before Jill realized that the entire show was for her: a surprise wedding shower. There were gifts from tutors and students and parents. Towels, a Crock Pot, a Pendleton blanket with an Indian design. The Tribal Council gave her a beautiful Indian drawing. And there was a card signed by everyone present.

The teachers at the Bishop Elementary School also gave Jill a shower. There were 45 to 50 people there, and Jill was very much moved because she felt she was a newcomer at the school. There were many, many presents, and Anna Kinmont opened them for her. A rotisserie. Four beautifully appliquéd dish towels from the hope chest of the grandmother of one of the teachers. A salad bowl from the superintendent of schools.

The following week Linda and Audra Jo gave Jill a shower, and Jill spent a day in Los Angeles shopping for wedding clothes. The most difficult item was a blouse for the matron of honor, Audra Jo. Jill insisted on one that would match the roses.

The press got wind of the wedding, and both newspapers

208

and magazines wrote or telephoned, asking if they could come. John and Jill talked it over, and they were in perfect agreement. They talked to the editor of the local paper and asked his help in turning away the press from Los Angeles and other cities. "It's not just John and me," Jill said. "We are all sick of the flashiness that's been going on. Everybody knows now that, whatever the reason for it is—namely *me*—everyone else gets pulled into it. Every time a reporter comes, it hits Bob and Josie and Vikki and Linda and all the others."

"It's just plain time to say *no* and go on about our lives," John said.

They kept the location of the wedding a secret as well as they could, and they refused the photographers' requests to "just wait outside the door." Eric Baumgarth volunteered his services as sentry to keep reporters and photographers out if they did happen to show up.

June was too busy planning the reception to dwell on what Jill's marriage would mean to her, but she talked with Jill about it. "I'm so happy," she said. "Both for you and for my own freedom. But I'm sad, too, because it means you and I are . . . well, getting divorced. It's lucky we're such very good friends, on top of everything else."

"We all face some big changes."

"I hope you know, Jill, I've surely changed my feelings about John. He is absolutely solid. And anyway, I've gotten to like him."

"I'll probably still come running when things get bad," Jill said.

"I hope so, Jill. There are so many little things that I know just from being with you for twenty-one years. Maybe it's an ego thing, but I worry some, too. If I see a sore on your bottom, a lot of doctors don't know how it could develop. I do know, and I know what's the effective cure."

"It's a lot more than the physical stuff, Mom. It's when I've been upset and could come talk to you, or call you in the middle of the night. That time I was sick and so thirsty . . . remember? I had bad dreams. I couldn't sleep. And you sat and read me those beautiful fairy tales."

"I remember," June said. "Well, we've both got a lot of work to do if we're going to be ready for the day after Thanksgiving."

Lee Baumgarth had a problem because his son Eric was playing in his high school football team's big game in Los Angeles the night of the wedding and wanted Lee to be there.

"I don't know quite what to do," Lee told Jill.

"Lee, *I want you at the wedding!*"

Lee nodded and went to the phone. He talked Gary McCoy into flying them down to Los Angeles at 3 p.m. The wedding ceremony was scheduled for 2:30.

"Are we going to be outside or inside?" Audra Jo asked.

"I love the yard," Jill said, "but you know how cold I get. We'd better have it in the living room. Too bad, with the weather like it is." The weather had been very bad or very good, depending upon who you were. For brides it was good. For skiers, especially for the owners of resorts and motels and ski shops, the weather was absolutely abominable—clear blue skies day after day. No snow at all. It was a tense month in the business. Dave McCoy alone felt okay about it. He had told Linda, "Every now and then God does this just to show us who really runs the mountain."

The wedding day dawned stormy and drear, and the skiing people were ecstatic. The Baumgarth living room was cleared. Bob and Jerry set up four dozen folding chairs. There was tape on the floor so there would be enough room left at the front for both wheelchairs. Flowers had been wound around the posts at the entrance to the room.

The wedding guests were all family except for the Baumgarths, the Tikalskys, and Dave and Roma McCoy. They all found chairs except for the children, who sat on the floor, and there soon was no room to walk around. The telephone rang constantly—telegrams, well-wishers, reporters, friends from far away. The storm had worsened, and every time the front door opened, leaves and dust and sand blew in and telegrams and gift wrappings were

210

swept onto the floor. "It's getting so bad you just have to relax," Jill said.

Audra Jo took the telephone off the hook, and the ceremony began right on time—probably because everyone remembered Lee and Eric had a plane to catch.

Jill wore a two-piece, off-white Chinese silk dress with a high neck and long sleeves. It had satin ribbon and lace on the bodice. She made a point of wearing something old (her grandmother's necklace), something new (a gold chain necklace John had given her), something borrowed (Audra Jo's bracelet), and something blue (her turquoise ring). John wore new Justin boots and a tan suit he had bought at Nudie's, a Western shop in Hollywood.

Lisa Baumgarth played the wedding march on the piano, and she made a mistake. Jill said, "That's the way I wanted it, Lisa." There was barely room for the two wheelchairs, and children sitting on the floor near the entrance had to pull back their legs to make room. Two of the children, Jill Tikalsky and Jill Lamkin, were namesakes.

"This is a joyous occasion," the Reverend Bee Landis said, "for we gather here, in the Presence of God the Eternal Spirit of Truth, to witness the joining of John Boothe and Jill Kinmont in the delightful unity of marriage. There are no ties on earth so sweet and tender as those you are about to assume."

She quoted Kahlil Gibran's *The Prophet*. "Love one another, but make not a bond of love; Let it rather be a moving sea between the shores of your souls." Bob and Jerry were standing behind Jill, and when Bee said, "Who gives this woman to be married to this man?" they both said, "I do."

John said, "I, John, give myself to you, Jill, to be your husband, to love and to cherish, and thereto I pledge you my faith." Jill said, "I, Jill, give myself to you, John, to be your wife, to love and to cherish, and thereto I pledge you my faith."

Champagne was opened, and Bob proposed a toast. "To Jill and John, may your life be full of gentleness and adventure."

211

Everyone went to the McCoys for the reception, although Bob and Jerry stayed behind long enough to fold the chairs and replace the Baumgarth's living room furniture. Five couples were already there when Jill and John arrived. Jill and Audra Jo combed their hair—the storm had been a tangler—and settled by the fire with John. A table was bountifully laden with hors d'oeuvres, and a champagne fountain bubbled nearby. Within half an hour, 140 or 150 guests had arrived, and the storm kept the overflow from spilling outside into the patio.

John and Jill were too busy greeting new arrivals to mingle themselves. The families were also busy, Bev serving punch, Vikki taking photographs, Anna in charge of the guestbook, Ben handling coats and gifts. At 4:30 Lyn cut the cake.

Jill tossed her bridal bouquet toward her cousin Cheryl, but 9-year-old Jill Lamkin leaped into the air and snagged it for herself. At 5:30, Jill and June went into a bedroom. Jill exchanged her wedding dress for a plaid skirt and green velvet blazer while John went out to start the van and turn on the heater. Then he came in to say goodbye.

John carried Jill out into the storm. Ben had sneaked out with a can of shaving cream to write JUST MARRIED on the van, and rice was flying everywhere, along with the sand and leaves.

John and Jill drove to Death Valley in a freezing dust storm, their car covered with shaving cream and rice: JUST MARRIED . . . JOHN AND JILL . . . HAVE FUN.

They stayed at the Furnace Creek Inn in a beautiful room with a fireplace but no other source of heat. The room was utterly romantic. Someone brought firewood to the door. John made a fire and took Jill to bed. As for what followed, Jill wrote in her daybook: "As we were kissing and caressing and letting each other know how much we loved each other, the smoke began coming into the room. The strong winds were backing it down the flue. Between loving and carrying on sweetly and gently, John had to open the door and windows to get the smoke out. It got colder and smokier, and finally he threw water on the fire. It is a lovely place. Furnace Creek Inn. All meals included in the price."

Their wedding day, it turned out, was the only stormy day all fall. The next day, Saturday, was clear and brisk and bright. They wandered around the outdoor museum and the geological museum, visited Scottie's Castle, where John had to carry Jill up and down many, many stairs, and returned for champagne on the veranda at sunset, high on the bluff with Death Valley spread out before them.

13

The Script Committee

John and Jill Boothe moved into John's house on Elm Street. They hired a local woman, Michele Smith, who kept house, got Jill up in the morning, and was willing to be on call whenever John had to go off on a long trucking haul.

Roy and Bev were living in the front house. June stayed on at Grove Street waiting for minor alterations to be completed on her "new" house on Sunland. Jerry was building kitchen cabinets and a deck, and Bob was panelling the living room. John and Jill's Sunland house would not be ready until May, since the changes they contemplated were more extensive: building a new bedroom with a bathroom door wide enough for a wheelchair, re-doing the kitchen and guest bathroom, tearing out a wall in the living room, painting inside and out, and building decks, ramps, and walkways.

Newspaper clippings about the wedding were coming in from friends everywhere. Jill and John were surprised that the event had attracted so much publicity. Now they were besieged by the reporters and photographers who had respected their privacy during the ceremony. The interviews were less hassled than interviews had been in the past, and they were all very much alike.

When John was asked the predictable question—what is it like being married to such a special person?—he answered, seriously, "Nothing special." When they both were asked what special adjustments they'd had to make, John usually answered that one, too. "Basically, no different from any two people coming together. Everybody has to make adjustments. They're different adjustments. If you can't handle it, you don't do it. If you can, you do it. That's all. The question doesn't require any special answer." Asked about their differences, he said, "Politically, we lean in opposite directions, but we hold hands in the middle."

How did Jill feel about being married? She said, "John has an extraordinary ordinariness that is pleasing to me. Some people gain freedom from leaving a husband, or they are even exhilarated. I realize I get the same feeling from gaining a husband. I have a sense of well-being, and I feel a new dimension because the decisions I make are not made just for me."

Doug Stewart called several times to ask about Jill's teaching career and to keep Jill and John posted on the progress of the script. The first call was cheerful enough, but after that, Doug sounded discouraged. He had completed a draft he liked. A treatment, he called it. He saw it as a serious love story with great integrity, but Feldman had a vision of joy and light, and it seemed that everyone wanted to capitalize on *Mountain One*.

"It's a hard pull," he said, "because people see it *only* as a sequel." Feldman apparently had thought the audience wanted to see a lot more of Jill than they did of John. At any rate, Doug was into a major rewrite.

Jill and John were sympathetic and slightly anxious. They felt Doug would have written a good, honest screenplay, and they wondered why it had been rejected.

215

They never saw the first draft, but they received a copy of the second one a few days after New Year's.

John was off work early the day it arrived, and he read it while Jill was still at school. *The Other Side of the Mountain, Part 2, The Continuing True Story of JILL KINMONT*. It opened with the big screening of *Mountain One* at Universal. John was amused by an early scene in which Doug had Jill—in some miraculous and unexplained way—maneuvering a wheelchair-on-skis through a slalom course made of old tires laid on the snow. Dave had indeed once put Jill's chair on skis, but there was no way of controlling it.

The first two-thirds of the screenplay was largely flashbacks to Jill's rehabilitation days, with a few scenes of her frustrating attempt to become a teacher. Then John came to the part of Jill's life he knew about personally, and he read that John Boothe rode a bull in the rodeo and had a brutal fight with a drunken Indian, tackling him, pinning him, and slugging him until he was half unconscious.

"I can't believe it," he said when Jill returned home. "Doug talked so much about making it honest. And all those things he asked me and we talked about, they aren't here anywhere."

Jill read the script. She was dismayed to read about herself saying to a date, "I'm one of the world's great kissers, you should try me," and she wasn't at all happy with the dream Doug had written for her, "Oh, Mom . . . it was just horrible, horrible . . . those crabs . . . crawling through me . . . I was just a head . . . a head without a body . . . and these little crabs like you see at the beach were eating my eyes and crawling through my skull."

What upset her most was John's fight with the Indian and a flashback scene in which her father, on his deathbed, is made to say, "Hell, Honeygirl, I was a partytimer, a big glad-handing fool with the luck of the Kinmonts and none of their character . . . until you gave me a chance to grow up." Just before that, Doug had him hallucinating about a naked girl named Naomi on the

216

ceiling. Bill's line was, "Honeygirl, what does that nubile, young, oh-so-full-breasted vision of pleasure say her name is?"

Jill was taken aback by the fact that much of the screenplay was not factual, but she also found many parts she liked. "He has some really nice things," she said. "That whole truck trip to Tonopah."

"Except that you weren't ever in the truck."

"I know we were only in the pick-up, John, but the whole feeling of it is so right." She was also pleased to see at least *something* in the script about her trying to teach in Watts and being turned down by the school board because she was in a wheelchair.

"How'd you like where I'm introduced to Frank and I say to him: A shrink, huh?"

Jill laughed. "You never said that."

"No, but I wish I had."

What disturbed both of them was that the very thing that was now important to them—appreciating the simple reality and ordinariness of daily life—was the very thing the movie people didn't want. Jill couldn't be in love with an ordinary truck driver. John had to come off as a new John Wayne. It was a wonder they hadn't made him a gunslinger; he couldn't just notice a deer jumping a fence; the deer had to get caught and he had to go save it. He was being made into a false hero.

"My teaching is only mentioned," Jill said, "and it's a terribly important eight hours of my life almost every day."

John took the script from her and tossed it on the table. "It has nothing to do with life, or with our life, either," he said. "And here we really opened and let Doug in to who we were. And I liked him. He wanted to show things as they really were, and there's hardly anything *in* it that's true."

"It's not that bad, John."

"He didn't have to see us at all, Jill. He already knew what he was going to write. He just took us for a ride. I feel ripped off."

217

They telephoned Doug. Jill said, "Well, I got it and read it and there are some parts I like, but it's sure not what I expected, Doug. There sure is a lot of fiction." Doug sounded very much disappointed by her reaction. "I don't like being sixteen, still, and I would like a little more truth. Where did you get that about my father being a loser?"

"From Linda and Dave."

John said, "Doug, I just never *did* rodeo stuff." Doug said he had asked John if he could take dramatic license and make John into something of a cowboy, and John had said okay. "Well, maybe I did," John said. "But not a *rodeo* cowboy."

"This is what they want," Doug said unhappily. "If you only knew how hard Ed fought for honesty. He really had our interest at heart." Jill made clear her objections and gave Doug a list of specific suggestions for dialogue that was more true to her life.

"Well," she said afterwards, "he's working for Universal, not for us. He's their puppet."

They talked with Doug a number of times during January, and Jill began to feel better about the prospects. Doug was writing a third version of the screenplay. Feldman and Universal both had been turned off by the fight with the Indian. The people at Universal Pictures apparently hadn't liked the script. They wanted a love story. A dramatic one. They wanted John brought into it more. Doug was also afraid that Universal was going lukewarm and the project just might die.

"I'm going to have to beef it up," he said. "We had to go back and say there's not going to be a movie unless we fictionalize a bit. To some extent. So I need a situation leading to a crisis so Universal can see the drama in the story. Something tangible. We could change it later on, once they've bought it." He said he needed a scene that involved danger to John and great anxiety for Jill, and he asked John for help. John said the only danger he might really encounter was coming upon a cow on the highway, or a car pulling out and forcing him off the road.

If that should happen, he said, he would probably call Honeybear on the CB. Doug asked how that would make Jill anxious. John said, "There really wouldn't be any danger, but I suppose if I lost radio contact with Honeybear for some reason, then she might get anxious and get in touch with Jill."

Doug apparently was on the hot seat all this time, getting it from both ends. He made some reference to meetings at Universal's black tower where, Jill gathered, everyone was acting crazy, was screaming and hollering. Jill, too, was hollering—hollering for more truth and less manufactured drama at the same time that somebody *up there* was hollering for more fiction and melodrama.

* * *

The third draft was completed late in February. At least, Jill noticed, it was entitled *The Continuing Story of JILL KINMONT*. The *"True"* had been dropped.

On the first page, Jill appeared as "an attractive, broad-smiling girl in her late twenties. "That was four years ago, and I was thirty-seven," Jill said to John. "Doug knows that!"

"I sure don't want a teeny-bopper for a wife."

Jill leafed quickly through the manuscript and found with relief that Doug had eliminated John's riding a bull, John's fight with the Indian, and Bill's hallucinating about a naked woman. Bill was still there calling himself a glad-handing fool. Then she came upon a shocker: a flaming crash of a school bus full of children, with John stopping to rescue them as another truck comes careening down upon them all, slamming into John's parked semi and blowing it up, "FILLING THE SCREEN with violent color." Plus a long sequence in which Jill goes into a delirious coma for four days because she thinks John may have been in a wreck.

The whole thing was unbelievable to Jill. "This script is *worse* than the last one," she said to John.

"They want a blockbuster," John said, "and they don't care how they get it."

Jill decided to telephone Feldman and ask for a big script conference and demand that the bus crash and the coma be cut out. But she was afraid this might be too aggressive a move to make at this particular time. She asked Vikki and June to read the screenplay to help her clarify her position in her own mind.

Vikki was more upset than Jill had been. "There's nothing about your everyday relationship with students or with John," she said. "Nothing about how John changed because of his relationship with you. It could be a wonderful film if it had these things in it. Are you just going to let it go by without getting these things in it?"

Jill said, "I don't feel I can say that to them. It's like boasting."

"It's not boasting. It's just taking responsibility for it."

June said, "The bus thing is terrible. There's been no violence in your life for twenty years."

"I guess they figure if there's no violence, what can they write about," Jill said.

"And there's no growth or development of you," June said. "Not even over the first film. You're still just a *girl,* like Doug calls you. A girl in her twenties."

"You have a social responsibility, too," Vikki said. "A responsibility to all the people who *could* be positively affected by a film about your life and family and teaching."

June added, "A *lot* of people in wheelchairs want to know how you've managed all you've done, and this movie is *not* saying it, how you did it."

Jill at the moment just wanted to escape. "It's a *movie,* Mom. Vikki. It's all about the past. It's not *my life . . . now.* I don't want to spend all that energy it would take to make the movie right."

"But you've got to take responsibility for making the film the way you want it," June said. "This time, at least, we know what to do, and we know to do it early. You've got to *handle* it."

"It's a cop-out," Vikki said, "when you and John only

make little changes like colloquialisms and ways you wouldn't have said things. The real issue is the making of false heroes and not capturing what your life is really about. John gets to be a big hero on a white horse, and you just come off *flat*."

June said, "If you go to Doug and Ed with all this, how's John going to feel?"

Jill had been pleased, in a way, that John's role was so flattering. She was afraid it would be putting him down to ask that his character be changed in the film. "I'll have to ask John," she said. John had said very little about this third script, and perhaps he wasn't so critical of it. She waited a day before telling him what Vikki had said because she was afraid of hurting his feelings.

Her fears about John couldn't have been more misplaced. John said, "I *hate* what Doug made me into in that script. I absolutely hate it. And I hate him keeping you as a bouncy little teen-ager instead of a wonderful, forty-year-old wife. But I didn't say anything because I thought it was flattering to you and that you liked it."

Jill was pleased by this, but she was discouraged. "I just hate the thought of gathering together enough energy to fight this stupid thing," she said.

June wrote a letter to Doug. She objected first of all to the violent school bus scene and to Bill's saying he was just a glad-hander. "It's as if he didn't have any sense at all until Jill's accident created a situation th~~ made him grow up." She continued:

I can't imagine *why* you would write anything like that. Bill was a lovable city man who brought his kids to the country. A whole guy. Certainly no~ a loser.

Jill's career is not written about. You've got John bigger than life. He's not. He's a very ordinary guy. It's ridiculous. You didn't develop Jill as a woman. She's still a teen-ager. She has accomplished a great deal in the past seven years.

Vikki also wrote a critical letter to Doug Stewart, but then she decided not to mail it. She felt that her feelings were not all that important in this situation, and she knew that Jill didn't want her to rock the boat. But then she said to herself, "If *my feelings* aren't important, then what *is?*"

She didn't want John to see her letter because she thought it might hurt his feelings, but she showed it to Jill. Jill approved of it and suggested that she also send a copy to Ed Feldman. "You might as well send a copy to Ned Tanen, too," Jill said. "He seems to be at the top of the chain of command." So Vikki mailed the original to Doug, with copies to Feldman and Tanen.

March 10, 1977
Hello Douglas!
No!
Just read the script and have to respond, because I feel so strongly.

It's a good script—but: why did you write it like that? Is it because of Universal Filmways and its influence? I feel like you're missing the most important point in Jill's life since the accident and that the film won't satisfy the public in their want to know "how Jill does it." *Constancy* is certainly a big part of it. You made John the hero of this movie and Jill's life of tragedies a continued one, when it's not true. Somehow, you didn't pick up on the incredibly subtle everyday ordinariness that Jill sees as "the whole thing," and this is how she can appreciate a man who is not a hero, like John, and everyone needs to recognize this in themselves in order to appreciate life like Jill does.

Jill and June make the smallest detail in life very meaningful and from day to day—and this is what America wants and needs now. Getting up in the morning, every minute detail of it, eating breakfast and going to school *every day,* all of those years— and through it all, a thread of "let's see what we can do with what we've got," instead of going from "orgasm" to "orgasm." And such positiveness! This is what pulled Jill and John together. John was having a hard time, feeling down on himself in many ways, and Jill has helped John a lot to recognize who he is. He's getting happier and happier. And it's Jill who can relate to him in every way—her purity, clarity and ability to relate to the smallest everyday detail has helped him—which in turn helps her—she's contagious. It's through these small successes that life grows. Did you know that we die many times a day? Why did you have to make the movie so crass? Jill's life is subtle and beautiful and hard. It's the everyday events that should be the highlights—not false over-dramatizations. I feel like my next tour of Universal Studios, we'll round a corner in the trolley and see John's diesel in flames and hear Jill's and the children's screams only to find out it's a special effect crew.

You did such a beautiful sensitive job with the "Bubble"—what happened? Are you afraid that "feminine qualities" in a feminine person could be that powerful?

I'd like to talk to you in person or even on the phone, if you care to call.

Try again!
Vikki Kinmont

Feldman responded at once to Vikki's letter by telephoning Jill. "Who is Vikki Kinmont?" he said. "Is she all right? Is she in an institution or something? That is the most vindictive letter I've read, ever, in my life!"

Larry Peerce saw the letter and said, "What she says is bullshit, straight-out bullshit. She makes me crazy."

Jill talked with Vikki and Bob about Feldman's reaction. "They're at a pretty dramatic place in doing the picture," she said. "The letter made them jump, and it made them put you down, Vikki. The women speak up, and the Hollywood types tell them they're crazy."

Jill realized, nevertheless, that she should be asserting herself and that, in this situation, she didn't know how to. Essentially, this is why she had encouraged Vikki to do the asserting. But Vikki had no power. Only Jill had power, since it was Jill who had to sign the contract, and Feldman knew how to handle her. Bob said, "Feldman is a real pro. He is so sophisticated and clever that he is extremely capable of manipulating you."

"I admit I go along with the pro's," Jill said. "They are so convincing and bright. I say *yes* and do it their way."

"They are absolutely remarkable!" Bob said with reluctant admiration.

Jill telephoned Feldman to say she and John wanted a meeting with him and Doug Stewart in Bishop. Feldman said fine, he was coming up for a ski weekend with his family around April 17th and would talk with Jill then.

Unfortunately, Jill and John had agreed to appear on the Easter Seals telethon in Los Angeles that weekend. Feldman suggested that she meet with Doug in Los Angeles after the telethon. John vetoed that proposal. "No way," he told Jill. "It's not Doug who has the last word, so we want to see them both. And we want to meet on our ground, not theirs." Feldman said the two of them would come up to Bishop soon after the telethon.

Linda Tikalsky phoned Jill from Mammoth, where she was working for Dave. "We've had an accident up here," she said. "An eighteen-year-old, Christine Richer. She lost control skiing on one of the intermediate slopes but kept riding the tails of her skis instead of falling. She gained momentum and eventually flew off a small embankment. Broke her neck at C-6 and C-7."

"Would it help any if I wrote or phoned or something?" Jill said.

"I think so, Jill. I felt almost sick to my stomach, and I ached because of how it reminded me of you. Almost exactly the age you were. Same weight, same height. I thought, what can I do to help her, and I remember you had said one thing that helped you was that all those stupid ski fans cared about you, so you just had to carry on."

Christine was in the hospital in Reno, and Jill wrote her and sent her an autographed copy of her biography. Jill and John were in Reno a short time later and stopped at the hospital, but Christine had been sent to a rehabilitation center in Irvine, California. Her mother answered Jill's letter and gave her Christine's telephone number. Jill called. Christine said, "Chris's pad. Who's this?"

"Jill Kinmont."

"Oh, boy," Christine said, "wait till everyone hears *this!*" Jill asked what level Christine's fracture was at and what she could do. Christine, who had normal biceps and some use of her triceps, could move her arms and wrists and had some use of the fingers of one hand. She was in a body cast and would begin physical therapy as soon as the cast was off.

"I thought of you when the ski patrol picked me up," Christine said. "In fact I even mentioned it to them. Could you give me your number? I'd like to call you sometime."

• • •

There were two Easter Seals telethons—a national show hosted by Michael Landon and a local show with Luci Arnaz. Jill and John were scheduled for the national program first. They were herded into the little greenroom where, among the crowd waiting to appear, they found Larry Peerce and Marilyn Hassett. It was a hearty reunion, and Larry launched right into a discussion of the scripts and what was happening about them.

"We're really upset with the school bus scene," John said.

"That scene is *out,*" Larry said. "Don't worry, that scene is *out.*"

"And I'm still not a woman in this last draft," Jill said. "I'm just not developed as a mature person."

"I'm with you," Larry said, "and that's not how it's going to be."

225

"We've got to *do* something about it, my dear," Marilyn said, throwing her hands up in the air. "We've got a teen-ager here and . . . well, I won't sign on for the role unless changes are made in the script."

The little room full of people was extremely noisy, so the four of them had to lean forward with their heads close in order to hear one another. Marilyn was working with her hair. It was in a large knot at the top of her head, clean and lovely. When a production assistant came in to give them five minutes' warning, she took out one large pin and let the hair cascade down. She leaned forward so the hair hung between her knees, and she brushed it. She was wearing velvet knickers and dark brown boots, a tweed blazer, and a green turtleneck sweater.

"In *Mountain One*," Marilyn said from beneath her beautiful veil of hair, "I had to gain weight in order to look like you, Jill. This time I have to lose weight to look like you."

"Thank you," Jill said.

They continued to talk about the script. Marilyn kept relating events in the script to experiences she and Larry were having in their own relationship. Certain things just would not have happened as they were portrayed in the script, she said.

Marilyn, Jill, and John went on camera together. They had been given a list of the questions they were to be asked, and in the end almost none of the questions ever came up. Landon started with John. "I understand you're married now, John. Well, what's it like?"

"Well, it isn't that different. We make adjustments just like anyone who gets married, and—"

"John and Jill are the subjects of a forthcoming motion picture," Landon said, interrupting John. "It's called *The Other Side of the Mountain, Part 2.*" And that was the way things went.

On the way out of the studio, the four of them met Joni Eareckson, the young quadriplegic who had learned to write and paint with her teeth and who had just completed a book about her experiences. Her sister, who was with her, recognized Jill and said, "Aren't you Jill Kinmont?"

Jill said, "Yes. About two years ago, Joni drew a picture of me skiing, and a mutual friend sent it to me."

"Oh, you remember!" Joni said, delighted.

Joni was worse off than Jill physically, but she was very much on top of things, full of life, bright and pretty. She had no previous claim to fame before she was injured in a swimming accident. She had since then made a name for herself by writing the book, drawing greeting cards, and publicizing her art work on the *Today* show. However, she now acted as if Jill were a star of some kind. She carried on like a teen-age fan. Jill realized for the first time how a young actress might react if she were to meet Bette Davis.

• • •

Larry, Marilyn, John, and Jill went to a nearby Denny's for lunch. The waitress brought a tray of water glasses and was about to put it on the table when she recognized Jill. She did not recognize Marilyn, which was strange, since she identified Jill only from having seen Marilyn in the movie. John said to her, "And *this* is Marilyn Hassett, who played the part. It's going to be quite a day for you." The waitress promptly spilled the water and, while wiping it up, asked hesitantly for autographs.

"I guess I know which one of us is famous," Marilyn said to Jill. "How's your fan mail?"

"Not bad, as a matter of fact. It was fifteen letters a day for a while, but now it's down to five."

Marilyn asked, "Do they all get answered?"

"Most of them by me personally. But no repeats. I throw it away if it's a second letter—unless it's something really important.

"What do they say?"

"Most of them are from young people between ages twelve to sixteen, and really, these kids' letters are so

227

great! Mostly predictable, but I got a marriage proposal last month. From a thirteen-year-old boy. At the end he said, but who'd marry a thirteen-year-old?"

Jill told Larry she was planning to meet Feldman and Doug with her list of suggestions and objections. She said she was afraid she wouldn't have the courage of her convictions, since Feldman was so capable and so persuasive.

Larry said, "I was intimidated by *you* when you came to us with your list in the first film, so I know you can do it. You just look at Feldman exactly as you're looking at me now. Tell him we can't have this scene, we can't have that scene. Tell him you don't want to be a teen-ager, you want to be a woman. Tell him that the violence is ridiculous. Let him know."

"Have you seen the letters my mom and sister-in-law wrote? They caused quite a stir."

"I heard about them!" Larry said, raising his eyebrows. "It's just those people reacting to something you want that they don't want."

The talk drifted from the film story to reality, and Jill discovered that she and Marilyn had a great deal in common as far as their love lives were concerned. Both couples had only been living together for a short time. Both women had had serious reservations before finally committing themselves. Both had learned, as Marilyn put it, that it's not smooth as it's pictured in the moving pictures. "Relationship," she said, "is made up of arguing and anger and caring, and I wish the film could demonstrate that more. Like me screaming at Larry from the kitchen and he screaming back."

Jill had been very much aware of the fact that the two themes which had been running her life for three years—her relationship with John and the two films—had been working at cross purposes, tugging her in opposite directions. Today for the first time she felt some connection between the two. It was not something she had expected, and it made her feel good.

Marilyn said she had not until recently been sure that she wanted to do the second film. "I didn't want to be in a wheelchair for the rest of my life," she said. Also, Jill gathered that Feldman had been worried that Larry and Marilyn's living together might have an adverse effect on the production, so for a while he hadn't been certain that he wanted her in the role again if Larry was going to direct.

"It was extraordinary," Larry said. "Marilyn never wanted to do a sequel. It had been almost too much with *Mountain One*. When she read the first version of the script, I thought she was going to have a heart attack. I mean she went bananas."

"I had my doubts at first, too," John said.

Marilyn said her trouble was that she had grown so much during the past two very difficult years that she couldn't imagine identifying again with the Jill Kinmont of the first film. "Before we started work on this film," she said, "I ran into someone who held out a copy of the paperback—*The Other Side of the Mountain*—wanting me to autograph it. There I was, my picture on the front with a round face, real innocent. You know, camera left, camera right. And I had gone through two horrendous years of feelings with myself since then, feelings I was going through in therapy, a lot of emotional pain, and coming out of it and falling out of the pits, so to speak, getting myself back together again. And that is when I realized I was not going to go back to playing the Jill of that first picture."

"What all good actors are doing," Larry said, "is that they take their own reality and filter it through the overlay of the character. But they do share with you their private pain or joy, all of their emotions. You cannot *be* the person you're playing, but you have to find common grounds. Not simply the common ground that Marilyn was in a wheelchair for a year, but the common ground of pain, of love, of joy, of sadness, of depression, of elation."

There was a quiet moment. Then John said, "At first I didn't want another picture, but now I *want* it made because I'm in on this one with Jill. I'm not on the sidelines this time." He added, "I want it made, and I want it made *right*."

The conversation would have gone on and on, and they all could have welcomed it. Larry said they would get together again soon because he and Marilyn had to visit Bishop to scout for locations. He said Doug still hadn't come up with a script that he, Larry, was willing to tackle, but he and Doug were getting together, and a fourth and final script should be ready before long.

After John and Jill had left, Marilyn and Larry talked about them. "John just knocked me out," Marilyn said. "A couple of years ago he seemed to be just part of the robot system around Jill, who was sitting up directing the whole scene."

"An enormous change," Larry said. "This extraordinary thing has gone down between the two of them. This man who couldn't look me in the eye when I first met him. And Jill Kinmont, in my opinion, is playing out the woman's role for the first time since she was hurt."

"Jill's looking like a *woman*," Marilyn said. "A softness in her face. She's vulnerable. She doesn't have all the answers any more."

They were both affected by the changes. "It gives me faith," Larry said. "It makes me realize that you can grow and you can move forward."

John and Jill, after they had left Denny's, talked about Larry and Marilyn. "You know, even *I* get a little confused, John, like the waitress. Was that *me* in the first picture? No, it was an actress. But Marilyn is sure it was Jill Kinmont. She sees herself acting the part, or feels herself acting the part, and she believes it. So of *course* she sees huge changes. Of *course* she doesn't want to be the Jill Kinmont of the first film again."

"Even Larry's remark . . ." John said. "That the part has to do with Marilyn as much as it has to do with you. Or more. That she takes her own reality and filters it through the character. I think they're the ones who have changed."

"They have. Like they said. So their perceptions have

230

changed. The way they see us has changed. So who knows how much of the change they see in other people is their own?"

Jill received a letter from a girl in Maine who was even more confused than the waitress had been about which Jill was real and which was the screen version. "I hate to bring this up," she wrote, "but you skied so good, and you're so pretty. And in every picture in the book you looked so different."

•   •   •

John telephoned Jill from outside of Tonopah one day to say a friend of his had just been killed. John had come upon the wreck shortly after it had happened. Packrat was already there. It was a tanker, and John was afraid Jill would worry if she heard that a Bishop man driving a tanker had been killed near Tonopah.

14

Infight

Ed Feldman and Douglas Day Stewart flew to Bishop at the end of April. John and Jill picked them up at 10 a.m. at the airport. Feldman was wearing dungarees, looking very relaxed, and Doug had his shirt unbuttoned, with his gold necklace and tanned chest apparent as usual. They were both terribly friendly and casual. They both kissed her. They all went back to John's Elm Street house to discuss the script. Feldman and Doug sat on the couch, each with a briefcase. Jill sat facing them. John sat in his chair. Doug took out a pen and clipboard.

Jill pitched right in. "For starters, I hate the coma, the crash, and being a teen-ager at thirty-seven," she said. "But let's go through the script page by page. Or shall I start with the general overall ideas I don't like? Or the little picky ones?"

Doug took notes, and he was more resistant than Feldman to the changes Jill and John suggested—undoubtedly because it was he and not Feldman who was going to have to do the work.

Jill went through dozens and dozens of relatively minor suggestions and criticisms. "Jill says . . ." she said, reading from her copy of the script. " 'Daddy, oh, Daddy . . . I don't know what to do to make them like me . . . like a woman.' Sounds weird to me, Doug."

Feldman felt strongly about this, Jill could tell. He said, "I want that in. I love the wonderful father-daughter relationship that's created there."

Jill was touched by his feeling, and this made her a lot less resistant. "I guess it's okay," she said. Doug nodded.

"And the crab dream," Jill said. "Let's forget the crabs!"

"Jill, you told me about the crab dream," Doug said.

"I did? I don't remember." Jill went on, "This business of John seeing his first wife and Bev says you never see her with the same boy twice. Now that's just—"

"We're already rewriting that whole tavern scene," Doug said.

"And the coma business . . ." Jill said. "I babble in a soft delirium? That is truly carried too far! And next page, I get desperately sick as soon as I hear there was an accident. It has to go, Doug."

The discussion was not so smooth when it came to whole scenes. Feldman explained why they were doing what they were doing with the melodramatic material near the end. The film had to be dramatically interesting to an audience. They had to create a certain amount of tension in order to build toward something. "If we dealt with it as just ordinary, the film would be very blah," Feldman said. "Not dramatic. We have to show it. Maybe you communicated with each other, or with June, about things without words because you were able to read the signs. But we have to have conversations about it so the audience will be able to see it, even though you wouldn't actually say these things."

It was easy for Feldman to be convincing. He explained

233

also that they didn't want to expend the energy it took to make any big changes. Jill tried to understand. These men were both professionals, and she felt the pressure from them.

"There's more specific things," she said. "You have me telling John, *I'm a bad luck charm. Every man I love dies.* Why am *I* coming off a loser? I'm not a loser!"

Vikki telephoned twice during the session to ask how things were going. She wanted to be sure Jill stuck to her guns. Honeybear called also! "What are you doing?" she asked. She knew perfectly well what they were doing because John had told her on his last trip that the producers would be here today.

"Sorry you're not here," John said. "I'm sure they'd like to meet you."

Feldman said they had decided not to use the teaching scene at Hawthorne.

"Well, I'm certainly disappointed about that!" Jill said. "Teaching is such a part of my life, eight hours a day every day. It seems there should be something about my teaching."

"No," Feldman said. "We'll probably take that out."

Jill didn't insist. She brought up the business of her still being under age.

"I'm already working with Larry," Doug said, "and we're removing all the *golly gees* and other parts that make you sound immature."

"Okay. And now about the school bus and the crash and the explosion and all."

Doug defended the scene.

John said, "Why, on top of the frightened and injured children and everything, do you even have to have second truck screaming up behind and blowing everything up?"

"Don't forget, John, you wrote that scene," Doug said.

"*I* wrote it?" John said. "I told you there might be cow in the road and that if I lost radio contact with Honeybear she might call Bishop and that could make Jill anxious. That's all I 'wrote.'"

"You did tell me there could be a crash, John."
Jill interrupted. "The audience is faced with believing the kids are going to be hit. It's absolutely horrifying to think our film has to put an audience through all that, and it isn't even one ounce true!"

Doug said he wanted to show John's sensitivity and courage and compassion. Feldman said he understood Jill's point and that the scene would be out of place in this film.

"That makes me feel a lot better," Jill said. "Now, as for the *coma*. That is absolutely ridiculous. It has to go."

John said, "If Jill reacted in that way to what she feared had happened to me, she surely wouldn't be the kind of person who could have ever functioned up to this point in her life."

Doug said, "Isn't it true that when you had these other tragedies, Jill, earlier, that your temperature went up and you got sick and had to call a doctor?"

"Maybe that could happen. My nerves. And I might get sick. But a coma just really didn't happen. That's the way *you* would react in that situation, maybe, Doug. It's not the way *I* react."

In the end, Jill and John felt that the meeting had been extremely worthwhile. Both Feldman and Doug had been so sincere, agreeing with many of the suggestions, really listening all the time. They all went to The Copper Kettle for a late lunch before driving to the airport.

Jill felt she was very much in the middle, her friends and relatives on one side and all the movie people on the other. But she realized Doug, too, was in the middle.

"The letters sure helped," John said. "Vikki's and June's. I don't think they would have bothered to come up otherwise. They were scared you'd back out or someone would bring a lawsuit."

"They do listen," Jill said. "And Ed is a tender-hearted guy. Very bright. He knows the film industry and he knows how to cause something to happen. The picture really means a lot to him, personally, I can tell. He has been so great about keeping me informed all along the

235

way. After the first film, I bet he called me every week to let me know the response at the box office and what Bea▪ and Marilyn were doing."

"It isn't hurting his wallet any."

"Well, I feel a lot better after talking with him."

.　　.　　.

The final draft of the script arrived early in July. It wa▪ much better than the third draft, and for the most part Jill liked it. Still, it left a lot to be desired. She noticed that Doug had put back the word *True* on the title page *The Continuing True Story of . . .*

John did not like it. He felt Doug had somehow be▪ trayed his trust. "Now he's even got me telling you▪ brothers that Nixon didn't destroy the tapes because he'▪ an honest man. That would be the dumbest guy in th▪ world, to say Nixon is honest."

"When Doug was with us," Jill said to him, "he wa▪ being as sincere as he could be. Then, I think, he wa▪ forced to deal with what *he* could create . . . that *Feld*▪ *man* wanted him to create . . . that *Universal* woul▪ accept . . . that *Larry* would agree to direct . . . that *w*▪ would be happy with, too. He's torn between us and hi▪ career. After all he *is* working for them. He plays int▪ their hands, of course, doing what he thinks they want▪ So everyone in the story gets to be bigger than life. I'▪ afraid they're losing the qualities that matter to us."

June had stopped fighting against the scenes she didn'▪ like. She was not completely satisfied, but she was be▪ coming philosophical about it. "Really," she said, "ou▪ lives are not what movies are made of. They haven't bee▪ that dramatic. It might just not be possible to make ▪ movie that's dramatic and successful and have it be th▪ way our lives are."

Larry and Marilyn came to Bishop a week later to loo▪ for locations, and they spent time with Jill and John. Th▪ four of them talked mostly about the final script. The bu▪ crash had been eliminated, and Jill appeared to be mor▪

236

f a woman. Jill was upset that Doug had not changed the
dream about crabs eating away at her eyes.

"It makes me uncomfortable, too," Marilyn said. "It
just can't *be* that way. And it won't." She threw out her
arms. "This dramatic crab scene *won't* be in it."

"Near the end," Jill said. "The departure scene. I go
running off to L.A. and John comes steaming after me.
It *has* to be toned down. John wouldn't be crying and
all that extreme emotion. He may have tears in his eyes,
but not carrying on like that."

"It won't be that way," Larry said. "That's how it was
written by the writer, but that's not necessarily the way
it will be acted."

They talked about the first film, and Larry said that
working on it was what had brought him and Marilyn
close in a way that could never have happened except
by working together.

"A lot of people didn't know what we were doing,"
Marilyn said. "Larry and I, the way we were going to
play a scene out, we were sort of conspirators. These
lurking hawks around us, just waiting to say *no*. We were
like in a combat zone. There wasn't time . . . once we
realized what we had to do together, we couldn't do it
separately. He became my best friend after the film. So
now, for this film, it's going to be a little curious to see
what will happen with the film, in a professional sense,
now that we're living together. Right? How do you . . .
how do you handle your professional life with someone
you're living with? If you get into a big argument?"

After Marilyn and Larry had left, Jill said, "I'm so
glad about those two. They're on our side. Except that
we know they have to have us on their side, so that's at
least part of their motive. I wonder what *they* have in
mind to show as our relationship."

"Probably an X-rated movie," John said.

• • •

A few days later, while Larry was looking for more
locations, Marilyn came to school to watch Jill teach and

to ask questions whenever she had the opportunity. Most of the time she simply watched how Jill moved around in her chair. Marilyn would be in an electric wheelchair throughout the film this time, and she realized that Jill was moving with noticeably greater grace and skill and speed than she had three years before. She wanted to know how Jill was feeling at various times during the day, what things made her feel good and what things bothered her. She asked about Jill and John, and she spoke again of her own relationship with Larry.

"You are so different from how you were when we did the first picture," Marilyn said.

"Really? How?"

"At ease all the time, and moving around a lot. Using your arms and hands in a way . . . a graceful way . . . that's a lot different." Later she said, "It's like you're a golden quadriplegic. Look at you. You look like a model. It's not until I sit down with you that I realize there's a wheelchair there."

•   •   •

Filming was less than a month away, and Jill remembered how upset the family had been with the casting of Nan Martin as June. She called Feldman and said, "Nan Martin doesn't have to play Mom, does she? She just isn't right."

Feldman said Larry would have a fit if he suggested changing Nan. "He has to have this continuity with the characters in the first film."

Jill also called Larry, but Larry wouldn't re-cast the part. Larry in fact felt that Nan's on-camera facade represented what was going on inside June, under the surface. He didn't say this, of course, but he had thought a lot about the masks we all wear. "I wear my Larry Peerce mask, and Marilyn Hassett wears a Marilyn Hassett mask, and when you peel those masks away, as a rule there is a lot different self going on underneath."

•   •   •

238

John and Jill took off for Washington, D.C., where Jill was keynote speaker at a dinner for the President's Committee for the Physically Handicapped. John said she was the only one there who didn't look as if she belonged in a wheelchair. They made a point of being back in Bishop in time for Mule Days.

Jill and the town ramp committee, which included Audra Jo, had prevailed on the Fair Board to build a special box for wheelchairs in the fairgrounds bleachers. It was not a simple job, since the approach ramp ran under the grandstand and crossed a gate leading into the arena. Part of the ramp had to be built so it could easily be removed. Boys from the Mammoth Detention School built the box and the ramp, and the Lions Club and the Mule Days Committee put up the money for it. The fairgrounds director had pointed out that this project was being done for only two people, so Jill was delighted, on the opening day of Mule Days, when eight wheelchairs showed up. The box would only accommodate six of them.

Meanwhile, the curb ramp program had accelerated, and there were ramps at the principal intersections on Main Street plus another 24 on other corners around town. The Indian Athletic Association had sponsored one of them, and the Fourth Grade at the Bishop Elementary School had baked and sold cupcakes every Wednesday until, at somewhat over 2,000 cupcakes, they had amassed the necessary $200. The price of ramps had gone up during the course of the cupcake program.

June was already settled into her new house on Sunland Drive, and on Memorial Day John and Jill moved in next door. John quit driving trucks so he wouldn't be on trips half the time. He bought an equipment rental business out on West Line less than a mile from home.

Both houses faced due west, looking out across the high school farm's pasture at Mt. Tom and the 13,000-foot peaks up behind Bishop Creek. The back yard was a small pasture inhabited by three fast-growing calves, one of which belonged to John and Jill. Behind that was just one house. It was owned by a neighbor who kept the Boothes well supplied with vegetables from his huge garden. The new bedroom in the Boothe house was large and sunny, with windows west and north and a sliding glass door opening onto a backyard deck. The wide bathroom door accommodated Jill's chair with room to spare, and so did the door to the shower. A special small, high basin was positioned so Jill could back up to it in her chair for hair-washing. The front room had a Franklin stove, as yet without a stovepipe, and an alcove with John's desk in it. Mt. Tom was neatly framed in the front window. A wide door led into the kitchen, which had a wide back door with a ramp running down onto the lawn. June's house was 20 yards south and also had ramps at the front and back doors.

Jill had a new wheelchair, actually an Everest and Jennings prototype which was not yet on the market. It had a lot of power, two speeds forward, a gimballed battery housing that kept the battery from falling out on a steep slope, and oversized rubber tires. The big tires made it possible for Jill to travel easily on grass and rough pathways, even out in the field, and she discovered that she was able to water the plants around the outside of the house. All she needed was someone to turn the hose on and off for her. She could also handle a sprinkling can.

Cast and crew members drifted into Bishop all through the first week of June. Filming was to begin on Wednesday, June 8th. On the 6th, John, Jill, Marilyn, Larry, Doug, Rick Waite, the chief cinephotographer, and actor Timothy Bottoms all had lunch together at Whiskey Creek. Doug said to John and Jill, "I haven't heard yet. How did you feel about the final script?"

Jill didn't want to have to talk about it with Doug. She said, "You know, I did call you a couple of times, but you were off at the Cannes Festival. The script is fine. We all made compromises."

Larry said, "It's going to be a bitch to shoot—one sitting and one standing all the time."

Later Jill felt badly about Doug and asked John whether she shouldn't tell him it was a really good script. "It's too early now," John said. "Wait till you see the film. You already told him it's fine. Don't tell him again. Wait till you see the film. If you think it's great, write and tell him you think it's great."

• • •

On Tuesday, June 7th, June ran into Nan Martin in the supermarket. June was upset by the encounter. She told Jill, "I just can't stand having that woman appear as me."

The entire family felt so strongly about the issue that they called Ed Feldman over to the house to ask that Nan be replaced. Since it was the night before production, they settled for asking that Nan try to come closer to June's character than she had in the first film.

"They paid so much attention to getting the stripe just right on Jill's van," June said afterwards. "I'm a short, fat woman, and they have a tall, thin woman playing me." After thinking it over, she said, smiling, "Well, maybe Nan Martin can *act* fat."

15

Life (bigger than)

Filming of *The Other Side of the Mountain, Part 2*, began Wednesday morning on Main Street with "Jill" returning to Bishop for the summer of 1973.

Marilyn and Jill were much closer than they had been at any time during *Mountain One*. Both of them had changed a lot. Jill was at ease and not worried about every little thing that was happening on the set. It was the second time around, having a film made about her. And, this time, she knew Larry Peerce. Marilyn was confident and had lost most of the nervous anxiety that had once been so typical of her off-camera personality. Marilyn this time told the wardrobe people what she wanted instead of taking whatever they handed her. She decided how she would have her hair fixed. She chose a denim skirt different from what either Jill or the wardrobe people suggested. She had found and bought a pair of beaded moccasins, and she was very excited about them.

Marilyn was happy to be working with Jerry again, and

she had many questions for Jill. She knew pretty well what Jill was about, and the questions were of a very different kind from those she had asked during the shooting of *Mountain One*. She wanted to understand how it was that Jill had become more confident, how her manner had become more open and relaxed. Was it just John? What was it in the relationship that made her so feminine now, and vulnerable? The ways in which Jill had *changed* across the past three years were extremely important to her, for she wanted this to show on the screen. She still asked small questions like "How do you like the outfit?" and "Do you like the way the hat is?" but these were incidental.

The townspeople were somewhat confused by the mixing of myth and reality along Main Street. Many people said hello to Marilyn while she was practicing in her duplicate wheelchair on the sidewalks, assuming she must be Jill. Jill's van was seen far more frequently than usual, sometimes in dulicate, even in triplicate. Aside from the original van, which John usually drove, there was an identical van used in shooting most van shots in the film, and a third identical vehicle with a camera platform in front that was used for shooting close-up travelling shots of Marilyn and Tim driving.

The best news, as far as John and Jill were concerned, was Timothy Bottoms, the actor cast as John Boothe. He was slightly shorter than John but slim, with broad shoulders and sharp features. He was blond, and he had a dimple in his chin. "What a sweet guy," Jill said. "And a good actor. No affectations. He's not Hollywood at all."

Tim and John liked each other at once, and they talked about their families. Tim's family was very close. He had a ranch and was comfortable with horses. He was familiar with the kind of life the Boothes lived. He was a good fisherman. He and his wife were staying in a motor home up on Bishop Creek rather than living in a motel. Also, he had a gentle way with people that reminded Jill of John.

Tim studied John carefully and was soon imitating his

walk and his mannerisms. He even showed a reserve that was typical of John but had not been indicated in the script. John was watching Tim rehearse on the second day, and he shook his head at the way Tim sauntered across the sidewalk, head down, hands thrust into the front pockets of his jeans. He said to Jill, "What's going on? *I* don't do that." Jill glanced at John's hands and smiled. John then realized he was standing exactly as Tim was now standing, a bit slouched, head down, hands in his pockets.

John was self-conscious for some while after that. "Hell," he said, "I don't know what to do with my *hands!*" People told him, "That actor sure has your walk down pat." He said to Jill, "I'm starting to worry that people will think I'm imitating Timothy Bottoms."

The Universal public relations man had been appearing intermittently to ask questions and set up interviews for Jill and John and Marilyn and Tim. He always began, "I'm sorry, but . . ." and he always interrupted himself midway to say, "Are you sure you don't mind?" Marilyn said, "If he'd just tell us and not keep apologizing." He asked Jill if she and John would mind spending part of the day with the *Los Angeles Times*, which had promised to give their story a big spread. Jill said okay.

The *Times* team appeared a few days later. Mary Frampton, the photographer, was a great person to be with, and she noticed at once how different Jill and John were from the scenes that were being shot with Marilyn and Tim. The reporter was something else. William Overend. John and Jill first met him while they were sitting in the van at the Rocking K watching a scene with Marilyn and Nan driving into town. John was in the front seat. Overend and Mary Frampton got in back with Jill.

Overend was aloof. He began with questions about Jill and John's relationship. "Do you argue?" he said.

"You're damn right we do, sweetheart," John said, hoping the quote would get into the article.

Overend asked how they felt about the film and whether it had changed their life. He asked what it was like being married. He asked John about his first marriage.

"I wasn't exactly happy in it, as you might have guessed," John said.

"Did you have lots of girlfriends before Jill?"

"No, not a lot."

•   •   •

John didn't see much of the filming, but he made an effort to catch Tim's scenes. Two of his favorites were watching the wild horses from the truck and rescuing the deer caught on a barbed wire fence. Both scenes were shot on the old highway north of Bishop. John talked with Tim while the tame deer was being made up with "blood." Someone recognized John and asked if he would really rescue a deer caught in a barbed wire fence. "No," John said. "I wouldn't be so dumb."

Tim said, "How come you don't spend more time on the set?"

"I did the first day, but I don't enjoy it. One thing, though, Tim. I like the way you're doing the job. I like the way you're portraying me, so I don't feel I need to check up on that." Tim was wearing a scrunched-up straw cowboy hat and John, in his CAT hat, said, "Tim, you should be wearing a CAT hat."

"They wanted me to wear a *cowboy* hat."

"At least they aren't making you ride bulls."

•   •   •

John and Jill held a big party at their new house on Sunday after the first week of shooting. John cooked a ten-pound roast on the rotisserie and Dudley took charge of the fish-fry—60 trout. Marilyn had mentioned that she loved trout, and Dudley had said, "We'll try and get something together for you." He brought the big camp stove down from the pack outfit, and he also built a campfire out back.

Feldman was there, looking like a jolly Dutch seaman, with his assistant, Donna Dubrow, and Rick Waite. All the Boothes and Kinmonts came, bringing salads and casseroles and bread and wine. There were two Johns and two Jills and two Dudleys. Marilyn sat with Jill most of the time. Nan Martin had gone home for the weekend.

Tim's whole family was there—his wife Alicia Bottoms and his son, Bartholomew Buckeye Bottoms, his two brothers, who had happened to be passing through Bishop at the time, and his father, Bud Bottoms. Bud was not an actor, but he had been cast to play the role of Dudley Boothe.

Bud and Dudley were more alike in their natures than in their outward looks. Dudley was six feet one, clean shaven, with black hair. Bud was shorter, with gray hair and a gray beard. Dudley stole the show when he walked up to Bud and said, "Jesus Christ, you're not going to disgrace me with that *beard,* are you?"

"I'll shave it off if you want."

"Yes, I do."

Larry was rather upset by the episode. "Let John's father have a beard in the film," he said to Marilyn. "What the hell does a beard have to do with it?"

"Well, Dudley'll go crazy, because shaving is important to them."

"I know," Larry said. "I was raised in a family where that was very important. Despite the fact there was a lot of yelling and screaming, the facade was all-important. Everything had to be great outside. I really got to understand Jill in those terms. I was raised by a star. Opera singer Jan Peerce. It doesn't matter that he was an opera star, it could have been . . . well, Jill's a star, too. The problem with those people. I always felt, is that they never let go. That pressure builds up, it had to be a nightmare."

● ● ●

Dudley went to the pack outfit to watch the big scene between father and son—between Dudley and his son John, acted by Bud and his son Tim. Bud still had his beard. Dudley walked up to him, whipped out his pocket knife, and pretended he was going to cut it off. Bud was wearing a hat with the brim down at the front and sides, and Dudley said with disdain, "That looks like a farmer's hat." He re-shaped it for Bud, turning the sides up and crumpling it a bit. "There," he said, returning it. "This is how your hat *should* look."

According to the script, John and Dudley are feeding the mules and the mood between them is tense. Dudley says, "All right, it's none of my business." John says, "I'm glad you understand that." Dudley says, "Your mother and I can see now, after Elana, you might look for someone more—" John cuts him off and says, "Hand me some more feed, will you, Pop." He adds, "Don't worry about me, Pop. Not this time." And they finish their job in silence.

Since both Tim and Bud were so at home in their roles, Larry had them ad lib the scene. They simply went into it as a father and son who had a deep underlying respect for each other.

Tim was rolling a cigarette as he and his father sat against a railing of the tackroom. "I think Grandpa took so much time rolling these things because he didn't like to smoke 'em," Tim said.

Bud said, "I know it's none of my business, John . . ."

"I'm glad you realize that."

The telephone began ringing down at the house. Bud said, "But I . . . you know, your Mom and I, well . . . Jesus, John, I mean we know she's been really kind to you and we know how you feel about her . . ."

"Why don't you answer the phone and make some money?" Tim said.

A short while later, saddling horses together, Bud said, "Don't you think you'd be taking on a pretty heavy load, son?"

"I'll be all right."

The warm feeling between the two of them was becoming obvious. Then, spontaneously, they embraced. "Hell," Bud said, "anything that happens, we still love you."

Larry had spoken several times of the great difference between a screenplay and the film that could come from it.

Jill and John only began to understand what he meant when they saw the difference between the written scene with John and Dudley and the scene as Tim and Bud played it out at the pack outfit. Another scene that revealed what film can do that words-on-paper cannot was the hospital scene after Linda broke her collarbone racing.

In real life, Linda had broken her collarbone at the Winter Olympics in Squaw Valley. In the script, Jill watches Linda racing and re-lives her own accident as she sees Linda fall. Jill and Dave visit Linda in the hospital, and Jill says, "Smooth move, Exlax." Linda answers, "Yeah, real smooth," and Dave says, "I've got to call the rest of the team; I'll be right back." Finally Jill says, with emotion, "Oh, Meyers, can't you do anything original?"

Marilyn and Larry talked over the scene and tried to work out how they would handle it. Larry told Marilyn, "You'll come into the hospital room sort of bubbly and say ..."

"Not smooth move Exlax, for sure."

"No. You come in and see the coach there, going through the same reaction he had years ago after *your* accident: *God I did it again, I pushed her off the hill.* It's real scary. You're sitting there looking at Linda and seeing yourself in the bed. You're looking in both relief and horror because you're saying to yourself, here I sit in the chair for the rest of my life, and there you are and all you've got is a broken arm."

Marilyn was upset already. She was choking on her own words. She said, "Larry, I can't play that! Don't be crazy. What am I going to do with *that?*"

"Okay, then, don't," Larry said. "Don't do that at all. All you do is go into that room and you let it all show. Let all of it show. You let all of it show, the fear, the horror. . . ."

"The guilt."

"The guilt, the jealousy."

"The guilt."

"Yeah," Larry said. "The way you get to the truth is by letting the real emotions flow."

They didn't tell anybody, but when the camera started rolling, Marilyn was totally into the situation, and she just walked in and ad libbed it. Doug might turn gray when he saw it, but it was a great moment. Marilyn came in crying. Real crying. The only line she said from the original script was, "Can't you do anything original?" With scarcely a word, she had caught the underlying feeling that was playing between herself and Dave and Linda.

•   •   •

One of the more complicated shots in the movie occurred during a Kinmont family picnic at Hot Creek near Mammoth. The idea had come from Burk Uzzle's photograph of Bill, June, Bob, and Jerry carrying Jill in her wheelchair across a rocky beach near Seattle in 1964. The movie version called for the family to lower Marilyn down a cliff face by means of an ingenious rigging of pulleys and ropes. Jerry tickles Jill's face with a feather. Jill yells for him to stop but he keeps on tickling her, and John rushes up and grabs the feather. During the rehearsal, everyone was laughing, and June said to Feldman, "It's not a bit funny. Why would you think I would think that funny?"

While they were running through the scene again, elaborately and loudly moving Marilyn to the family's picnic site, Jill herself was wheeling up to a footbridge in her own chair a short distance away. The footbridge had steps at her end. Some people were standing nearby and she quietly asked them to lift her chair up onto the bridge, which they did. The difference between the way the two Jills were being helped was painfully obvious.

•   •   •

The *Los Angeles Times* article came out on June 22. It was a big spread entitled "At Long Last Love: Jill Kinmont—a New Chapter." It began, "This is a story of two wounded people," and went on to say that their kind of love "is the gentle kind a lot of other wounded people would like to find." The relationship was thoroughly

249

analyzed in extensive quotes from Larry Peerce, Marilyn Hassett, and Doug Stewart. Feldman was quoted as saying, with a laugh, "I was ecstatic when I heard they were going to get married. We needed a finish." The reporter himself called John a man "who never had much luck with women before."

The article ended with a long quote from Doug Stewart. "The script deals with her fear of trust. I think she's still learning that. As far as trusting John, she really couldn't believe he would stay with her if confronted with the reality of taking care of her. A trip to Canada together changed that. John was pretty well shattered by some things that happened to him earlier in his life. In a sense that made him just like her. It really is a fairy tale. If they hadn't met each other, there really wouldn't have been anybody else for either of them."

"Jesus Christ," John said, "I'm never going to talk to another reporter! Makes you and me out as the number one and number two losers of the world. It plays right along with the script."

June said, "That *sounds* like Doug. He probably really believed it."

Jill was upset that Doug had said she couldn't trust John to take care of her. "It's totally the opposite of that," she said. "One of the attractions was just that John was so easy about taking care of me. But in the film I'm afraid a big part of Marilyn's doubts is whether he can take care of me and handle the situation."

On the set, the public relations man asked Jill what she thought of the article. All she could say was, "It'll help the movie." When she talked to Donna Dubrow about it, Donna said, "Sometimes it's hard to read these truths in print." Jill said to her, "We all have our inadequacies."

Jan Mason wrote from New York about the article. "This business of the illusion makers having delusions themselves . . . Feldman is probably so wrapped up in making his own fairy tales that he starts to believe them. He's the one who read our article and said he loved the girl but the article stank. What does *he* know about *my* truth about Jill?"

•   •   •

Larry and Marilyn had a fight one evening while they were filming Marilyn and Tim at a local fireworks display. Marilyn was having fun with her wheelchair, and the script called for her to almost run down a pedestrian. A lot of Bishop people were watching.

The scene was supposed to be funny, but it wasn't working. It wasn't entirely clear to anyone else what the fight was about—perhaps not even to Larry and Marilyn— but it erupted in yelling and screaming.

"I don't care what you want!"

"You'd better care!"

"Larry, that's bullshit!"

The crew was walking on eggshells, holding their breaths. The yelling got sharper and louder. Somebody whispered, "Oh my God, the director and the actress!" Marilyn stalked off. Larry went back to his dressing room.

When Larry came out, everybody had left. He walked back to the motel thinking, this is terrible; is it going to destroy our relationship? He walked into the room, expecting the fight to erupt again. Marilyn was there, expecting the same thing. But Larry was no longer the director once he got inside. He surprised himself. He said, "Would you like a drink?" and he smiled. They hugged each other.

John and Jill were having a small fight of their own about the same time. They knew their differences were real, and they knew they could not remain intimate unless they expressed their antagonistic feelings when they came up. "The same thing happens each time," John said to her. "Afterwards, a new closeness develops."

The two final days of filming in Bishop were spent on the south fork of Bishop Creek. The last time Jill saw Larry and Marilyn, they looked exhausted but somehow exhilarated. The film was going well. "There was much more to be done and said in the second film than in the first," Larry said.

251

Talking with friends later, after Jill had left, Larry said, "That woman, Jill Kinmont, is not the same woman as three years ago. She is a complete human being on the set now, and a woman, not some ballsy thing sitting in a chair plopping people over the head."

"She was like a producer in the first film," Marilyn said.

"It's rough on Marilyn," Larry said. "There's a kind of paranoia that comes from an actor playing a role and looking up and seeing the person he's playing going *hmm hmmph* or *hmm hmm hrumph*. But this time she's been loose and comfortable."

Later, when Jill heard about Larry's comment, she said, "I wasn't aware of acting like a producer. I was just watching everybody and wondering and being amazed and loving it. Where do you suppose he got the idea I've changed so much?"

"From knowing you before?"

"We had no communication at all, John, except three brief times. Judi Rosner introduced him one afternoon, he went over the script with us at Feldman's, and he was with Marilyn up at that press conference at the school and talked about what a time he had with Elizabeth Taylor in *Ash Wednesday*. I never saw him again except on the set."

"Maybe he just noticed that *you*, today, are different from how *Marilyn* was in front of the camera three years ago."

"I've changed *some*," Jill said, "because I've been through it all before and because the second film just wasn't that important to me. Also, I've had this sense of well-being since we've been married. It's all part of the myth, I think, some big dramatic change."

"I'm sure we *are* different to them," John said. "We've really felt related to them in this film. The first film, well, they were strange people to us, and we weren't at ease."

•　•　•

The last ten days of filming were in Los Angeles and British Columbia, and Jill and John had to rely on Jerry to sample the results for them. They shot a scene on the

252

Santa Monica pier in which Jill and her father dance. A ballet, really, Jill in her wheelchair spinning and turning and holding her hand up to Bill, who danced with her and around her. Marilyn had liked doing it. "It gave a closeness Jill didn't have with anybody else. She wouldn't have asked anyone to dance with her. She wouldn't have trusted that."

Jerry said Larry had had a hard time personally with the scene where John tells Jill off, tells her he is not about to help her until his coffee is ready. Larry had said, "I still have to face up to a guy standing up and having a lover's quarrel with the woman he loves and saying to her, Go to hell. She's sitting in a wheelchair and can't move. Marilyn Hassett sitting there in her goddamned wheelchair and he walks away on her!"

Jill asked Jerry how the love scene in the motel came off. "They did a fine, sensitive job with it," Jerry said. "They didn't pull any punches, and yet it was tasteful and very loving."

"Is it really going to be Jill Kinmont up there on the screen?"

"I think they have a different lady than you are," he said, "but it is a great love story, and it's real. How do you feel about it?"

"I told Lee I was pretty sick of all the nonsense," Jill said. "He told me, don't knock it, it's paying your way."

"But are you happy about them? The two films?"

"I don't know if they've made me happier, Jerry, but they've added another dimension. I like my life to be full."

16

Meanwhile, Back at the Ranch

It was a relief to have the movie people done with Bishop, done with everything except putting the pieces together. It was a relief to have an end to meetings and decisions. The film wouldn't be out of the editing room until early spring, but meanwhile it was comfortably out of sight and out of mind. John and Jill settled into the summer, consciously trying to live down the myth, trying to get their own real life separated from the movie.

It didn't just happen, for there were many strings still hanging. Reporters kept calling. John usually handled that, since he was the one who knew how to say *no*. People around town were always asking how the movie was coming along. Jill said she didn't know, and at the moment she didn't care. A little girl stopped her in the doorway of a card shop and told her at length how wonderful she was, how much courage she had, how everyone should know someone like her.

Life at home on Sunland Drive was what Jill had

always wanted, and she gave up her summer job at the Indian school so she could thoroughly enjoy it. They had only been in the house since Memorial Day, and the movie had pretty much dominated their lives since then, except for Jill's teaching and John's business. Now Jill was beginning to savor what she most loved about being married. For the first time in her life, she was planning her own meals, shopping with John for her own food, setting her own table, putting her own silver away in her own silver drawers. She had never realized before how many things June had always done, simply because June had always managed the house. Now Jill herself was directly responsible for how her house looked and for what went on the table and into the refrigerator. She loved this. She liked making sure there was always beer and cheese and ham in the refrigerator for John and that his sandwich was ready when he came home for lunch. She remembered that June had always had a meal or coffee ready for Bill, and she liked the custom.

The Boothes hired Rachel Howlett, the wife of a ceramicist living and working at Bob's new studio, to work from 6:30 until noon five days a week. Rachel got Jill up in the morning, cleaned the house, drove Jill to town or at times ran errands, and handled any other chores that Jill needed done. Before she left, Rachel usually took the meat out of the freezer, and she often mixed a meat sauce or salad dressing that Jill had planned for dinner. Jana, a local high school girl, came for an hour in the late afternoon to put out the dinner, under Jill's supervision. Jill wanted to make the house a pleasant and happy place, and she liked to have coffee or a beer ready for John when he showed up after work. She liked doing whatever she could for herself. She could water the flowers and help set the table. Kitchen drawers had been built for her convenience, so it was not difficult for her to get out place mats, napkins, silver, and salt and pepper shakers. John would hand her the plates and glasses. She liked to have the table fully set, even if they weren't planning to use everything.

John always cooked dinner. He liked to cook, and Jill liked to tell him how to do it, although she often had to telephone Audra Jo or Vikki or Bev or June to check out a recipe. "Hello," she would say. "Is this Dial-a-Cook? How long for a six-pound roast at 325 degrees?"

Jill also liked to hand out advice in the kitchen after dinner, and this didn't always sit so well with John. "Would you wipe that counter again?" she said one evening after he had finished the dishes. "Not just there, John, back along under the window." She found several other things to be done. John was already impatient, watching her as he worked. She said, "John, I'd just as soon see all the chrome polished on the sink. I can see the soap stains."

John simply hung up the dishcloth and turned out the light. "We're not going to go on like this," he said, walking past her into the living room. "I'm happy to do so much, but there's an end to it. If you want the chrome polished and the back of the counter cleaned, it's your business to have Rachel do that before she goes."

Jill was frustrated by all the things she wanted done that she couldn't do herself. "Please, John," she said from the dark kitchen, "just the sink. Just polish the chrome."

"Wait just one minute," he said. "Nothing has *got* to be polished." This angered Jill, and she spun her chair out into the living room. One wheel hit the coffee table and knocked a potted plant onto the floor, spilling dirt and breaking the stem. Jill backed off and wheeled right around the fallen pot. "Well, there's just certain things, John, that I want to get done," she said. "If they aren't done, I can't stand it. *I* can't do it. Rachel doesn't have time to do it. Then *you* should do it."

John stood before her with his fists on his hips, glanced at the fallen plant, and shook his head. Jill started to cry. John, after a moment, knelt beside her and put his arm around her shoulder. "I guess I know how you feel," he said, "but it's nothing to be all so worried about. I know how *I* feel, too, Jill. I've cleared the table, put all the dishes in the dishwasher, wiped off the sink and table, and put the pots to soak. It is absolutely ridiculous for me to stand back there polishing the chrome on the sink when we should be in here enjoying the evening."

Jill nodded. "Okay. Next time I won't follow you into the kitchen after dinner."

The next evening John went into the kitchen to clean up the dishes. When Jill started to follow him, he turned and stuck his head around the door frame. "You're not coming into the kitchen," he said. "Remember?"

He loved having her in the kitchen while he was preparing a meal, however, and he was pleased when June popped in to peek into his pots. She came while he was cooking a beef heart late one afternoon. John and Jill always got the heart when the Boothes butchered an animal, since nobody else cared for it. June lifted the lid. "Smells good," she said. "Different. Must be a Grandma Rosie recipe. What are you steaming?" It was zucchini. "A real home supper. Your own garden vegetables and meat from the ranch."

John put Jill to bed every night, tucking her in carefully so she felt cozy and comfortable. He usually left her watching television while he took a shower. He refused to leave her electric blanket going for more than a few minutes at a time for fear they might forget about it and Jill would get overheated.

The worst arguments of the week usually came on Sunday morning between the hours of six and seven. Jill had to depend on John to get her up on Sunday mornings, and it was the one day John had a chance to sleep in. Jill, on the other hand, was awake and ready to go at six or 6:30.

One Sunday, Jill set a goal of seven o'clock. She waited until 6:30, and then she said, softly, "John, it's 8:30." This didn't really fool him, but at least he had to open one eye in order to check the clock. Jill then began to think of all the things that she could ask John to do during the day. She said them aloud, slowly. "These are the things that John has to do today."

Finally he spoke. "If you keep that up, I'm not going to get you up at *all*." It was long after eight when he crawled out of bed, stumbled into the kitchen to put on the coffee, and finally came back to get her up.

"I think . . . the hardest time . . . is waking up in the morning," Jill said, quoting the opening line of the first film. "Those first . . . vague moments . . . before I fully remember who I am."

Every Sunday after that, Jill said, "I think the hardest time . . . is waking up in the morning." But one day she said, "John, what time do you really want to get up on Sunday?"

"Eight o'clock, but that may be pushing it."

"Okay, John, eight o'clock. I'll hold out until eight next Sunday." He came over and kissed her.

"The Sunday after that, I don't know," she said. "We'll negotiate."

•   •   •

John and Jill usually went shopping together in the Safeway. The big shopping day was Friday. They always started at the meat section and worked straight through the store from there. Jill had a master shopping list that she had started the weekend before and to which she and John and Rachel had added, day by day.

At home, either Jill or John paid the bills, whoever had the most time. When Jill wrote the checks, John stuffed them into the envelopes for her. John kept a separate account for his rental business. Since he had given up his trucking job, they were living on Jill's income and putting John's income back into the business. He was hoping to buy the gas station next door to his rental yard.

Jill had been drawing and painting a lot more than usual since the end of school and the end of movie-making.

John was excited about the precision of detail in her beautiful sketches of the mountains they could see from the house or from up at the pack outfit. He borrowed his favorite—a drawing of Mt. Tom—and used it as the background for his business card.

Hi-Mountain Rentals
Tools and Equipment
for
Homeowners • Contractors • Gardeners

He also had the drawing reproduced on the door of his pick-up.

The biggest thing John was able to do for Jill was to shield her from the unthinking demands of the outside world and allow her to let down her guard. It was as if she no longer had to be responsible for protecting her energies and time, since John was now able and willing to do it for her. She alone could not have resisted the requests and demands people made of her without feeling guilty. John kept people from taking advantage of her, and he helped her not to feel guilty about guarding her privacy. Consequently, Jill was becoming less aloof with her friends and more willing to do things with them and for them.

Linda put it the other way around. "She can afford to be less self-centered now," she told Frank, "and as that happens, she finds her well-being is the center of someone else's concern."

Jill was still vulnerable, however. June said to her, "It's good to see John dealing with all this nonsense that's going on around you."

". . . Or dealing with Jill dealing with it," John said. John also shielded Jill in direct, physical ways. When she said she could wheel herself to school, which was on the other side of West Line Street, John said, "They drive like maniacs on Line Street, and you have no business there."

He drove her to the eye doctor one day in his pick-up. When she came out, Jill said she would just wheel home under her own power, and she started along the sidewalk behind a hedge which, from John's point of view out on the street, hid everything except her head. He called across

259

to her, "If you don't mind my saying, when you're going by behind that hedge . . ."

She wheeled out of earshot before he finished his sentence. He shrugged and drove off, circling the block since he had been headed the wrong way. He forgot all about Jill until he realized he had just driven by her on Line Street. She was in fact stopped—stuck in a shallow ditch where a new driveway was being made.

John turned around and drove back to help her. He turned around again and followed her. At the traffic light a block from Sunland Drive, she was stuck again because she couldn't push the WALK button. John stopped the truck, got out, and pushed the button for her. She wheeled off again with an air of defiant independence.

When they reached home, John leaned out of the window of the pick-up and called to her. "As I was saying, when I was so rudely interrupted . . . if you don't mind my saying, when you were going behind that hedge you looked kind of comical. Reminded me of one of those targets in a carnival. You just see the head going by behind the rosebushes."

Having the entire summer free was a luxury Jill never took for granted. She painted every day. She started a little flower garden of her own in a big pot on the back porch. She spent a lot of time with Beverly Boothe trying to devise schemes for getting John and Roy to do the yard work she and Bev wanted done.

"I think they'll love it if we approach it in the right way." Jill said. Her eyes were lively and very blue. "They've got all these fun tools to use over at John's shop."

"We'll buy some beautiful plants," Bev said. "I know they'll love to plant them."

Jill and Bev bought plants for both their houses, and Bev outlined future garden areas with rocks so it would be absolutely clear where the turf was to be cut. The idea was a good one, but it did not meet with enthusiasm. It took Roy over a week to get around to planting anything, and it took John longer than that.

260

Bob Kinmont was in and out all summer helping Jill with her painting, seeing that she had the right paint, the right brushes. The brace that held her brush was like her pen brace, but making a fine line with a watercolor brush was a far more delicate operation than with a ballpoint pen.

"Hey, where'd you get *this*?" Bob said, examining one of her new brushes. They were on the back deck, and Jill had her bare feet in the sun. She was wearing a white T-shirt and cornflower blue skirt printed with small white flowers. She had delicate gold hoop earrings, and her heart-shaped locket hung from a fine gold chain around her neck.

"Jan Mason gave it to me," she said. "She got it in England."

"You can't even buy them like that any more. I wish I had one."

Bob came by once or twice a day, sometimes with Vikki, sometimes with one or more of the kids, and he helped his mother with her painting, too.

"I love being alone and having time to paint and sew with no interruptions," June told Jill. "Bob said, with your new big windows, there's no end to the paintings you can paint."

Seth and John were still the best of friends. They went out to get wood one Saturday morning and John said, "Ain't you got your coat, Seth?"

"You don't use that word," Seth said. "It's *don't* you got your coat!"

Bob was painting a lot himself. He often went out in the fields in his pick-up and rigged a blanket to give himself shade. He always stopped to see Jill on his way out or on his way home.

Jill's favorite subject was mountains, and she painted both from "life" and from photographs. She completed a painting of the mountains above South Lake one morning just as Bob arrived. "You're right in the ballpark," he said.

"In the ballpark? Bob, it's all done!"

He shook his head. "You can still do a lot of things." Jill wasn't sure she wanted to. "Your mountains are right.

261

Just right. Your color on the near ridge is just a bit more intense. Just right."

"I hadn't even thought about that."

"No, it's an innate thing. Now you just have to continue the same thing in the foreground. The lights lighter, the darks darker. The rock is too flat. Show the volume of it."

Bob was always seeing just a little more than she had noticed. He made her acutely aware of the dimensions of objects, of the relationship between lights and darks in the foreground, of the need for more volume. "It needs more contrast. You want to carry the eye into another area here. The foliage has to come forward. You've seen willows. Look at the color, how one group shows in front of another. The color, the softness, volume."

"I do have trouble with the trees," she said. "The greens always come out too blue."

Bob's home in the desert was completed, and it was everything he and Vikki had planned. They called it "Coyote." The kitchen and living room were small, but each of the three children had a room.

Bob had built a small attached studio for himself and a separate building, a *zendo*, in which he, Vikki, and several friends meditated every morning before breakfast. There was a thriving garden fertilized with scrapings from irrigation ditches. Several hundred yards north of the house were the workshop-studio and students' quarters. Brian Howlett and three others were in residence for the summer.

•   •   •

Jill had a visitor one day, a wealthy rancher whose 40-year-old daughter had been a quadriplegic for 14 months, following an automobile accident. She was discouraged, he said, and he offered Jill $25 if she would telephone her from time to time.

Jill didn't know what to do with the check, but she called the woman, Carol Wiley, the next day. Jill was amazed at how little the woman knew about her own condition and about how to take care of herself. She had been in two different rehabilitation centers, and they had told her nothing about what to expect once she was out on her own. She didn't know about the urgent need for regular urinalysis. In fact, she thought that the sediment in her urine was normal for quadriplegics. "The doctor said anyone with an indwelling catheter will have a chronic infection," she said.

"That is not normal," Jill said, "and you had better get it taken care of *now*."

Carol was full of questions. She didn't know how to keep her feet from swelling. She'd never heard of drinking cranberry juice. She didn't know that a good corset would make breathing a lot easier. She was a teacher and had been given a two-year leave of absence. She would have to begin teaching again in September 1978 in order to keep her job, and she was worried because she tired so easily. She even asked Jill how to get and keep a good housekeeper. She had gone through eight during the past several months.

Jill had many letters from other quadriplegics and from victims of multiple sclerosis and cerebral palsy and other crippling diseases. Some were self-pitying, but most of them were remarkably self-contained. Among the few letters Jill saved were these three.

Dear Jill,

I can really relate to your situation because I was born with Cerebral Palsy and spent a major part of my life in hospitals. While watching the movie I felt I had known you all my life . . . I am trying to decide what I would like to do with the rest of my life. This is where your movie came into the picture—providing me with inspiration. Thank you for showing me life is only what you make it.

> Paula Hardy
> Scottsdale, Arizona

P.S. I typed this letter myself

• • •

Dear Ms. Kinmont:

I am a senior at Alvin High School, Alvin, Texas. Recently I became involved in a program in which I go into the classroom and help teach. The program is basically set up for future teachers, introducing them to the problems and responsibilities of a teacher. I entered the course, at first, just for the credit; but after working with this type of situation, I have grown quite interested in this type of work. Since I am a quadriplegic I have encountered several things that I do not know how to do. Little problems such as putting up bulletin boards, mimeographing work for the students, and writing on the chalk board are just a few.

The class which I aid in is a Learning and Language Disability class. There are only eight students ranging in ages from 8 to 12 years—they are just super. They have adapted to me in their class fantastically, which I did not honestly expect. And if anything, I have learned from them.

I read of your marriage in People Magazine; it seems as though you've got it all together and I congratulate you.

Any help or tips you could give me would be greatly appreciated. Thank you for your time and consideration.

Sincerely,
Glen Baker, Jr.

• • •

Dear Jill,

My name is Martin McNerney & I'm a quadriplegic too. I saw "The Other Side of the Mountain" last night & decided it was about time I thanked you for all that you have done for me.

A friend of mine & I were walking around after a Saturday night party, & a police car stopped us. We panicked & ran. In climbing over an eight-foot fence, I fell on my head & broke my neck. I went to a junior college after my accident but dropped out a year later. I couldn't and wouldn't accept my limitations. I wallowed in self-pity, & my self hatred reached an unbearable intensity. Something had to be done. I wanted to live but was afraid to. Then I saw you on "60 Minutes," & you gave me the inspiration to live, to be myself, to accept myself, & not to waste so much of life worrying about what I couldn't do. It was my decision to live or die & I had to make it, but you helped me so much by just being there, by being yourself. In you I saw myself freed. A simple decision to live and love or waste away & die a little more each moment . . .

You showed me that it isn't what you lack that is important, but what you possess. You were the missing link to life that I desperately needed & so gratefully found. You acted as a catalyst, bringing everything together, which allowed me to open up to life & myself. Thank you so much, Jill. I love you very much.

Love,
Martin McNerney

• • •

The *National Enquirer* sent a reporter, Barbara Sternig, to Bishop for a story. The interview was a long one, but it was refreshing to be asked intelligent and sensitive questions and to have all of your answers understood. Barbara was also impressed by the great animation in Jill's face and by the way her curly hair bounced when she tossed her head.

Jill wanted to correct the impression left by the *Los Angeles Times* article which had ended with Doug's quote, "It really is a fairy tale. If they hadn't met each other, there really wouldn't have been anybody else for either of them." So she made a point of telling Barbara that her life with John was good but not always smooth, and certainly not a fairy tale. "I don't think of it as being a fairy tale," she said. "It's just good. We argue, and that's exciting to me, too, working these things out, knowing each other better. That happens every day. It changes and grows in all kinds of directions. Rather than a fairy tale, what we have is a real life."

The article appeared in late August under the headline "FAIRY-TALE ENDING TO SKI CHAMP'S TRAGIC STORY." This was through no fault of Barbara's, whose opening paragraph began, "I don't think of my marriage as being a fairy tale, declared Jill Kinmont, whose heart-breaking story was told in the 1974 movie, *The Other Side of the Mountain*."

"You can't win," John said.

The article prompted a letter a few days later from Fort Wayne, Indiana, with the following address written on the front of the envelope:

> Mr. and Mrs. John Boothe (respecting page 4 featuring your picture and article by Barbara Sternig National Enquirer Aug. 30 1977 issue—true God is Love—I know, for Mom was an invalid from 1951–59 —body afflicted but mind alert, she died 5/11/59 age 89 I was married Thanksgiving 11/26/59 age 52 My good husband died 9/10/77 I say there is No Poor Widow, but a Blessed widow, his Spirit is with me)
> Bishop, California, 93514
> (thank you Mr. Postmaster for making proper delivery I have no better address)

An easier fan letter to answer came about the same time from Randy Wells in Whittier, California.

> I am a 13-year-old boy who once wanted to be a professional skier. Even though I now want to be an airline pilot, I would still appreciate your autograph.
> Thank you very much.

The new movie meanwhile was coming together in Eve Newman's editing room under Larry Peerce's watchful eye and Ed Feldman's periodic review. Larry was pleased with the substance of the footage because both Feldman and Universal had once been concerned about the material— was there enough there to carry the film? Would a love story hold for an hour and a half? "Ed Feldman and I have an extraordinary relationship," Larry said. "He leaves me so much space to work in. One of us has to keep some distance from the film, because when you begin to get immersed in it as a director, it starts to get boring and you hate it and you begin to rip it to shreds. Now he stays away and he says, when you're ready I'll take a look. And when he looks, he says *blimp!* He gives his opinions and feelings, and then I take it away again and the editor and I work on it. It's finally starting to look like a film."

Larry was particularly pleased with the opening. "We did something I think is going to work fabulously," he said. "It opens with Jill standing in the chute getting ready to go down that race in Alta, Utah. We follow her right down and nobody says anything. *Boom* out she goes and off that cliff she goes. And she falls *ballum boom boom* and stops. And as she stops we dissolve through to Jill being pulled out of a van backwards by her mother and turned right around at the camera in the wheelchair and the film begins. And she's going to be presented the award of Woman of the Year."

Larry had at one time planned to shoot a few flashback skiing scenes at Mammoth in late November, but the plans were changing. In the process of editing, the film was coming to deal more with the on-going relationship between John and Jill and less with Jill's past. Doug was back at work rewriting a scene that hadn't quite come off and would likely be re-shot. He was very pleased with the way the film was turning out. "I've been trying to do a more realistic film than the first one," he said, "and I think I'm going to end up with that film. But it has had to grow into that. You can tell a lot more about who Jill really is behind many of her strong coats of armor."

John and Jill were disappointed when they heard of Doug's remark about armor. "Those days when he was here," John said, "we really opened up our armor. We didn't pull any punches. The writing he's done since then doesn't reflect much of what we let him in on."

•   •   •

In November, June went to Anaheim with Jill to attend the annual conference of the California Reading Association. John had wanted to go, but he had just contracted to buy the service station next to his rental business, and he had to stay home to follow through with the negotiations.

It was another of the trips, like those to Edmonton and Washington, D.C., that June enjoyed so much. There were hundreds of speakers and seminars at the four-day conference, and they covered everything you could imagine about reading. June sat in on many of the talks. She felt as well-informed as most of the teachers she encountered.

The most exciting session for Jill was a talk by Herbert Kohl, the author of *Thirty-six Children*. Kohl talked about using the local resources that exist in every school district to provide unique learning experiences and material of value to the entire community. Jill asked herself what Bishop might have in the way of unique resources. She thought at once of the Paiute Indians and their cultural heritage, which was fast dying out. If she could find a way of providing her Indian children with portable tape recorders, they could begin a systematic recording of tales and traditions and tribal history. The children could talk with their grandparents and seek out the oldest men and women in the tribe and ask them to talk about whatever they could remember of their own early days as well as tales and myths they had heard as children.

Jill telephoned Christine Richer shortly before Thanksgiving. Christine had been home a week, after eight months in hospitals. She was living with her mother, brother, and sister in a newly rented house. She had gotten the master bedroom. "I can only use the fingers on one hand," she said, "but my arms are strong, so I can get onto the toilet from my wheelchair and even dress myself, except for shoes and socks. The pants are pretty hard, though." Christine's break had been one vertebra lower than Jill's, and that extra inch or so of spinal nerves made a huge difference.

"Is it hard being home?" Jill asked.

"Just at first when I started unpacking my boxes. All those things reminded me of skiing, and it was a little depressing."

"So what are you going to do now?"

"Some form of counselling. I'm going back to school in January. I have almost a year's credit from before the accident."

"If you have a problem, get in touch with me," Jill said.

"Thanks, Jill, but things are going well. I think I can work it out myself. It's so good hearing from you. I'm dying to see your new movie."

Jill had a dream that night. She dreamed she was an Oreo cookie with a bite taken out of it.

Jerry and Lyn arrived from Canada to spend the winter. They had a place to live at the Rocking K, where they would act as caretakers, and Jerry had a job in town as a carpenter. The entire Kinmont family was in Bishop again. It was like old times, but it was very new.

Jerry was the only one around who had seen most of the filming of *Mountain 2,* including all the scenes in Los Angeles and in British Columbia. Jill asked him, "How's the movie going to be?"

"It's really a hell of a movie. The big crazy story was told in the first film, and now this one's about people."

"Is this one going to be better?"

"It's a better picture," Jerry said. "Some places are typical Hollywood—for dramatic reasons—but the development of the relationship between John and Jill is really something to see. I think you'll think it's a good picture. Of course, it's an editing problem now, but the material is sure all there."

There was another potluck—this time at Bob and Vikki's—with the old Mammoth gang. It was the best one yet. They played catch and pitched horseshoes. There was less talk about Mammoth and the old days, and John and Ben won at horseshoes.

Life was simpler than it had been for many years. What it meant to Jill and John now was planting a garden, cutting

269

wood for June, having friends over for a barbecue, paying the bills, teaching, running the shop and the gas station, all those things which are fairly ordinary. "But it all has a focus when you love someone," Jill said to Jerry. "Everything else seems to radiate from that."

BOOKS OF DISTINCTION FROM WARNER BOOKS

HANTA YO
by Ruth Beebe Hill   (96-298, $3.50)

You become a member of the Mahto band in their seasonal migrations at the turn of the eighteenth century. You gallop with the warriors triumphantly journeying home with scalps, horses and captive women. You join in ceremonies of grief and joy where women trill, men dance, and the kill-tales are told. "Reading *Hanta Yo* is like entering a trance."   —*New York Times*

DEEPER INTO MOVIES
by Pauline Kael   (93-525, $2.95)

Pauline Kael's latest volume brings together more than one hundred and fifty pieces of criticism from *The New Yorker*, written between September 1968 and March 1972. The author considers it to be a "record of the enteraction of movies and our national life during a frantic time when three decades seem to have been compressed into three years." *Deeper Into Movies* is the only book on movies ever to have won the National Book Award (Arts and Letters, 1974).

FAGGOTS
by Larry Kramer   (95-153, $2.75)

It is a novel with precedent. It is an odyssey, not of a Greek adventurer, but of a fortyish writer, a homosexual looking for a lover, looking for a permanent relationship. It is explicit in sexual detail but funny and compassionate, too. "*Faggots*, for all its excesses, is frequently right on target and, when it is on target, is appallingly funny."   —*Edward Albee*

THE CHANGING LIFE OF THE CORPORATE WIFE
by Maryanne Vandervelde   (91-180, $2.50)

Until recently the answer has been a resounding no! But women themselves are beginning to change the pattern to fight for their own identity. Maryanne Vandervelde, a corporate wife for 16 years, conducted an extensive survey of the Fortune 500 companies chief executive officers and their wives to determine current attitudes and presents the sometimes shocking results.